Soundbitten

Soundbitten

The Perils of Media-Centered Political Activism

Sarah Sobieraj

NEW YORK UNIVERSITY PRESS
New York and London

NEW YORK UNIVERSITY PRESS
New York and London
www.nyupress.org

Substantial portions of chapter 4 originally appeared in
Social Problems, vol. 57, issue 4, under the title "Reporting Conventions:
Journalists, Activists, and the Thorny Struggle for Political Visibility."

References to Internet websites (URLs) were accurate at the time of writing.
Neither the author nor New York University Press is responsible for URLs
that may have expired or changed since the manuscript was prepared.

Library of Congress Cataloging-in-Publication Data

Sobieraj, Sarah.
Soundbitten : the perils of media-centered political activism / Sarah Sobieraj.
p. cm.
Includes bibliographical references and index.
ISBN 978–0–8147–4136–8 (cloth : alk. paper) — ISBN 978–0–8147–4137–5
(pbk. : alk. paper) — ISBN 978–0–8147–8386–3 (e-book)
1. Public relations and politics—United States. 2. Mass media—Political aspects—
United States. 3. Communication in politics—United States. I. Title.
JA85.2.U6.S66   2011
324.7'30973—dc22   2011006177

New York University Press books are printed on acid-free paper,
and their binding materials are chosen for strength and durability.
We strive to use environmentally responsible suppliers and materials
to the greatest extent possible in publishing our books.

Manufactured in the United States of America

c 10 9 8 7 6 5 4 3 2 1
p 10 9 8 7 6 5 4 3 2 1

For Esther and Ruth

Contents

Acknowledgments

THIS RESEARCH HAS been made possible by the kindness, support, and patience of many people to whom I am profoundly grateful.

First and foremost, I thank the inspiring activists and remarkably candid journalists who shared their experiences with me. The writing of this book had its ups and downs, but gathering the data—spending time watching these fascinating people do their work and listening to them share their stories—was one of the best experiences of my life. The bits of data I did not gather were expertly culled by my former research assistant, Elizabeth Kulik, who spent a summer carefully completing and evaluating the news archive described in chapter 4.

This research received financial support from Tufts University and Initiatives for Women at SUNY Albany, and I also thank Sandra Sobieraj Westfall, who let me sponge off her expense account and wriggled me into all the good convention and debate spots, from parties and pressrooms to motorcades. Thanks to her I had great company and a really nice meal once in a while. Thanks also to my father, John McGuire, for allowing me to turn his home away from home into my own personal writing refuge. Writing there, with him, was wonderful.

I am incredibly appreciative of the time and care invested by the anonymous reviewers of this manuscript. When I read their reviews, it was apparent that I had hit the jackpot: the gift of being read closely by scholars at the top of their field. The book benefited tremendously from their insights, as well as from the guidance of Ilene Kalish at NYU Press.

I am also grateful to my colleagues in the Department of Sociology for making Tufts such a welcoming and pleasant work environment. Their collegiality, wit, and encouragement kept the work of writing from feeling isolating, and they reminded me that I would "get there" eventually. Many of them graciously read parts of this work or offered feedback during our departmental colloquia. Thanks in particular to John Conklin, who, even amid his responsibilities as department chair, provided extensive, detailed feedback on this manuscript. I am also deeply indebted to Jim Ennis, Paul Joseph, and Susan Ostrander, who talked some sense into me at a difficult time, and to Vickie Sullivan for helping me to find the balance that allowed this book to come to fruition. Thank you, thank you, thank you.

There have been several colleagues outside my department—too numerous to name here—who provided feedback or guidance about writing and publishing. I thank Myra Marx Ferree, Tina Fetner, Dana Fisher, Bill Gamson, Dave Grazian, Kieran Healy, Doug McAdam, David Meyer, Joya Misra, Gwen Moore, Charlotte Ryan, and others who gave their time to help a newbie find her way. In particular, I am grateful to Ron Jacobs, whom I turn to for advice more regularly than is reasonable. If he were not right so often, I might leave him alone. Jeff Berry has also been an indispensable mentor. Although our work together has been on a different project, I have learned a great deal from working with him.

For the last five years I have been fortunate enough to be a part of a miraculous writing group whose members strike just the right balance of incisive critique, pointed questions, and enthusiasm. Thanks to the fantastic Chris Bobel (just typing her name makes me smile), Frinde Maher, Julie Nelson, Susan Ostrander, and Anna Sandoval for both their priceless Friday afternoon contributions to the evolution of this book and their friendship. Thanks also to former members Paula Aymer, JoAnne Preston, and Jyoti Puri, who helped me unearth what exactly it was—in all these data—that I had to say.

I must also acknowledge the funny and freakishly wise Tina Fetner for pointing me to the "magic book" and instigating an ongoing series of video chats about writing as a process, during which she, Jessica Fields, and I strategize about how to protect our writing time, even if it requires spreadsheets, odd hours, and Internet-blocking software.

Between chapters, I have enjoyed magnificent breaks that kept me sane, especially fabulous meals and bona fide relaxation at the farm with John, Brenda, and Maddie McGuire, who make everything feel special; holiday poker and virtual scrabble with Jeb McGuire; beach vacations with the Sobieraj family; and laughter with many friends, particularly Sue Aman, Melissa Burress, Tracy Holleran, Kristie Kapusta, Jenny Keys, Krista Siringo, Kristin Stainbrook, Heather Sullivan-Catlin, and Kristen Wallingford.

Constant contact with my mother, Laurie McGuire, meant that I had lighthearted breaks even in the heat of the writing. Her frequent calls to discuss pressing issues—good deals, her grandchildren, leisure reading, and reality television—kept me connected to her across state lines and, I think, to all that is best in life. Thanks, Mom, for everything, always.

Heather Laube deserves the key to some spectacular city for having the great misfortune of being both my closest friend and a sociologist, as it meant that she felt obligated to listen to me work through intellectual questions *and* talk me off the ledge during moments of panic. No one should have to do both, but this book exists only because she did.

Finally, I thank Jim, Quinn, and Graham Sobieraj. My three bright stars contributed to this book in many ways, particularly Jim, who has sacrificed often and without complaint to support the project. I am grateful beyond words for their vivaciousness and generosity, but I am even more appreciative of the way they make something as substantial as a decade of research and writing appear so conspicuously insignificant.

1

What If the Whole World *Isn't* Watching?

Activism, Presidential Campaigns, and
the Thorny Struggle for Visibility

DURING THE 2000 Republican National Convention (RNC) in Philadelphia, a network of activists from across the country used human blockades reinforced with PVC piping and steel to close down five major traffic arteries for nearly two hours during rush hour. As I observed, a school bus filled with police officers in combat gear arrived, a gas truck rolled in, and loud, low-flying news helicopters hovered overhead while officers worked to dismantle the human roadblock. Activists who were not part of the blockade filled the streets and faced the barricade of protesters, dancing, drumming, and playing makeshift musical instruments in the hot, late afternoon sun. Some entertained the crowd with offbeat political street theater. Still others threw confetti and lent exuberant voices to familiar protest chants. The classic activist refrain, "The whole world is watching! The whole world is watching!," was imbued with a new layer of meaning as it came from the mouths of activists brandishing camcorders, indicating to the police that any brutality would be documented. Amid the revelry, some participants were designated to provide medical care (one offered me sunscreen), and others disbursed bottled water to those embroiled in the lockdown. A handful of reporters crouched in front of the conjoined activists, posing questions and taking notes. Others watched from the sidelines, updating editors via cell phone, as they peered around the bystanders who filtered through, despite police efforts to disperse the crowd and secure the surrounding area.

Riot-gear-clad police, marching rhythmically in long lines with military precision and demeanor, worked to contain the boisterous crowd. The marching officers transitioned seamlessly into four rows, took the shape of a square around the intersection, and then turned to stand shoulder to shoulder, physically enclosing the protesters and supporters in the intersection. If this confinement bothered the activists they certainly didn't show it, but I felt trapped. The once-celebratory political expression seemed distant, as the delicate boundary between well-mannered standoff and adrenaline-propelled conflict began to feel increasingly vulnerable. I wandered inside the square constructed by the rigid lines of stoic police officers with shielded chests and faces, moving through a crowd dense with clusters of emboldened activists, many marked by piercings, tattered shorts, and surplus-store messenger bags embellished with political buttons, patches, and pithy slogans rendered in uneven ballpoint ink. A smattering of notebook-wielding journalists, wearing running shoes and sporting layers of credentials around their necks like Mardi Gras beads, lingered within and beyond the square, watching and waiting. Over the course of a tense hour and a half, police detached the activists one at a time, binding their wrists with plastic handcuffs and dragging them to the school bus despite passive resistance. By the end of the long, disruptive standoff, more than 400 people had been arrested.

Amid the turbulence, I was certain this was a historic moment. I envisioned my family watching CNN as the events unfolded and feared they would worry. Yet I soon discovered that the drama in which I was immersed had slipped almost completely under the radar. The *New York Times* gave the event a single 640-word story that was buried in the paper's late edition. The account was descriptive and accurate but never mentioned what had compelled so many people to do something so dramatic. A group named Disrupt[1] had planned and carried out this complex, illegal action because its members felt they had something exceptionally important to say that was relevant to the election. That "something" went unheard.

This book works to reconcile this puzzle, showing how activism erupts around the perimeter of presidential elections, unraveling why activists' efforts remain largely invisible, and looking at what activist groups lose in the process. Early in my research, I thought this would be a book about how activist groups use presidential elections as moments of political opening, but as I spent time with activists engaged in campaign-related work I came to realize that first and foremost this is a story about activists and the news media.

· · ·

Nearly six months before Disrupt's civil disobedience, during the presidential primary season, a minor story in the Metro section of the *New*

York Times caught my eye. The two leading Democratic candidates, Al Gore and Bill Bradley, were scheduled to appear at Harlem's Apollo Theater, in the only face-to-face debate prior to the New York primary. Two days before the debate, the International Alliance of Theatrical Stage Employees (IATSE), the union representing the Apollo Theater stagehands, threatened a walkout if management would not give them a signed contract. With representatives from both campaigns vowing that their respective candidates would not cross a picket line, the union's demands were met the next day. IATSE alleged that theater management had been refusing to negotiate in good faith, and they approached the high-profile debate as an opportunity to end an uncomfortable five-month standoff. It worked.

IATSE's ingenuity in using the debate as leverage on an issue unrelated to the election led me to wonder if other groups approach key campaign events as windows of opportunity. What opportunities do activists see in election years, how do they choose to respond to them, and what transpires as a result of their efforts?

This book emerges out of these questions and the search for answers that ensued in their wake. I immersed myself in activism around presidential debates and nominating conventions in 2000 and 2004. After following the work of 50 groups engaged in campaign-related activism and talking at length with their members, I resurfaced with paradoxical answers. Although I was propelled into the research by IATSE's instrumental use of the debate, not one of the groups I studied enjoyed this level of success. In fact, in the final analysis, the brief, politically impoverished news coverage of Disrupt was one of the most noteworthy outcomes for any of the groups I studied. How do we make sense of IATSE's success as we compare it to the challenges faced by Disrupt and its peers? If Disrupt is the most successful organization with which I worked over the course of two campaign cycles, what does this say about political activism? How do we reconcile Disrupt's quite sizable mobilization with its inability to influence (or even enter) campaign-related discourse?

I will show that a tremendous amount of robust political activism emerges around presidential campaigns, but the story beneath the rallies, teach-ins, protests, and petitions is considerably less encouraging. We will see that unlike IATSE, whose action made targeted demands of its management, most groups drawn to major campaign events focus on more nebulous goals. In particular, they are mobilized by a perceived opportunity to shape mainstream political discourse via the news media, and they channel their energies accordingly. This rampant media-centrism proves ineffective and in some ways even destructive. Activists' often-outrageous attempts to lure journalists politicize public spaces in memorable ways, but for most groups the pursuit of media attention is largely futile, brings with it important organizational costs (including missed opportunities to connect with one another and with the people they encounter in the course of their work), and comes at the expense of other political activities.

These outcomes are problematic for the groups I study, but they also signal larger issues that require attention. Because the mass media serve as the "master forum" in which political debates are waged, the activists' inability to become news is about more than fifteen minutes of fame; it is fundamentally about who is able to participate in discussions about social and political issues.[2] The proliferation of media-centered activism, then, reveals a chasm between civil society and the public sphere—concepts I will explore in this chapter—that both limits associations' ability to live up to normative visions proffered by existing theories of civil society and raises troubling questions about the inclusivity of American democracy.

Media-centrism was not limited to civil disobedience collectives like Disrupt. Indeed, there was a range of groups active around key campaign events. Some were social movement organizations, but there were also religious organizations, large national citizen groups, and nonpartisan civic organizations. The organizations examined in this book reflect the diversity of the associational universe. In light of this, the umbrella term "voluntary association" and its sibling "voluntary organization" most accurately honor these groups' varied forms and uniting principles. I use these terms frequently throughout this book, but in the interest of readability I also take the liberty of using quasi-synonyms that are overly broad (e.g., "groups") and overly narrow (e.g., "activist organizations"). In all cases, I use these varied and imperfect terms to refer to collectives that are nonfamilial, intentional, and freely entered, and which do not exist as a result of state coercion or for the purpose of generating profit. The breadth and diversity of the associational universe was visible when I stepped into the field. Presidential campaigns serve as catalysts for much of civil society, including, but by no means limited to, social movements.

What's So Special About Presidential Campaigns?

Presidential campaigns provide an inviting atmosphere for activism. The campaign context is viewed by scholars of both civil society and social movements as presenting a special opportunity for voluntary organizations. There is research in the social movements literature that addresses elections as political opportunities, such as the work done by Blee and Currier (2006), Earl and Schussman (2004), Goldstone (2003), Meyer (1993, 2005, 2007), Meyer and Minkoff (2004), and Van Dyke (2003). In the civil society literature, Tocqueville ([1835] 2000) viewed elections as politically mobilizing, and Habermas (1996) clings to elections as moments that heighten the level of influence civil society has in the public sphere. Elections create opportunities for groups that are explicitly organized around political issues, as well as for organizations for whom political interests are secondary, and even those that normally focus their efforts elsewhere (e.g., the Apollo Theater stagehands union). Presidential campaigns are compelling to these groups because of their unique clustering of attributes: breadth, significance, liminality, geographic dispersion, periodicity, and publicity.[3]

Breadth refers to the multiplicity of issues that are open for debate during presidential campaigns. As an ever-increasing number of issues once understood as private (e.g., sexual behavior or domestic violence) have been thrust into the public sphere, presidential campaigns have become venues for open discussion of virtually all matters of common concern. It is difficult to imagine another arena in which immigration, environmental issues, the death penalty, public education, same-sex marriage, health care, trade agreements, tax policy, and stem cell research are all deemed relevant. This abundance of potentially salient issues renders the campaign context pertinent for an overwhelming number of voluntary associations. Some mobilize because candidates raise an issue central to their organization, while others attempt to force politicians to address an issue that is not on the agenda.

With respect to *significance*, presidential elections are consequential; the winner will be imbued with arguably more power than the victor in any other election in the world. The outcome will have local, national, and global effects. Thus, pro-choice and pro-life groups may be more active during a presidential campaign than a local campaign, because of the president's control over Supreme Court nominations. The weight of these elections serves to increase the perceived importance of participation and heightens the incentive for association involvement.

The uncertain outcome of a presidential election confers campaigns with a *liminality* that presents a political opportunity.[4] By empowering a new set of leaders or re-sanctioning the incumbents, elections present political apertures during which activists can attempt to assert influence through a variety of mechanisms, including, but not limited to, offering candidate endorsements, making campaign contributions, protesting, publicizing candidate records or proclivities that please or displease them, and working to shape party platforms. In some instances liminality may prove mobilizing because it produces a sense of anxiety (as opposed to efficacy), leading groups to seek control of the outcome.[5] Either way, this vulnerability, this political openness, prompts engagement.

Presidential campaigns are also *geographically dispersed*, moving politics outside Washington. Nominating conventions and televised debates take place beyond the Beltway, and candidates make countless stops across the country to give stump speeches, patronize neighborhood eateries, visit classrooms, and make themselves available to civic organizations. Hart (2000) argues that the campaign process brings candidates in closer contact with the public than they are likely to experience again once they enter the White House. The presence of candidates in local communities is an attractive opportunity for organizations hoping to have their political concerns addressed.

Presidential campaigns are also *periodic*. That is, they happen every four years. This regularity enables associations to anticipate and prepare interventions in a way that other major national events with the aforementioned characteristics do not. Natural and man-made disasters (e.g., Three Mile Island or Hurricane Katrina) and other crises (e.g., 9/11) bring politicians out of Washington, present moments of great uncertainty, and render many issues salient, but they occur without warning. The predictable lead time offered by presidential campaign events (e.g., conventions, debates, inaugurations) gives activists ample opportunity to mobilize, choose tactics, and make necessary preparations, such as securing permits, renting equipment, soliciting donations, and publicizing their efforts.

Finally, presidential campaigns bring with them *publicity*. The national press pool that follows each candidate, and the throng of local news personnel that joins them at each stop, create myriad perceived opportunities for associations to garner publicity. In addition to responding to journalists' questions and distributing unsolicited press releases, activists can stage events designed to capture the attention of the news media. Dayan and Katz (1992) explain that the prospect of sending a message to a national or international audience makes media events vulnerable to "hijacking" by outsiders in search of publicity.[6] The belief that they will be able to attract coverage is compelling to activists who hope such attention will help them reach candidates, voters, and political parties as well as potential new members, contributors, and supporters.

This uncommon clustering of qualities inspires activists but does little to explain the unsatisfying outcomes experienced by the groups I will introduce in the pages of this book. Turning to the literature on civil society and the public sphere, we are left scratching our heads. While some argue that civil society is dead and others see it as vital, none really explains this peculiarity. What if we have a civil society that is robust and participatory but also invisible and inefficacious? And if this is true, why is this happening?

Civil Society, the Public Sphere, and Mobilization

Civil society is the arena of public group life, the terrain of voluntary associations. Although the term *civil society* has a long history in political and social theory,[7] I use it in the contemporary sense, to refer to that sector of society that is analytically distinct from the state, the market, and the realm of the family.[8] In their myriad formal and informal incarnations, the groups that populate civil society connect people to one another and channel individual energies, interests, and talents. They are the skeletal underpinnings of civil society and serve as a locus for civic engagement in both its episodic and enduring forms. In association, participants may discover common interests, develop community, attempt to influence public opinion, and seek to initiate or maintain public policies consistent with their definitions of a good society.

In many ways, voluntary associations can be understood as the infrastructure of civil society. As such, they are indispensable but not infallible. Many have romanticized voluntary associations and the civic engagement that they facilitate, but a growing body of research suggests that the results of involvement are contingent on context and may fail to live up to, or may even subvert, normative ideals.[9]

While Habermas argues that at least temporary consensus can be reached in healthy civil societies through rational-critical discourse, this process of articulating and asserting the public will is complicated by frequent conflicts over what constitutes the good society and how it should be approximated. Thus, while the will of the people theoretically emerges through the development of shared interests and unconstrained communication, in reality the public interest is defined in innumerable ways. In addition to political interests and group identities, cultural meanings and taken-for-granted assumptions are often created, negotiated, and challenged within civil society.[10] The coexistence of competing concerns, views, and objectives manifest themselves in constant pressure for and resistance to political and cultural change on an array of fronts, from minor community disputes to issues of international significance. The ebb and flow of these struggles contribute to the ever-changing dynamics within and between voluntary associations, as well as those between civil society and non-civil sectors. As a result, civil society is best understood not only as a stable and homogeneous space characterized by consensus and solidarity, but also as a fluid and heterogeneous space of contest and conflict.

The term *public sphere* refers simultaneously to the practice of open discussion about matters of common concern and the public spaces that serve as settings for such dialogue, such as parks, e-mail lists, community centers, newspapers, and plazas. The public sphere thus refers both to public dialogue about matters of general concern and to the places where these discussions transpire. This incarnation of the concept stems largely from Habermas's (1989) *The Structural Transformation of the Public Sphere*. For Habermas (1996), publics can range from the episodic, accidental gatherings found in coffeehouses or taverns, to prearranged events such as conferences and church congregations, to abstract publics of dispersed readers, viewers, and listeners connected through mass media. Particularly relevant here is the argument made by Hallin and Mancini (1984, 2004) that as local publics deteriorate, mass-mediated publics take on increasing importance.

Habermas (1996) argues that the networks of associations, organizations, and social movements serve as barometers for how private individuals experience social problems because they filter and present these experiences in the public sphere. While he makes clear that these associations are not the most visible bodies in a public sphere dominated by mass media and professional public relations entities, he sees them as the critical organizational foundation for citizen-generated public discourse on matters of common concern. Thus, while the sphere of group life and the practice of public discourse should not be conflated, civil society and the public sphere are deeply entwined concepts, with associations often serving as micro public spheres that foster dialogue among those with shared interests and influence public discourse beyond their borders.

As I explored the relationship between presidential campaigns and voluntary associations, I looked to the civil society literature for insights into potential opportunities and obstacles encountered by mobilizing organizations. Instead, I found a literature ill-equipped to address such questions. Contemporary theories that address the relationships within civil society, and between civil society and other sectors, bring a variety of issues to the fore, including those of boundary formation and social solidarity,[11] discourse ethics and new social movements,[12] visions of community and equality,[13] and questions about what constitutes a political community.[14] Some of this work explores the relationships internal to civil society, those that take place within and between its multiple, overlapping publics, while other research explores the relations among civil society, the state, and the economy. What remains unproblematized is the prevalent notion that these varied relationships, both internal and external, are consistent and continuous. The stagehands union and the many associations introduced in this book suggest otherwise.

While none of these scholars explicitly argue that action and engagement are staid, there is a silence around issues of differential mobilization. Cohen and Arato's rich theoretical work on civil society serves as an excellent example of this silence. For these scholars, agency abounds and is utilized; civil society is an active terrain. Indeed, much of their work examines new social movements and the role of civil disobedience in democratic societies. They explain that "civil society, beyond all functionalist and pluralist models, should be seen not only passively as a network of institutions, but also actively as the context and product of self-constituting collective actors" (1992, xviii). The institutions of civil society are molded by the efforts of the multiple formal and informal organizations that inhabit this space. The reader is left with the image of a vibrant, contest-filled, and productive sphere of group action.

This image evokes the energy implied by the term *mobilization*, but variation in energy level—the shifting between different levels of activity—is unaccounted for. In *Civil Society and Political Theory*, Cohen and Arato explain that civil societies may vary in character: "There can be different types of civil society: more or less institutionalized, more or less democratic, more or less active" (1992, 17). But the implication is that this level of activity varies from society to society, rather than from time to time *within* a given society. In other words, they argue that civil societies of different natures exist, and that one civil society may be more active overall than another. Their argument is strengthened by attentiveness to the ever-changing, historically specific, social context. They posit that the nature of a given civil society is neither intrinsic nor fixed, but rather is fluid and expected to change in character over time.

We must extend this historical specificity to a more finely grained discussion of the ways in which the engagement and activity levels of a particular civil society may fluctuate on a smaller scale—not just with long-term historical transitions, but also from day to day and month to month. Further, it is critical to look not only at variation between different civil societies across time, but also at variation within any specific civil society at any given historical moment. A cross-sectional snapshot taken at any particular moment would reveal that the diverse associations within a society's civil sector are not simultaneously at an equal level of activity (or institutionalization or democratization for that matter), but rather that each association has a unique composition that may at one moment be very active and at others lie close to dormant. Even in unusually thriving and particularly repressed civil societies, the diverse coexisting groups are unlikely to sustain equivalent levels of (in)activity. Conceptualizing the associational landscape in this way, then, provides a useful analytic tool as we work to understand voluntary association activity around presidential campaigns.

In *The Structural Transformation of the Public Sphere*, Habermas (1989) depicts an image of civil society that stands in stark contrast to the vibrant realm of activity described by Cohen and Arato. He describes the contemporary public sphere as bleak and depoliticized. Habermas argues that the once-vital public sphere was re-feudalized by the development of a mass consumer culture, the intrusion of bureaucratic associations, the development of the welfare state, and the withdrawal of individuals into isolated worlds of work and leisure. The consequence, he argues, is that contemporary civil society has been reduced to an apolitical realm: it is devoid of the critical activities of public discourse, and has deteriorated to the point that groups associate purely for social reasons. Habermas's depiction of a public sphere dominated by advertising and consumption does not assume that these degraded associations and passive individual actors can be stimulated into increasing dialogue or activity. The lasting impression is one of non-reflexive individuals who have retreated into family and occupational life and of bureaucratic organizations that seek nothing more than symbolic representation. We see no rise and fall of meaningful interaction in civil society. Instead, Habermas paints the nineteenth- and twentieth-century public sphere as one free of the sparks of life that ignited the bourgeois public sphere of the eighteenth century.

These visions of civil society diverge along one axis and merge along another. The divergence is striking: where Cohen and Arato find energy and agency, Habermas finds passivity and inefficaciousness. Yet both theories foreground consistency. Cohen and Arato describe a civil society that remains in motion, while Habermas describes a civil society mired in inertia. The activity around a presidential election cannot be explained by either of these accounts. Civil society needs mobilization as a key concept if we are to understand voluntary association activity as something more than weekly meetings at the Moose Lodge or monthly newsletters circulated to geographically dispersed issue adherents. In his more recent work, Habermas (1996) is more optimistic about the role of civil society; in fact, he points toward the presence of textural variations, arguing that *crises* and *elections* can alter the social landscape such that the relationship between civil society and the state changes. In the end, however, he describes variation in the balance of power rather than changes in associational activity itself.

In order to understand how it is that an activist group like Disrupt can bring a city to its knees and yet go virtually unnoticed beyond the local paper, it is critical that we think about mobilization and its constraints. But mobilization as a concept has been applied almost exclusively to social movements, rather than to the broader spectrum of groups that engage in activism. This is an oversight, as even anecdotal reflections on voluntary organizations quickly reveal that associations are not static entities. Events that produce great excitement and concern can generate new groups and increase the activity and membership levels of existing organizations. For example, new organizations arose in response to both the Iraq war (e.g., Iraq Veterans Against the War or Code Pink: Women for Peace) and the devastation of Hurricane Katrina (e.g., Katrina's Angels or Katrina InfoShare Collective). For associations already in existence, activity can be intensified by such events. For example, the National Rifle Association increased its activity and attracted numerous new members after the backlash against the private ownership of guns instigated by the spate of school shootings in 1998 and 1999.[15] These examples suggest that civil society is a fluid and responsive arena rather than a smoothly operating assembly line.[16]

Existing theories of civil society overlook these fluctuations in association activity, implicitly depicting the arena as either persistently engaged or disengaged. This oversight is puzzling since the literature on social movements is grounded fundamentally on the notion that collective action—which most often takes place in the realm of civil society, even if this is not explicitly stated—is *not* continuous. McAdam, McCarthy, and Zald (1996, 7) highlight this point as follows: "Understanding the mix of factors that give rise to a movement is the oldest, and arguably the most important, question in the field. Moreover, virtually all 'theories' in the field are first, and foremost, theories of movement emergence." Though social movement theories differ considerably and I make no claim to be a social movements scholar,[17] it is clear that they share a central concern with a core question: what sparks collective action?[18] The understanding that group action ebbs and flows is implicit. Those interested in civil society and the public sphere need to ask this question as well.

Transferring the knowledge about mobilization gleaned from the study of social movements to civil society is helpful, though it is limited for two reasons. First, while civil society is the terrain of social movements, social movement organizations are only one of many types of associations existing in this arena. In other words, knowing why social movement organizations mobilize and what their outcomes are may not translate to our stagehands union, a cultural organization, or a religious group. It would be reductive to collapse the diversity of the associational spectrum into one type of organization.

A second challenge is that social movement researchers have traditionally addressed mobilization primarily in regard to instrumental actions aimed at attaining economic, political, or cultural goals, which directs them away from asking some of the questions most salient to those interested in civil society. Debates in the social movements literature explore which types of mobilizations are likely to generate political gains—particularly with regard to policymaking, but also in the acquisition of rights and the impact on electoral processes—focusing on whether and under what conditions social movements have political consequences.[19] This is a critical question, of course, but it means that this research is less concerned with asking questions such as: What does the act of engaging or participating do for group life? What are the outcomes of mobilization, not in its political or economic impact, but in terms of social solidarity, democracy, and civic engagement? Certainly there is attention paid to culture in social movements. Indeed, it has been incorporated into most aspects of social movement studies through explorations of phenomena such as collective identity, framing, cultural repertoires, and cultural innovations, but as Kurzman (2009) argues, meaning making has primarily been assimilated into a cause-and-effect-based analytic framework rather than treated as foundational.[20]

Mobilization has important consequences for voluntary associations, separate from goal attainment. This is not to say that exploring effective strategies for goal attainment is unimportant to those studying civil society, but rather that the act of associating, in and of itself, is a lesser-order question for those researching in the social movements tradition. Exploring activism from a civil society framework involves the assumption that associational life exists and persists, not necessarily because there is an issue that needs to be addressed, but as a direct result of the shape of modern democratic society. As a result, I borrow questions about mobilization from the social movements research and broaden them in order to introduce this vital concept into the literature on civil society, which stands to gain considerably. In mobilization, we can expect to see civil society's greatest strengths but also its limitations. Said another way, voluntary associations' concerted efforts to engage tell us a great deal about what such groups—so often romanticized—can (and cannot) accomplish and how this work shapes group life.

For the concept of mobilization to be meaningful in the broader realm of associations, it must capture not only the *level* or *intensity* of activity (which is perhaps what first comes to mind with the term *mobilization*), but also the shape that the activity takes, the *mode* of action. A distinction is often made between those social movement efforts that are visible to outsiders, such as rallies or protests, and those that transpire in preparation for this external engagement. These behind-the-scenes activities, such as creating websites and securing meeting space, are often invisible to both the public and most participants. This is a useful distinction, but a third analytic category is necessary to highlight the myriad activities created by and for members, without external engagement, such as conferences, workshops, and social gatherings. Without this third category, these communal efforts are rendered invisible at worst and residual at best, as the default presumption is that behind-the-scenes activity is secondary, mere preparation for external engagement. While this would be an accurate assessment of the way behind-the-scenes activities are viewed by some organizations, it would be a gross misunderstanding of the standpoint of others. Imagine, for example, a religious organization that serves primarily as a space for

TABLE 1.1.

Voluntary Association Activity Classification Scheme

Fundamental: Behind-the-scenes endeavors that facilitate the coordination of the group (often unseen by the majority of the membership).
Communal: Activities run by and for members without the intent of reaching a broader audience.
Demonstrative: Externally focused activities intended to be highly visible (may or may not involve the majority of members and are directed toward non-members).

Sample use of spectra for a hypothetical environmental group:

Activity Mode Spectrum

		FUNDAMENTAL	COMMUNAL	DEMONSTRATIVE
Activity Level Spectrum	TYPICAL	Newsletter Preparation	Monthly Membership Meeting	Annual Earth Day Rally
	MOBILIZED	Generation of Urgent Email Alerts	Retreat or Celebration	Series of River Vigils

Level of visibility ⟶

socializing, discussing shared values, and pursuing charitable goals. Such an organization may rarely be concerned with engaging a broader audience, yet it could conceivably choose to do so if it perceived it as relevant (e.g., if a salient community issue arose). It would be inaccurate to interpret most of this group's activities simply as preparation for public engagement.

These activity types are arrayed along the horizontal axis in table 1.1. On one end of the spectrum are *fundamental activities*, which include behind-the-scenes endeavors that the majority of the members do not see, but that facilitate the coordination of the organization and its membership. At the center of the spectrum are *communal activities*, those run by and for members, without the intent of reaching a broader audience. At the other end are *demonstrative activities*, which are highly visible, externally focused endeavors that may or may not involve the majority of the membership and are directed toward nonmembers.

The terms demonstrative, communal, and fundamental refer to distinctive *modes* or types of action rather than to distinctive *levels* of action (e.g., mobilized vs. typical). Looking at the vertical axis, *typical activities* are those that organizations engage in routinely. In contrast, events that involve a notable break from routine and an atypical investment of resources are considered *mobilized activities*; such activities are a "big deal"

and require explanation even for regular participants. The distinction between these two levels of activity is relevant for all three modes of action.
For example, communal activities may be designed for mobilization (e.g.,
a special party to celebrate an accomplishment) or be part of a standard
mode of operation (e.g., a monthly potluck dinner). Certainly many group
activities have dual foci;[21] this heuristic device is simply intended to facilitate thinking about the variety of potential choices available. Considering
the range of alternatives, and the options that exist *within* each category
(activities within each of these six broad categories can take many forms),
helps to place media-centricity in context as one particular variant of demonstrative mobilization.

The Research

This book is based on my ethnographic fieldwork at voluntary association
events during the 2000 and 2004 Democratic and Republican nominating
conventions in their host cities: Los Angeles, Philadelphia, Boston, and
New York City, as well as during the three televised presidential debates
of 2000 in their respective host cities: Boston, Winston-Salem, and St.
Louis.[22] I observed civil disobedience collectives, local single-issue groups,
large national citizen groups, labor unions, social movement organizations,
religious organizations, and broad, multi-issue coalitions, among others.
These groups focused their energies on a wide array of issues, ranging from
the environment and global justice to abortion and war opposition. Most
of the organizations I encountered identified as progressive or nonpartisan,
with a smaller number identifying as conservative, libertarian, or anarchist.
The rich palette of organizations whose colorful stories grace these pages
reflects my assessment of diverse activities in these environments and my
earnest interest in attempting to represent them as fairly as possible.

Other researchers have spent months and years immersed in voluntary
associations and produced exceptional ethnographic accounts of association life, or used extensive interviews to create rich case studies of individual organizations.[23] This book is different; I provide a wide-angle lens to
capture the breadth of activity around a handful of mobilizing events. My
mural of 50 groups brings to life the extraordinary range of organizations
active in this environment, and also highlights their various interests, tactics, and outcomes. For example, large national mailing list organizations
differ significantly from anarchist collectives in their campaign activism.

This broad view enables me to draw out commonalities and (sometimes counterintuitive) patterned differences that emerge among these organizations as they mobilize. Seeking this breadth made traditional ethnography logistically impossible. Instead, I use my ethnographic work as a foundation on which to build snapshots of these 50 associations, as well as to develop an intimate understanding of the social context in which their events transpired.

The groups in this book transform the cities that host national nominating conventions and televised debates into political festivals quite rare in the United States. Because these circumstances are fleeting and the mobilizations are circumscribed in time and space, I augment my ethnographic explorations with more than 125 in-depth interviews with association representatives (at least one "lay member" or "participant" and one "key member" or "leader" from each group) and political reporters who covered the events. Their stories and my relatively brief ethnographic excursions are complemented by news coverage of key events, association literature, website archives, and a small selection of association e-mail list discussions.[24] It was a fascinating challenge to weave together these threads, to assemble the pieces of the puzzle in a way that captures the hopes, experiences, and consequences of association activity in the context of presidential campaigns. The picture that emerged revealed a great deal about the relationship between activist groups and presidential campaigns, but it revealed even more the relationship between activism and the media.

Media-Centered Activism

As it turns out, the activism that originally piqued my interest was remarkably unique. The Apollo Theater stagehands leveraged the Gore/Bradley debate to negotiate a contract by pressuring their management. In contrast, most groups that mobilized around the campaign events had broader objectives and a considerably larger target audience; they approached these events as opportunities to participate in or shape mainstream political discourse.

This emphasis on shaping public discourse led them to adopt a demonstrative, outward-looking orientation that generated activities intended to communicate with or be visible to nonmembers. What is even more interesting is that this desire to intervene in public discourse almost always translated into a dogged pursuit of mainstream media attention at the expense of other approaches, such as canvassing or holding open meetings. Despite a range of available action alternatives, the groups narrowed their range of action twice: once by focusing exclusively on visibility, and again by treating the mainstream news media as the best or sole means of becoming visible.[25]

As a result of this narrow interpretation, activism in the presidential campaign milieu is dominated by media-centric efforts that require extraordinary effort be devoted to public relations preparation and strategy. Organizations held elaborate media trainings, designed eye-catching photo opportunities, wrangled over the perfect slogan, sent press releases, held press conferences, and even broke the law with the hope of garnering media attention. One group even had members practice being interviewed aggressively on camera and then had the group review and critique their performances. Media training was not taken lightly. Yet success eluded them: the vast majority of associations received no meaningful mainstream news coverage.

In the worst-case scenarios, the publicity work not only fails, but also has deleterious effects on the organizations. The tireless pursuit of media attention hurts associations' ability to reach laypeople in several ways. Some association members appear unable to relinquish the marketing model designed for the news media, even when they talk *directly* with outsiders, face-to-face. I repeatedly heard activists respond to earnest inquiries posed by bystanders with sound bites, pithy slogans, and canned answers that sounded insincere, evasive, and, in some instances, dishonest. In other cases, I watched association members give interested bystanders the brush-off in order to follow a journalist or to make themselves available for interviews. Media-centrism created a barrier between association participants and potential supporters.

In addition, I found that the focus on publicity often shaped the internal cultures of mobilizing associations, transforming them into performance-oriented spaces designed for journalists. This transition stifled internal dialogue and led to the creation of rigid rules for members. Rather than the egalitarian spaces of community building and political discussion described by public sphere theorists, I found organizations with leaders who approached their members as potential liabilities, in that these individuals could potentially embarrass the group on camera if left to their own devices. In response, these groups worked to discipline their members' speech and behavior. Ultimately, for many associations, this public relations approach is not only ineffective, but also damaging to group life.

It is useful to juxtapose this research to Gitlin's (1980) classic study of the relationship between the radical student group Students for a Democratic Society (SDS) and the news media during the antiwar movement of the 1960s. Gitlin artfully shows that the creation of news is a complex and mutually dependent social process. We take away from his text the knowledge that those who are covered in the news are not powerless, but also that the balance of power between journalists and activist groups is imbalanced. He demonstrates, for example, that news coverage of the student movement often trivialized its efforts, distorted the activities of the organization, and created celebrities out of members (which proved more divisive than galvanizing). *The Whole World Is Watching* chronicles the unraveling of SDS under the media spotlight. But the media environment today is not the media environment of the 1960s. In many ways, this book tells a story that is the inverse of Gitlin's: where he lays bare the organizational costs of media attention, I find associations derailed by their often-herculean attempts to attract that gaze.

Reaching the Public:
Does It Matter If the Whole World Isn't Watching?

Disrupt's dramatic efforts to shape political discussion around the Republican National Convention in Philadelphia culminated in a remarkably low level of visibility, but most groups that I studied, even those that aggressively pursued news coverage, received even less media attention. Despite the crescendo of activity in civil society around key presidential campaign events, the impact of association attempts to influence broader political discourse is minimal. How do we make sense of the disjuncture between these groups and the mainstream public sphere? Does it even matter that there is a disjuncture?

Although Habermas's early work depicts a single public arena and prioritizes rational-critical discussion of general rather than particular interests, scholars have since challenged this conception for its historical accuracy as well as its normative desirability. Historical evidence demonstrates that the bourgeois public sphere Habermas described was indeed a public sphere, but it was one of many. Competing publics taking different forms (e.g., non-rational, non-liberal, particularistic) or those comprising participants formally and informally excluded by the bourgeois public sphere (e.g., women, the illiterate, non-whites, the lower class) are absent from

Habermas's account (Eley 1992; Fraser 1992; Ryan 1991). Further, although he believed a single, communal public sphere to be the ideal, this single-public model has been criticized as a step away from democracy in stratified societies, since the majority may oppress those of subordinate status because participatory parity is unachievable (Benhabib 1992; Fraser 1992; Mouffe 1999; Young 1990).[26]

Fraser (1992) and others point toward and value the existence of multiple public spheres, suggesting that they provide spaces for articulating marginalized interests and viewpoints, building group solidarity, and establishing alternative interpretations of existing arrangements, and act as staging grounds for the development of strategies to inject these interests and views into mainstream public discourse.[27] The coexistence of multiple public spheres is understood as a step toward building more inclusive democracies, broadening public discourse, and facilitating participatory parity. This is grounded in the notion that smaller publics enable group members to experience solidarity as they share interests with like-minded individuals and develop strategies to amplify their voices when they enter mainstream public arenas. In other words, to the extent that voluntary associations serve as micro public spheres, they are vital because they provide safe havens and support for marginalized groups or viewpoints, and also because they allow participants to work together to expand mainstream discursive space to create room for their issues and concerns. These micro publics, then, serve both as valuable enclaves and as incubators for engagement with nonmembers.

Since writing *The Structural Transformation of the Public Sphere*, Habermas (1989, 1996) has acknowledged the presence of multiple public spheres in no uncertain terms, making clear that multiple associations, organizations, and movements can provide spaces for public discourse. He seems to conceptualize the role of these publics in much the same way that Fraser (1992) envisions them, as spaces in which marginalized groups build community and work to engage the mainstream public. The experiences of the voluntary associations explored in this book complicate this optimistic vision by demonstrating that while such strategizing does indeed transpire, attempts to expand mainstream dialogue are profoundly limited. Most associations are narrowly focused on wooing or shocking the news media; when coverage does not materialize or fails to circulate their preferred message, the groups find themselves stranded in the margins, as spectators to, rather than participants in, discussions about political issues and choices that will shape their lives.

This involuntary enclaving has obvious consequences for the associations that flounder, but it also has consequences for society at large. In 2000, for example, with candidates Al Gore and George W. Bush largely aligned in their support of the continued expansion of free trade, news readers and viewers heard little about the potential costs of free-trade agreements. Meanwhile, groups organized around global justice in general and fair trade in particular were quite active in the broader campaign environment, offering radically different interpretations and arguments than those delivered by the candidates. For many, their arguments may have been unpersuasive, but for others they may have shaped their viewpoints, priorities, or behavior in the voting booth or in the marketplace.

If a disjuncture exists between voluntary associations and broader publics, it is a consequential one. Although seen as a vital element of democracy,[28] civil society does not directly wield power in the political arena. Cohen and Arato (1992) explain that those in the civil terrain can acquire political influence but not political power. Because this influence is not institutionalized and remains outside the political decision-making process, they argue that civil society can directly transform itself but can affect the political system only indirectly (e.g., by pressuring elected officials or voting to change officeholders). Cohen and Arato take the possibility of "self" transformation for granted, but the ability to transform even civil society relies on the communicative structures of the public sphere, which are dominated by the mass media.

What is perhaps most perplexing about the gap between civil society and the public sphere is that theory suggests such gaps may actually be *narrowed* by elections. Habermas (1996, 373) states that "under certain circumstances civil society can acquire influence in the public sphere,[29] [and] have an effect on the parliamentary complex (and the courts) through its own public opinions." Given this vision of elections as crescendos of inclusivity, we might expect that marginalized groups working to shape political discourse would have better access to discursive arenas then they would in other circumstances.

The groups profiled in this book challenge this presumption, demonstrating that the realities of a public sphere dominated by the mass media and, equally important, the associations' mindfulness of this domination, render striving to acquire influence in civil society and the political arena a daunting challenge. It might be tempting to interpret the disjuncture between associations and broader audiences as a simple function of media gatekeeping. Indeed, this is part of the story, but another part of this story is the association response to the presence of a public sphere dominated by mass media. Gitlin (1980) reminds us that the struggle over news is a lopsided negotiation between news organizations and news workers, on the one hand, and voluntary associations and members on the other. The struggles to define what will become news reveal a great deal about why association coverage is thin and ultimately favors logistical reports rather than considerations of substantive issues. This is an important negotiation that I will address in detail, but equally important is the recognition that other association responses to campaign events, including circumvention of the mainstream media, may prove more effective politically and less toxic to group life.

While the literatures on voluntary associations and the public sphere remain largely separate (see Jacobs 2003), I hope to narrow the gap by unraveling their relationship, telling the story of the creative fashion in which voluntary associations attempt to enter political dialogue, the paradoxical way their approaches often undermine their success, and the deeply limited accomplishments they accrue. These complexities highlight the associations' limited ability to live up to normative visions, such as those articulated by Fraser and Habermas, and cast shadows on the legitimacy of American democracy. Many have romanticized voluntary associations, but without access to circles of discussion they are dispossessed of their most vital strength (the ability to shape public opinion and transform civil society) and their potential indirect influence over the political system. Even more fundamentally, a meaningful democratic process requires that citizens have adequate information to make informed decisions on their own behalf. If the voices of many are rendered inaudible in mainstream political discourse, despite strenuous efforts to be included, and if alternative views on political issues or new ideas about what is defined as political are not deemed legitimate, then the presumption of an informed citizenry is untenable. It is also critical to consider the implications of a civil society that is debased by the frenzied pursuit of such inclusion.

Plan of the Book

In the chapters that follow, I explore the process of mobilization, particularly media-centered demonstrative mobilization, in the campaign context and lay bare its consequences for the associations under consideration. Chapter 2 describes the rarely seen political carnivals that emerge in the cities that host national nominating conventions and debates. It explores why the associations choose to heighten their activity surrounding these events, and the remarkable consistency with which associations opt for mainstream media outreach as their focal mobilization strategy. Chapter 3 offers three extended case studies that illustrate the tactics most often used by associations trying to lure journalists, as well as an example of what a communal mobilization might look like. Chapter 4 shows how infrequently these elaborate tactics bear fruit, looking at the amount and character of subsequent news coverage. The remainder of the chapter documents the complex negotiation between journalists and activists over what will become news. Drawing this struggle out, I show that association members fail because they work strenuously to conform to the set of professional practices that are in place for political insiders, which run counter to a second, invisible set of standards in place for activists. Chapter 5 demonstrates that in addition to losing the publicity game, associations' quest for mainstream media attention derails their efforts with real live people. I show that while media trainings abound, activist groups invest virtually no effort in training their members to engage pedestrians in productive conversations. In chapter 6, I show that campaign mobilizations are more than simply lost opportunities: they are association-altering experiences. While some changes are positive, such as the enhancement of members' feelings of efficacy, others, including the suppression of members' political speech, are disconcerting. I further use this chapter to examine what the association mobilizations offer our understanding of civil society, the news media, and presidential elections. Finally, I close the book with an epilogue that reflects on the 2008 election and examines the resilience of mainstream news media-centrism in the face of new platforms provided by web 2.0.

2

Campaign Events as Catalysts

The Politicization of Public Space

WASHINGTON UNIVERSITY IN St. Louis hosted the final televised presidential debate of the 2000 election. The night before the debate, a plane crash took the life of Missouri Governor Mel Carnahan. Stunned, many voluntary associations cancelled or toned down their planned activities in response to the tragedy. A smattering of protests, workshops, and panels went on as planned, but the relative quiet following the governor's death served as a poignant indicator of the elevated level of activity to which I had become accustomed. This was the fifth host city I had visited in four months, and it was remarkably different. Where *was* everybody?

These thoughts ran through my mind even as I stood alongside a protest in the streets of St. Louis. How could I regard this situation as quiet? In my research up to this point, the convention and televised debate locations had been carnivalesque. Each host city designated official demonstration sites where groups gathered, and some organizations held parties at community centers, restaurants, and hotels. Political gatherings filled arenas, movie theaters, and college classrooms and poured outdoors into public spaces. Parks, town squares, parking lots, streets, and public transportation stops were used as places to convene, paint signs, and often conduct the events themselves (e.g., street theater, leafleting, marches, civil disobedience). When I walked through these cities on my way to activists' events, I inadvertently stumbled onto others en route. And when I didn't encounter the actual events, I found their graffiti: sunburned activists looking at a map on a street corner, footprint-flecked fliers upturned on curbs, women wearing Planned Parenthood T-shirts and pro-choice buttons talking in a hotel lobby, white spaceship-like news vans waiting to go live, droves of police officers, delegates on the subway chattering about the clever retorts they had made to passing protesters, political banners draped from downtown buildings. National campaign events are magnets for political activity.

What Are They Doing and Why?

The colorful political atmosphere that emerges around key campaign events says as much, maybe even more, about how voluntary associations understand and seek inclusion in the democratic process as it does about their political issues. This chapter describes that political circus, looks behind the activity at the groups that orchestrate these events, and examines the motives behind the outrageous publicness of their efforts. While mobilization is a common response to the rituals of the campaign cycle, the cavalcade that it produces is not inevitable. Instead, the political festival emerges from the activists' belief that an effective mobilization must capture the attention of the mainstream news media.

This chapter will show that the groups' motives for mobilization are quite diverse, but that their disparate aspirations do not yield different strategies. Instead, the groups almost universally equate mobilization with attempting to shape political discourse. I find exactly what Fraser (1992)

Figure 2.1. The presence of concurrent activist events often meant stumbling on them unexpectedly. Here, marchers in New York City during the 2004 RNC protest the Bush Administration's immigration policies.

Figure 2.2. In addition to activism in designated protest areas, public spaces such as parks and public transportation stations also become venues for political expression. Here, a group of activists sing songs and entertain the crowd at a T stop in downtown Boston.

anticipates: subaltern counterpublics attempting to intervene in the mainstream public sphere. While it is interesting that such an array of associations would interpret campaign events as opportunities to increase their visibility, it is even more intriguing that they almost unanimously sought a particular form of publicness—news coverage—while making little effort to reach outsiders via other routes, such as face-to-face interaction, direct mailings, educational events, advertisements, independent media venues, blogs, and, by 2004, other user-generated content tools.

Mobilization and the Politicalization of Public Space

I don't think I'm the first American to have read Habermas and wondered how he could construe a park or a plaza as a space that fosters the public discussion of matters of common concern. It is conceivable that such spaces could be used in this way, but my own experiences in public settings

Figure 2.3. The influx of activism also brings an influx of police. This cluster of police officers in New York City during the RNC in 2004 was one of many positioned along the route of the massive anti-war march described in chapter 3.

make this optimistic vision feel suspect—not only a counterfactual ideal, but an improbable one as well. Everyday talk often contains implicit and explicit political elements, but how many Americans have ever engaged in rational-critical deliberation over political issues with strangers at a park, as suggested by the Habermasian vision? Yet, in the campaign context, many public areas actually do transform into Habermas's unlikely public spheres. Rather than serving simply as spaces for social interaction (e.g., playing Frisbee or having a picnic), havens for solitary individuals (e.g., reading the paper or smoking a cigarette), or raw functionality (e.g., thoroughfares for pedestrians), many of these settings are politicized in the shadow of the conventions and debates. I offer a few snapshots to illustrate.

Snapshot I: Los Angeles, 2000

The designated protest space for the 2000 Democratic National Convention (DNC) in Los Angeles was a parking lot outside the Staples Center, where the convention was being held. A large stage was erected at the end of the parking lot closest to the convention center, and various voluntary organizations reserved time slots to use it, creating a revolving door of

Figure 2.4. In addition to marches, rallies, and delegates being shuttled to their venues, evidence of politicization around the debates and conventions abounds. I encountered political graffiti, banners hanging from buildings, people in political T-shirts, and discarded fliers regularly, as well as politicos and protesters en route to or from their events, such as this activist sleeping on the subway in New York.

activist voices. The nearby streets were equally interesting, coming to life as various groups, formal and informal, small and large, emerged. My observations as I meandered through the city on the third day of the convention illustrate the way these mobilizations bring politics into public space.

Down by Staples Center, the designated protest area teemed with people—some wearing matching T-shirts and carrying signs, some dressed in costume (I see a "chicken" on stage in the distance), some resting in folding lawn chairs brought from home, fanning themselves to cool down. Just beyond the parking lot, along the perimeter of the protest zone, was a path that delegates, journalists, staff, and attendees took to enter the convention hall. These credentialed guests were channeled through a security screening station not unlike those at airports, while small clusters of people without credentials convened along that very same path. As long as the activists kept moving and did not overtly disturb those trying to enter the convention hall, the police let them be. One group of young people held two large banners, each printed to look like a Washington DC license plate. The letters on the first plate read, "no taxation," the second, "without representation," and the protesters chanted this refrain while posing for pictures. Nearby, a few anti-abortion activists paced slowly, carrying oversized gruesome photographs of what they suggested were aborted fetuses. A small but well-known and very vocal group of protesters opposing homosexuality stood at the corner. One held a sign that read, "God Hates Fags," and another had a picture of Al Gore with a big pink triangle on his forehead. A third activist carried a giant photo of Matthew Shepard that read, "Matthew burns in hell." One shouted at passersby, "If you vote for Gore-Lieberman, you vote for homos!" A young man, about 22, sat at a lone picnic table at the edge of the protest zone, adjacent to the path. He had several magazines—*Time, Newsweek,* and so forth—each with Al Gore's photo on the cover. He looked at me and, nodding toward the antigay contingent, said, "They are frightening, aren't they? . . . These look like the same freaks from Matthew Shepard's funeral." He then asked a sweat-drenched man, who was wearing a welder's mask and carrying an antiabortion poster and a megaphone, why he was wearing a face shield. The man replied that he had to protect himself from "people like you."

To be in Los Angeles at this moment was to be transported from the routines of urban life in the United States to someplace unfamiliar and intriguing. That the protest zone and its perimeter were bubbling with political activity perhaps comes as no surprise, but the entire downtown was punctuated with political action. As I walked away from the man in the welder's mask and the man with the Gore magazines, a flatbed truck puttered by, carrying a passenger who used a megaphone to advocate for clean disposal of nuclear waste. The truck had a large, dumbbell-shaped object painted on it to represent nuclear waste. Shortly thereafter, I saw a truck with a tutorial on its side made up of images depicting "how a partial-birth abortion is performed." And perhaps most unexpectedly, minutes later in the heart of downtown, I found professionals and other pedestrians stopped, hands shading their eyes, looking up at the sky. An airplane was skywriting over downtown Los Angeles. Looking upward, I saw two unbelievably large, skywritten white letters—E and R—but had to take a few steps away from a tall building to read the entire message: "Nader." Politics really were everywhere.

Moments later, at the corner of Hope and Olympic, six police cars went by, sirens on, with officers in riot gear. Sirens were also coming from other areas. I asked a police officer what had happened. He told me that "something big is going off right now." I walked quickly once again toward Staples Center, toward the commotion, and found that Figueroa Street had filled with protesters in the few minutes since my departure. They were at a standstill: the police had formed a human wall between the majority of the protesters and the legal protest zone in the Staples Center parking lot, where the activists had a permit to stand and where the remainder of the group was clustered.[1] The protesters (about 800–1,000 in number) included the largest group of "black bloc" members I had seen, probably 20 of them.[2] They stopped and huddled for an impromptu meeting under their banner in the middle of the street. Looking around, I saw several police-themed T-shirts. One popular shirt was black with gold lettering that read, "Danger, Police in Area."

Standing in the street, amid the thwarted marchers, two men approached me with a portable tape recorder and a disposable camera. One lifted the tape recorder to my face and asked what I thought of the situation. I was taken aback, and before I could respond he asked my name. I told him I was a sociologist doing research and asked what he was doing. He said he was making his own unofficial report and he wanted to interview me. Six young women stood nearby holding two large banners. The first was black with bold yellow letters that read, "don't," and the second, "vote." As I negotiated my way through the crowd, a young man handed me a flier. He said it was for a student organization opposed to corporate control of politics and the economy and that I should check it out. I put it in my messenger bag, which was already littered with the fliers, organization newsletters, and other paraphernalia I had accumulated that day. By this point in the late afternoon, there were plenty.

Further up the sidewalk, a young man in his early 20s made a fake gun with his thumb and index finger and hollered, "Stop! Police! Don't Move!" to a passerby who didn't respond. He greeted the next passerby the same way. This one grabbed his outstretched "gun" and yelled back, "No! Don't hurt me, Officer, I'm nonviolent!" With that, two other young men joined the fake police officer, and all three pretended to beat the "nonviolent protester," throwing fake punches. The mock victim fell to the ground theatrically, calling out, "Help me! Someone call the police! Wait, these are the police!" as the three mock officers pretended to kick him in the stomach. A small audience collected around the four actors, and they began clapping and whooping for the performance. Finally, the "beaten" protester stood and all four took a bow. Then the instigator said to the mock victim, "Hey, gotta love spontaneous street theater," and they shook hands.

The streets around the convention center were politically charged, with interaction often finding me even when I did not seek it out. Although many pedestrians opted not to engage the activists in the streets, it would have been impossible to use this public space—to walk to work or run an errand—without confronting the political expression that had infiltrated these ordinary streets and sidewalks. During the brief time that I have described, small groups were out in the street, a large march came through, flatbed trucks were used to convey political messages, and even the sky was politicized as a skywriter captured the attention of those below. All of this happened during just 90 minutes of the four-day extravaganza.

Snapshot II: Boston, 2000

The University of Massachusetts at Boston hosted the first presidential debate of the 2000 election. The area closest to campus was awash with union members, global justice activists, and Green Party supporters of Ralph Nader, who was excluded from the debate. Even though the UMass–Boston campus is located quite far from downtown, public spaces in the city were still percolating with association activities. On the day of the debate, I took the subway downtown to find a march that was scheduled to take place, but long before I located the march I found clusters of activists.

I ascended the stairs to exit the Park Street subway station, and as I reached street level and began to see the light of day, I heard drumming. The sounds came from 100 or more activists loosely clustered in small, relaxed groups around the area. Some held large banners, and others greeted friends. It was a sunny day and the energy level was high, with people laughing, shaking hands, and chatting busily. About six people, some shirtless, played drums of various shapes and sizes, and a small crowd gathered in front of them. I saw a familiar group of satirists. They were with the group Inequality Forever and referred to themselves as "Wealth Warriors." Three men parodied the affluent in top hats and bow ties (one had a monocle), and three women wore elaborate gowns with jewels and satin gloves. One carried a picket sign that read, "Save the Tax Loopholes," and another read, "Wealthcare Not Healthcare." A mock debutante in a red dress distributed political buttons. Also within view was a large red banner, probably seven by eight feet, that read, "Socialist Alternative Supports Nader for President." Another banner read, "Rutgers Greens." Two women walked by, decked out in nonconformist garb—pink hair, glitter, tattered black-and-tan clothing. One held an American flag with the McDonald's golden arches painted across it. The women also had McDonald's logos painted on their faces. Many people carried preprinted, 11-by-14-inch signs that read, "Let Ralph Debate," in green capital letters, while a gray-haired man held a chalkboard that read, "Free Speech? Sold Out." A large, elaborately detailed cloth mural, comprising several smaller illustrations, was spread on the sidewalk. In one section of the mural two pig faces, each with dollar signs in their eyes, were united under one large top hat, which read, "Corporate Greed," on the band. A different portion showed a fisted hand and read, "Rise Up, Resist," while another said, "Planet for Sale," and yet another pictured Mumia Abu-Jamal and read, "Free Mumia. Free Leonard Pelletier." Another section depicted a marijuana leaf and read, "Dare to Legalize It." Behind me, people started to chant, "Let Ralph debate! Let Ralph debate!"

Most of the people with large banners, as well as several others, were on a grassy slope, while the rest of the group—the Wealth Warriors, the drummers, the Greens, and others—clustered on the flat sidewalk area below. I walked up on the slope and meandered. I saw a giant wedding cake made out of cardboard sitting on the grass. Nearby, two men and three women struggled to unroll long, vertical banners protesting the plight of the U'wa people of Colombia. The bottom of the posters read, "Land and Life Protection League." The setting reminded me of an art festival. Everywhere I turned, there were skits or musicians or big pieces of artwork. A man introduced as a law professor from American University and wearing a navy suit and red tie approached the center of the sidewalk and began speaking through a megaphone. Suddenly, the pavement where he stood felt like a stage and the grassy slope became a gallery. The professor said that the dominant parties were running the Commission on Presidential Debates, that they wanted to exclude challengers, and that therefore "our election is being stolen from us!"

The crowd yelled and applauded in support. He said the Constitution guarantees equal time to those with five percent of the vote.[3] He asked, "Where did fifteen percent [the requirement of the Commission on Presidential Debates to be included in the debate] come from? The stork? Santa?"

As I attempted to listen, a young man in a red T-shirt approached me, selling Socialist Alternative newspapers. As the law professor wrapped up, a skit began at the base of the slope. A 10-foot-tall puppet appeared, sporting two cardboard heads, one with a Bush face and another with a Gore face. A man operated the monster from underneath its fabric body. Someone screamed, "Eek! No! Bush and Gore, corporate puppets, go away!" The puppet then moved through the crowd pretending to attack people. A woman in a long blue dress faux-screamed through a megaphone, "Oh no! Bush and Gore, you're so scary!" as the giant puppet descended on her, reminiscent of a vintage horror movie.

Although it was several miles from the debate site, the area adjacent to the subway station had become an impromptu gathering place, a playful space where small groups of people from different associations mingled with one another while bystanders filtered through. Those convened were not necessarily like-minded, but they shared the perception that the debate presented an opportunity. Those who gathered to perform skits, distribute literature, make speeches, lead chants, and display banners showcased their issues and ideas in a public forum. At other times, people would gather in this area to meet friends, read newspapers, and eat lunch; what differed now was that the people who gathered in this space were activists talking about politics.

Snapshot III: The Sobriety of 2004

The campaigns of 2000 and 2004 occurred in very different historical circumstances. The events of 9/11 produced a chilly climate for political opposition, manifested culturally in the perception that activists were unpatriotic and legally in restrictions on civil liberties (e.g., the Patriot Act). This climate coalesced with national anxiety around high-profile symbolic gatherings—political (e.g., the presidential inauguration) and otherwise (e.g., the Oscars or the Fourth of July)—grounded in the concern that these events may present targets for further attacks. One by-product of the heightened fear of outsiders, the distaste for political dissent, and the concern about prominent national events was an unprecedented level of security around the 2004 campaign events. Delegates were ushered in and out of secure buildings far from the designated "free speech zones" that had been established for protesters who chose to follow formal permitting protocols.

Figure 2.5. A sign hanging in the widely criticized "free speech zone" established for activists at the 2004 DNC intends to call attention to violations of activists' civil liberties.

In Boston, the designated protest area for the 2004 DNC provided a telling example, particularly when compared to the debate activity that took place there in 2000. In 2004, the designated "free speech zone" was a rectangular area underneath the tracks of a defunct elevated subway line. The perimeter was surrounded by cement jersey blocks topped with an eight-foot-high chain-link fence on all sides, lined at the top with razor wire and enclosed overhead by heavy mesh netting. All of this contributed to a distinct cage-like feeling, which was exacerbated by the presence of only one entrance and exit. Armed guards stood looking down from the overpass above, and police with dogs circulated in the vicinity. Standing in the space was unnerving. The *Boston Globe* quoted U.S. District Court Judge Douglas Woodlock as saying it was an "understatement" to liken the space to an internment camp (Bombardieri 2004). Judge Woodlock also said, "One cannot conceive of what other design elements could be put into a space to create a more symbolic affront to the role of free expression" (Thomas Jefferson Center 2005). In the end, however, the judge neither moved nor opened the space, citing the need to balance free speech and national security issues. Protest post-9/11 was on display at the 2004 DNC, and these erosions of civil liberties became a focal point of critique for many activist groups.

The activists' primary response was to reject the use of the space and take their events elsewhere, even if it meant moving farther from the delegates. Marches wound through the Back Bay area and the financial district. Gatherings were held on Boston Common. Faneuil Hall housed political groups, while out front, MSNBC's *Hardball with Chris Matthews* taped from a 20- by 30-foot set arranged in the middle of the major tourist thoroughfare. The activity in Boston was farther from the convention site and less prominent than the activity I witnessed around either convention in 2000, or even at any of 2000 debates, with the exception of St. Louis following the death of Governor Carnahan. But just as I began wondering whether the climate for association activism was chilly enough to alter the public political landscape in a significant way, the 2004 Republican National Convention in New York City was greeted by the largest protest in the history of U.S. presidential elections, with an estimated 500,000–750,000 participants (described in detail in chapter 3). Despite the radically different political climate—activists in 2000 invigorated by the new energy and tactics developed at the Seattle WTO protests, and 2004 awash in attempts to suppress dissent (e.g., permit denials or increased use of protest pens)—key campaign events in both years infused public spaces with political talk and activity.

Activism and the Demonstrative Mandate

Many of the groups most visible in these ethnographic snapshots might be seen as voices of the ideological fringe, but these organizations mobilized alongside more moderate, large national citizen groups (e.g., organizations dedicated to women's issues, environmental concerns, and the like), many of which held sizeable (if less colorful) events open to the public. In addition to the dramatic gatherings in the public spaces I describe, activism also proliferated in less conspicuous venues (e.g., hotel ballrooms, concert arenas, academic buildings, churches).

As table 2.1 illustrates, 48 of the 50 organizations I studied held or participated in activities during the campaign events that required notable breaks from their usual patterns of engagement, though for some groups the break from routine was more dramatic than for others.[4] The two organizations whose campaign events did not represent an unusually heightened level of activity were the Young Adult Voters Association and GenNext. While each group held noteworthy events—one a concert/debate watch and the other a large debate watch party—that required significant planning and expense, both organizations' primary goal was increasing youth voter turnout, and as a result, they routinely organized around the presidential campaigns. The events were the largest of the year for each group, but they were not indicative of "heightened activity" in the organizations' broader context.

I found the widespread interest in mobilization unsurprising, in part because the presumption of this propensity attracted me to the site, and in part because activity was a baseline for inclusion in the sample, even if mobilization was not. But I was surprised by the degree to which the mobilization overwhelmingly took the form of *demonstrative* action. Of the 48 voluntary associations that mobilized around the campaign events, 45 held at least one event intended to be visible to nonmembers, and 39 of those 45 held *only* demonstrative events. In contrast, just two associations held *only* communal events.[5] Eight organizations created space for both communal and demonstrative events, although in seven of these instances, the demonstrative events were treated as the focal point of the associations' work (i.e., monopolizing preparation time and resources). There is a reason that political activity seemed to be lurking around every corner in the host cities: the activists wanted to be seen.

Mobilization almost always involved an attempt to communicate with outsiders, which is a little curious. These groups could have used the energy around the campaign event to draw geographically dispersed members together to concretize their shared social or political priorities and to develop face-to-face relationships. They could have held workshops or conferences. They could have thrown convention or debate parties or candidate information sessions for their adherents and members. They could have held party platform evaluation sessions or convention speech reflection groups to address how party priorities and messages may relate to the issues or constituencies of concern to their organization. They could have gathered members to strategize about get-out-the-vote efforts. The groups I examined certainly saw an opportunity before them, but why was this almost unanimously seen as an opportunity to reach out? Why was demonstrative activity *the* story instead of just a *part of* the story?

TABLE 2.1.

Association and Event Categories (Fundamental Activities Not Included)

ORGANIZATION NAME (ALIAS)	EVENT 1	TYPE	EVENT 2	TYPE
2000				
ABOLISH!	large permitted rally (co-organizer)		picket line	T/D
American Adult Network	bus tour	M/D		
Bootstraps	ethics hour	M/D		
Business Watch	information table	M/D		
Christians for Families	large permitted march (co-organizer)	M/D		
Citizens' Campaign Watch	alternative conference (co-organizer)	M/D	alternative conference (co-organizer)	M/D
DISRUPT	civil disobedience	M/D	participant trainings	M/C
Envirolink	panel of speakers	M/D		
Federation for the Freedom from Religion	permitted protest	M/D	dinner party	T/C
Feminists for a Socialist Future	permitted march (participant)	M/D	educational forum	M/C
GenNext	concert / debate watch	T/D		
Income Gap Attack	member trainings	M/C	alternative conferences (co-organizer)	
Inequality Forever	street theater / march	M/D	street theater	M/D
Land and Life Protection League	street theater	M/D	scaled building / banner drop	M/D
MassCares	debate watch	M/D		
National Union of Creative Artists	flyering	M/D	picket line	T/D
NC Citizens for Smaller Government	information table	M/D		
NC Parents Against Gun Violence	permitted protest	M/D		
Network for Peace	float in legal march	M/D	float and petitioning	M/D
Northeast Union of Professionals	permitted rally (co-organizer)	M/D	teach-ins (co-organizer)	M/D
Pro-Choice and Paying Attention (PCPA)	fundraiser	M/C		
Rights Now	large permitted march (co-organizer)	M/D	street theater party	M/D
School Choice, Family Choice	permitted rally	M/D		
Stand-Up St. Louis	issues forum	M/D	civil disobedience	M/D

ORGANIZATION NAME (ALIAS)	EVENT 1	TYPE	EVENT 2	TYPE
Students for Change	teach-ins (co-organizer)	M/D	permitted rally (co-organizer)	M/D
The Freedom and Equality League	panel of speakers	M/D		
United for Change	large permitted march (organizer)	M/D	dance / party	M/C
United Trades	flyering	M/D		
Young Adult Voters Association	debate watch party	T/D	participant trainings	T/C
2004				
Alternacheer	cheering / unpermitted march (participant)	M/D		
Boston Pacifists United	massive permitted march (participant)	M/D	permitted rally (organizer)	M/D
Boston Resistance	bazaar (co-organizer)	M/D	unpermitted march (organizer)	M/D
Chinese Cultural Freedom Collective	torture exhibit	M/D	permitted parade	M/D
Choice!	concert (co-organizer)	M/D	large permitted march (organizer)	M/D
Conservatives for Reproductive Rights	concert (co-organizer)	M/D	presentation to youth group	M/D
Electoral Gridlock	very small long distance march (organizer)	M/D		
End Contemporary Colonialism	bazaar (co-sponsor)	M/D	very small unpermitted march	M/D
Faith in Peace	public exhibit / memorial	M/D	symbolic walk (co-organizer)	M/D
Guts Initiative	progressive conference (participant)	M/D	puppetry events	M/D
Jews for Justice	massive permitted march (participant)	M/D	pre-march breakfast	M/C
Moms for New Leadership	commercial premiere	M/D		
National Peace and Equality Coalition	massive permitted march (organizer)	M/D	progressive conference (participant)	M/D
Pre-born Protectors	billboard truck drives	M/D	small permitted protest	M/D
Progressive Activists Coalition	progressive conference (organizer)	M/C		
Radical Grandma Chorus	singing / street theater	M/D		
Republican Freakshow	street theater	M/D		
Silled Trades Union	large permitted march (participant)	M/D		
Veterans Opposing War	public speaker panel	M/D	convention	M/C
Women Against War	press conference	M/D	unpermitted protest in convention hall	M/D
Wrath of Christ	small permitted protest	M/D		

M = Mobilized, T = Typical, D = Demonstrative, C = Communal.   Some associations held more than two events. The two most significant undertakings are listed here.

Why Reach Outward?

The most obvious answer is not the correct one. Activist groups had a variety of reasons for adopting an external focus during the campaign events, but attempting to influence the outcome of the election mattered to only a handful of groups I encountered, and *none of the associations chose demonstrative action as a means to help a candidate get elected.* Although swaying the election may seem to be the most intuitive reason why an activist group would mobilize around a debate or convention, the group members offered very lucid explanations for why such work was not of interest and, for some, irrelevant.

Election Outcome as Irrelevant I: Two Parties, Too Similar

For some groups, the Democratic and Republican candidates appeared equally unappealing. Roy, a core member of the Federation for the Freedom from Religion, a national association promoting the separation of church and state, explained that while the Democratic candidates might seem a logical choice for his organization, they offered little hope on his key issue:

> People equate Republicans with the religious right, but they don't stop to think about what goes on on the left, which, you know, for every Reverend Pat Robertson on the right, you got Reverend Jessie Jackson on the left. And people think that the Democrats or the left is automatically better on church and state separation issues, when in fact they are not. We were really disappointed. As far as at least the two major candidates go, both are unacceptable from a separation of church and state point of view.

Nina of End Contemporary Colonialism, a peace and racial justice organization, shared similar frustrations:

> There are so many peace groups tied to the Democratic Party and [many people] feel that, you know, the Democratic Party is gonna make a difference, that voting for John Kerry is going to be different and slowly they're seeing the similarities between the two parties. . . . Even though John Kerry is for the war and wants to send more troops there and also wants us to put more aggression toward Cuba and Venezuela. . . . We wanted people to speak out against the war machine. . . . The struggle on the streets is the answer and voting is not necessarily the answer.

Although these two voluntary organizations organized around very different issues, both felt alienated by the dominant parties and their candidates.

Critiques of party similarity such as those offered by Roy and Nina were fairly common in 2000, but in 2004, with the incumbent president George W. Bush's popularity exceedingly low and discontent over the war in Iraq on the rise, progressive activists expressed "sameness" critiques less frequently. Activists who expressed frustration with similarities between Democratic nominee John Kerry and President Bush often did so gently, intimating that a short-term alliance had been forged between many progressive organizations that might otherwise have been critical of centrist Democrats in particular and the Democratic Party in general. Critiques of the Democrats remained, but they were placed on the backburner in light of what many on the left understood as an unusually critical election. This sentiment was so entrenched that sometimes even those who disagreed with this strategy failed to speak out, because they felt it would be futile. Carter, from the eye-catching political cheerleading group Alternacheer, said, "There were so many people that were in this 'anyone but Bush' mentality. For me, it wasn't necessarily about swinging votes, because I feel a lot of people had already committed that they were voting for Bush, or that they were voting for anyone but Bush." He elaborated that as a result, his organization did anti-Kerry critiques, but not with the intent of changing minds or votes—Kerry was seen as only *slightly* preferable—but because they felt it was important not to jump on the bandwagon of people who no longer thought critically about the Democratic candidate's policy preferences.

Election Outcome as Irrelevant II: The Parties Need Changing First

Some activist groups argued that influencing voters was a fruitless exercise, because the dominant parties' platforms fell short of their needs or expectations. Instead, they hoped their public presence would influence Democrats or Republicans to move in new directions. For example, Jane from Conservatives for Reproductive Rights explained that her organization mobilized around the 2004 Republication National Convention to try to push the platform in a more inclusive direction. Some progressive groups focused on broadening the inclusiveness of the Democratic Party. Dean from Guts Initiative explained that their goal in Boston was "to urge that same progressive agenda on the Democratic Party, to suggest that it can be more inclusive by including progressives." In other words, while one might expect to find associations active in order to rally support for their party of choice, these groups were active in an attempt to rally party support for their particular issues.[6]

Election Outcome as Irrelevant III: The U.S. Political System Is Broken

Other organizations avoided attempting to influence the election because it was the electoral process itself they wished to interrogate. Millie, a member of Citizens' Campaign Watch, a national organization advocating for responsible government, explained that her organization intended to critique the national nominating conventions, which it understood as distortions of the democratic process: "Well, we certainly wanted . . . not necessarily to influence the outcome of the election, no, but just to let people know what's happening with conventions. Everybody's being bought and sold, and this was just a good time to bring this out." Citizens' Campaign Watch objected to the increasing influence of wealth in the electoral process; members were concerned about the advantage that affluent citizens have over those with fewer resources if they choose to run for public office, as well as the perceived impact of corporations' sizable campaign contributions to major party candidates. Since exposing the role of wealth in campaigns was the central objective of Citizens' Campaign Watch, the organization reached out in order to publicize campaign contributions to the major candidates rather than endorsing a candidate or working to support a political campaign.

The Land and Life Protection League, a national environmental and antiglobalization group, also used demonstrative action to critique the existing electoral process. Oliver explained the group's demonstrations during the RNC:

> It was more an act of community resistance. . . . They were not making demands on any of the Democrats or the Republicans. They were saying, "This system, that our political system, does not work. It is a sham. We will not obey. We will not participate and we will not be silenced." . . . People are trying to challenge really the system itself and they see these opportunities with the conventions to do that.

The group members could have resisted via boycott, but they chose to protest so that their frustrations would be visible to both parties as well as the general public.

In the same vein, during the 2000 election cycle, some associations protested the debate guidelines established by the Commission on Presidential Debates. They argued that requiring candidates to have a large following in order to enter the televised debates disadvantaged lesser-known candidates by depriving them of an opportunity to build a national following. I heard "Let Ralph Debate" chants in support of Green Party candidate Ralph Nader at multiple points during my time in Boston; and a noticeable, though less prominent, contingent of supporters of Libertarian Party candidate Harry Browne was present in Winston-Salem. At least rhetorically, these groups protested the system, advocating more for open debates than for specific candidates.

One organization offered a visual commentary about the exclusivity of electoral politics. Jill, a volunteer for the progressive coalition United for Change, described this contrast:

> Down there [at the convention] they are surrounded by police, you can't get in without a pass, it's mostly white, middle-aged people, wealthy people, and up here it's like anybody can come, it's free, there's so much—I mean, we had Tibetan monks singing, and had people from Haiti, it's very diverse, we had Native Americans, hip-hop bands, all kinds of the real things that the country's about, very diverse, very celebratory, very colorful, and fun and free. And that's a contrast to the stuff on the floor. All rich people trying to keep things the way they are, you know. We had puppets and guys on stilts. I like that.

This symbolic challenge reflects United for Change's understanding of the political process in the United States, and helps illuminate why electoral influence was not prioritized more often.

Not Irrelevant, but Illegal

Some groups were focused on election outcomes, but they were in the minority. According to the organization representatives I interviewed, *fewer than* one-fifth of the organizations holding demonstrative events supported a particular candidate, but not even these groups' efforts to reach the public involved handing out campaign literature or waving candidate signs.[7] Most groups with candidate preferences refrained from electioneering for legal reasons: organizations with certain nonprofit tax statuses face stringent restrictions on their political activities, and loath to risk losing their preferential tax status.[8] Susan, from NC Parents Against Gun Violence, explained the way her organization coped with this restriction:

> We cannot endorse candidates. We cannot actually come out and say we want you to vote for Al Gore. But what we can do is present both sides of

their positions. Like, we can pass out information and just say here are the positions of Gore and Bush so that you can make up your mind. It is kind of a sneaky way of endorsing, but we can't actually say, "Vote for Al Gore." You can't actually say that.

This "voter education" tactic allowed organizations to sidestep federal restrictions on electioneering by indirectly steering voters toward candidates sympathetic to the groups' issues of interest. As part of voter education campaigns, two groups produced and distributed "voter guides," which publicized each candidate's position and voting history on salient issues. Guides were distributed to members, posted on the association websites, and, in some cases, distributed to passersby. The less-than-subtle message of these guides was that those supporting the organization have a clear choice on Election Day (of course, such "voter education" also runs the risk of mobilizing opponents). This was the closest any association came to endorsing a candidate, but most 501(c)(3) and 501(c)(4) organizations were more cautious. Legal worries prompted these organizations to focus on other priorities, such as efforts to prompt voters to consider the substantive issues of the group when they evaluate their options in the voting booth.

Ultimately, none of the groups chose demonstrative action in an effort to get a particular candidate elected, even though individual respondents often "divulged" that they did have a strong personal preference for one candidate. In 2004, a handful of associations actively sought to prevent the reelection of George W. Bush, but they were clear that they did not *support* any specific candidate. Indeed, many disapproved of Senator Kerry or felt conflicted about their candidate preferences. For the overwhelming majority of organizations, other interests motivated their focus on communicating with outsiders.

If Not the Election, Then What? Why *Do* Associations Reach Out?

Most groups interpreted the key campaign events broadly as moments of political permeability, rather than as narrow windows of electoral influence. The organizations perceived conventions and debates as producing a dual opening, creating space for (their) meaningful participation, on the one hand, and increasing openness on the part of desired audiences, on the other.

Listen to Us: Voice and Inclusion

Many groups adopted an external orientation around major campaign events because they sought inclusion in the political discussions circulating during the campaign. Most often this meant having a stake in agenda setting, raising issues not being discussed by candidates or in the news media in the hope of forcing the issues to become pertinent during the election. Niles, a member of a regional labor union for professionals, explained:

> Our feeling is that labor isn't adequately represented in the political process. The most you hear about labor is that this or that union is backing the Democratic candidates. Very little is done to discuss either organized labor or just general labor issues; typically, the appeal is to the "working middle class," which actually isn't by and large the working population at all in the traditional sense. So . . . we thought it would be useful to have a voice of protest there to raise some of the issues that we knew wouldn't be raised in the debate. They weren't raised in the debate.

Similarly, Suki, a core member of the Young Adult Voters Association,[9] explained that the group's involvement around the debate was intended to encourage the candidates to think about youth issues: "The whole point is that our issues are not addressed. So, for example, the fact that we don't have health care when we graduate from college, that's not addressed. When they talk about health care, they talk about prescription drugs and that doesn't apply to us as much. In order to get our issues addressed, we need the candidates to hear that we want to be part of things." Efforts like these are more akin to raising a topic for conversation at the dinner table than to attempting to win a debate. In other words, the union and the youth group became involved with an eye toward thrusting their issues into public discourse—rendering them germane to the election—rather than hoping to influence the opinions of the public or the candidates.

Many activist groups had specific substantive issues, such as nuclear arms, morality, environmental concerns, and gun control, which they wanted the candidates to address. They hoped that the debate moderator or a political reporter would hear their concerns and pose related questions to the candidates. Robert, from the American Adult Network, a large national citizen group, offers an illustration:

We figured that this is the time to force our issues out there. If we make a big production that can't be ignored, then someone is likely to say, "Hey, Governor Bush, what do you think about prescriptions in Medicare?" Then he has to answer. He has to respond and then maybe Al Gore responds to his answer. This is just the place to be if you have an issue that you think should be in the platform or at least near it.

Other groups targeted issues that were *already* central to the election, hoping to shape the discussion by introducing their particular perspectives. This is what Graber (1993) distinguishes as agenda building, shaping not what issues are addressed, but how they are conceptualized and interpreted. Marissa explained that while the war in Iraq had received a great deal of attention, Faith in Peace, a national religious organization, hoped to deepen the dialogue. Instead of focusing on the success or failure of the "war on terror" or which candidate was "tough enough" to handle the threat of terrorists, they used a poignant display of soldiers' boots, one pair for each U.S. soldier killed in Iraq and Afghanistan, lined up like headstones in a cemetery to highlight the consequences of war, and to concretize the war's impact in a visually arresting manner. Marissa explained, "There was just so much national attention and so many people coming to the city. We wanted to raise consciousness about the real costs of war." She described the challenge in attempting to strike a balance between a fitting memorial to those who had died and introducing this emotional element of the story into the campaign discourse. This was their attempt to influence the way the candidates and the public thought of and spoke about the war in Iraq.

Representatives from well-established national citizen groups said that the election made the issues their associations work on year after year feel fresh and relevant, and hence offered a rare opportunity to get some traction. One of the American Adult Network's focal issues is health care for older Americans. The organization chose to be active during the 2000 campaign season because the candidates were discussing related issues. Sid explained: "These two key parties [Democrats and Republicans] have not been in harmony with social security, Medicare, long-term care, and the patient's bill of rights in managed care for several years, and since they brought these up during the campaign as items that need attention, then I think it was timely for the association to jump in." The discussion of health care in the election, coupled with disagreement between the major party candidates over this issue, created a perceived opportunity for the American Adult Network to weigh in. Similarly, members of Citizens' Campaign Watch felt the best possible moment to critique the role of wealth in politics was during a presidential campaign, when major donations and sponsorships could be publicized. Millie elaborated, "There was an unprecedented amount of money that was just going into these conventions. So, you bring that to light. It was just a very auspicious time to do it."

Capturing the Moment(s)

Person after person described their respective groups' motives for mobilizing in general, and seeking the attention of outsiders in particular, as attempting to "capture a moment" that they perceived as unique. But while many associations shared an interest in using the perceived opportunity created by campaign events, they conceptualized this moment in different ways.

Local and regional organizations sought to capitalize on the undercurrent of political interest and enthusiasm generated by the arrival of national politicians and campaign events in their communities. This influx brought with it perceived potential for interaction with candidates and a feeling of greater connection to the political process, as well as a qualitative shift in the mood and interests of those living in the host cities. Haley, a core member of MassCares, a statewide, campus-based environmental and consumer watchdog group, described the impact the debate had on the mood in Boston:

> I don't know the last time that a presidential debate was in our state and I definitely think that that galvanized the activist community, not just MassCares, and I think that it had a huge effect. . . . My god, we actually had the candidates in our state. And this is a state where Gore is just going to win, so there's not really any campaigning going on here to begin with and suddenly we had two presidential candidates coming and there were huge protests planned—what a tremendous opportunity. . . . It's a huge event already, it was already there and we knew we could just piggyback off that. . . . There's nothing quite like having the presidential candidates in your state. I think that was wicked empowering.

Similarly, representatives from School Choice, Family Choice, a statewide organization supporting school vouchers, explained that they had been attempting to get people in the community involved throughout the campaign season; they chose to organize a major demonstration during the DNC in Los Angeles because they knew people who otherwise might not have participated would be excited to come out and be a part of the big event. Serena, from the national reproductive rights group Choice, described her organization's similar perspective:

> They [Republicans] were going to be here in New York. . . . It's an opportunity. There were going to be a few thousand delegates, not all of them conservative, but many who are espousing this agenda, and I think a lot of people just latch onto that as an opportunity to organize around. I mean, that's really what it was, an organizing tool. You know, to get people out, to get people talking, to get people activated. It's like the election. It's something people can really grasp and understand and want to act around.

These groups leveraged the interest in national politics to prompt local involvement.

Rather than attempting to prompt the politically reticent to become active, some organizations sought to reach political enthusiasts already involved with campaign activities. In Los Angeles, the Freedom and Equality League, a national, multi-issue progressive organization, held a high-profile panel on the impact the new president would have on the future of the Supreme Court. The group decided to organize a major event during the DNC based on its knowledge that the convention would draw left-leaning delegates and donors from across the nation, and its belief that this setting would be an effective place to reach their target audience. Their goal was to motivate panel attendees, who had a high degree of political involvement already, to return to their communities and coordinate similar sessions. To further this goal, the league distributed organizing kits to each of the approximately 1,000 participants, containing information about how to coordinate forums of their own. The league used the convention context to reach potential leaders who could spread their message beyond the borders of the host city.

In 2000, some activists sought to capture a different moment, the one generated by the global justice protests in Seattle and Washington in November 1999 and in Washington again in April 2000. Rich, one of the Wealth Warriors from Inequality Forever, an organization concerned with economic inequality and the role of wealth in politics, facetiously described the conventions as the "next gigs on the concert tour." He and the other organizers of his group understood the conventions as the next logical occasion for mass mobilization, as well as an opportunity to keep the momentum of the antiglobalization protests alive. He explained: "It was Seattle, this new sort of global justice oriented movement around Seattle and sweatshops and this kind of stuff . . . what was sort of a white movement, a white student movement, linking up with more established, less white people and with a bigger chunk of the movement focused on bread-and-butter economics and political issues at home. It seemed like a very powerful, movement-building moment." According to Rich, the major pull factor for his organization was an interest in bringing the power present in the burgeoning movement to electoral politics. He believed that the conventions and debates provided a chance to use that momentum to gather strength via recruitment of new participants and supporters.

The Seattle protests, in particular, loomed large in the minds of many respondents, especially for those focused on civil disobedience. Perhaps more unexpected was that the perception of a growing movement also figured prominently in the minds of leaders of some of the more institutionalized voluntary organizations that typically engage in more conventional political activities. Charles, from Network for Peace, explained: "There were already going to be protests organized around the conventions because they were seen as kind of a follow-up to the protests that had taken place in Seattle and Washington around the WTO and IMF, the World Bank and IMF, and that it was seen as kind of a momentum being grown by progressive groups to protest a lot of policies that were mainstream for this presidency, and we felt like we had part of the message to lend to that." Thus a few groups understood the 2000 campaign events as an opportunity to further the antiglobalization movement that was first felt nationally in November 1999, rather than as a chance to affect the election or to gain access to candidates in new locales.

Tunnel Vision

The groups I encountered were motivated to mobilize by a wide range of factors. None of them used the campaign events the way the stagehands' union had, as moments of economic leverage; instead they sought to reach outsiders, and did so with diverse goals in mind. The most common objectives included weighing in on timely campaign topics, forcing new issues onto the agenda, reaching politically active people, critiquing the electoral process, and furthering the global justice movement. Given these diverse goals, we would expect associations to use a wide array of strategies. What is interesting is that with the exception of a few groups, primarily national mailing-list organizations (discussed in detail in chapter 5), this desire to reach out almost always translated into media-centered activism: a stead-fast quest for attention from the mainstream news media at the expense of other approaches, such as talking with bystanders, working with indepen-dent media, lobbying delegates directly, or (particularly in 2004) employ-ing user-generated content vehicles on the web. In effect, the associations narrowed the scope of their activities twice: once by focusing so intently on visibility, despite the range of possibilities (e.g., lobbying, increasing member awareness of campaign issues, convening distant members), and then again by treating the mainstream news media as the necessary path-way to this visibility.

This is not what I expected. I entered this research anticipating that different groups would see diverse opportunities embedded in these key events. If the stagehands' labor union worked to get a contract negotiated, what might an environmental group or a civic club do? The groups do see different opportunities, but these varied goals do not set activists on di-verse trajectories. Instead, almost all roads led back to the media.

Mainstream Media Mania

In 2000, there was a significant amount of buzz about Indymedia, which had been hatched around the anti-WTO protests in Seattle months ear-lier. Independent Media Centers, set up at both conventions, were chaotic, buzzing with people having meetings, participating in workshops, and ex-changing information on erupting conflicts between protesters and police. Still, the organizations virtually never described Indymedia as their target or as a potential vehicle for them to reach their desired audience. Instead, they focused energies on reaching the same "corporate media" or "liberal media" (politics depending) that most groups regarded with skepticism and, in some cases, vilification. Indymedia was valued, even valorized, by many progressive activist groups, perceived as a way to find information about what was going on in the activist community that might be invisible in mainstream news outlets. Yet when it came to their own publicity, the groups sought a mainstream audience, although their aspirations varied.

Most groups were interested in shaping the campaign event coverage, hoping that reporters would adopt their association's critiques or questions as their own. Many organizations believed they could transform national debates by using media work to redirect journalists and convince them to write stories on the activists' focal issues. While a sense of political efficacy or a "plausible promise" of success undergirds much political participation, this perceived media openness is quixotic, given (1) existing journalistic imperatives and work routines that compartmentalize reporting (e.g., coverage of debates or conventions and of protests or outside events are rarely the same beat), (2) cultural norms within the profession of journalism that fail to treat outsiders as legitimate political actors,[10] and (3) the geographical separation of campaign events and activist work. These factors make it unlikely that reporters will come in contact with the activists, consider them as relevant political voices, and include them in politically substantive stories, all of which are required for this vision to become a reality.

Some organizations had loftier ambitions and focused not on being *mentioned* in a story, but on—in the words of Dayan and Katz (1992)—"hijacking" the convention or debate news coverage by creating an irresistible lure. Davis of Pre-born Protectors provided an example of this type of approach:

> We got there a week early, in Boston. I mean, you had people, media, from all over the world and they were bored. They're standing around before the convention started. I mean, they're doing articles on contamination levels in the bay. They're doing articles on what people like better, Maine lobster or Florida lobster. I mean, the most inane, uh, you know the producers must have been sending these guys just off doing stories just to fill in their time. You know, we're paying you. We're paying your hotel rooms. Go find a homeless man and interview him. See what he thinks about John Kerry or something. You know, so you show up early and that's the story. I mean, we become the story and you have your message sent out over the airwaves.

Similarly, according to Mark from United for Change: "We wanted to utilize the fact that there were going to be, what we found out later was going to be 15,000 accredited media in town, and they're all going to be looking for stories. Not all of them are going to have face time with whoever the presidential nominee was going to be. So, they were all going to be looking for stories. Well, let's create some stories for them." This vision of bored journalists is at odds with the reality of a highly competitive news environment that is saturated with associations, party leaders, candidates, city leaders, and celebrities clamoring for attention, yet there is some substance to this idea. Many journalists described the conventions as tedious or scripted and questioned their newsworthiness; others derided the debates as over-rehearsed. In light of this, the outside stories—to the extent that they are not tedious or scripted—may be more enticing. Most news organizations sought coverage of both the campaign event and the story in the city, but I did not encounter a single journalist who opted to cover an activist activity—or any other event—*in lieu of* the debate or convention.

For some organizations, the drive for media attention was not only a key objective for their campaign-related activity; it was the only objective. Roy from the Federation for Freedom from Religion told me that his organization's interest in the Winston-Salem debate was actually in the event's ability to attract the press: "Anything that has to do with the campaign is naturally a magnet for the media. You got something to go out to the media; you go to where they are. It is that simple basically." The sentiment that activists who want to raise awareness about public issues "ought to be where the action is" was common, and I gradually came to understand that "action" referred more to the presence of the media drawn by the candidates than to the presence of the candidates themselves.

Who exactly do they hope will be listening, watching, or reading about them and their concerns? Representatives from Veterans Opposing War, NC Parents Against Gun Violence, and the Young Adult Voters Association expressed an interest in communicating with the candidates directly. Several organizations, notably Alternacheer, Christians for Families, School Choice, Family Choice, the Wrath of Christ, the National Union of Creative Artists, and Women Against War, wanted the ears of delegates and other political players on the scene. But most of the organizations sought political influence by reaching out to the "general public." Talia, from Boston Pacifists United, expressed this succinctly: "We don't care if Bush doesn't hear us. Anywhere we show up, we want the press to see us. We want to be seen on television. We want to let the world know that there is opposition to this administration."

Groups active around the campaign events saw reaching an abstract audience via the mainstream news media as the preeminent strategy for goal attainment. In some cases, media strategy and political strategy were conflated, as if coverage were the end goal. As a result of this circumscribed interpretation, association activity in the presidential campaign milieu is dominated by media-centrism, with extraordinary effort devoted to media preparation and strategy, which I detail in the following chapters.

It's Not About the Election, It's About the Media

Activist groups see presidential campaign events as an open invitation to bring their issues and viewpoints to a wider audience. In attempting to reach out, they create politically charged urban landscapes, showcasing an active citizenry that seems far removed from the oft-repeated, bleak descriptions of American political life. Standing amid the rush of activity, it becomes clear that politicians, commentators, and academics who wring their hands over citizen apathy and disengagement are missing a critical piece of the story: this doesn't look like apathy.

There is a lesson here to be learned about voluntary associations. They can and do mobilize, even if their mobilization is somewhat peculiar in the campaign context. In the shadow of the election, mobilization looks like a bewitching funnel in which a broad array of choices is increasingly narrowed, not as activists identify the best tactic to help them realize their goals, but as they decide how their goals might be addressed by what most have presumptively determined to be the required tactic—becoming news. This is true in two quite different political moments, one in which there was an enhanced sense of efficacy for those involved in outsider politics (2000), and another in which such activities were greeted with increased suspicion and police control (2004).

In all this, two themes emerge as particularly intriguing. First, given that voluntary associations regularly engage in a broad array of action alternatives, it is puzzling that nearly every group I encountered approached the presidential campaign events as moments to adopt an external orientation, to design events focused on nonmembers. While demonstrative activity in a politically turbulent environment is not an illogical choice, it would have been equally plausible for associations to respond to the campaign events by circling the wagons and reinvigorating bonds among members and between members and the group itself. Groups might also have used communal events to develop strategies based on political contingencies soon to be resolved by the election; to engage in critical dialogue about candidates, political parties, or the electoral process; or to build members' political skills. I was surprised by the lack of variation or even interest in internally oriented forms of engagement. In virtually every instance, activists prioritized outsiders, exhibiting a nearly universal focus on shaping public opinion by raising issues, providing contrast, critiquing the electoral process, or weighing in on issues open for debate.

The other puzzling discovery was that this desire was not motivated by an interest in influencing the election's outcome. The pervasive demonstrative orientation that I encountered would be logical, completely unsurprising in fact, if the activists understood their efforts as attempts to influence voter behavior. After all, it would be quite difficult to influence voters *without* communicating with them. What, then, could the groups have been hoping for in a presidential campaign context if not to shape the election outcome? If we understand these multiple formal and informal associations as partial public spheres, as spaces where issues of common concern are addressed, which may be involved with other similarly focused organizations, newspapers, bookstores, and spaces of dialogue, we see that the presidential campaign was interpreted as an opportunity to broaden discursive space, to expand the discussions circulating in these fragmented clusters. The diverse organizations' shared goal was to have a voice and influence public opinion, rather than to elect a particular leader. To wield this influence, activists seek to commandeer the attention of the journalists on location, and they deploy a variety of techniques to capture that interest. The politically charged streets of Los Angeles and Boston described at the beginning of this chapter hint at the approaches the associations use, and I explore them more fully in the next chapter.

3

Streets as Stage

The Many Faces of Publicity

WHAT DO ACTIVIST groups look and sound like when they attempt to court the news media? I have used adjectives such as "carnivalesque" and "colorful" in reference to the activity that swirls around national nominating conventions and televised debates. These descriptors are appropriate not because they capture playful iterations of attempts at publicness, but because they point toward the cacophony of approaches cobbled together in these geographical and temporal spaces. In fact, sometimes the tenor of the association efforts was anything but playful. The organizations used many techniques, creating some events that were comedic and others that were somber, melancholy, or confrontational. Their public appearances took many forms, from a performance titled "Republicans Gone Wild," featuring activists in Donald Rumsfeld, Dick Cheney, George W. Bush, and Condoleezza Rice masks, wearing toy missiles affixed as symbolic penises, dancing, and flashing plastic "breasts"; to a street march made up of several thousand union members supporting Al Gore; to procuring credentials to enter the convention hall and unfurling an antiwar banner from the floor during Governor Arnold Schwarzenegger's speech.

I have selected three key events to illustrate the most common approaches that associations used in an effort to interest the mainstream news media. While the events varied in size, location, scope, and mood, they all sought to lure the press. I then describe contrasting events, held by the two groups in my sample that utilized member-focused or communal action exclusively.

A Presence in the Streets

Attempting to establish a presence in the streets was one of the main strategies employed by the groups I studied. The day before the 2004 RNC in New York City, a coalition of more than 800 antiwar and social justice organizations sponsored the largest march in the history of U.S. presidential conventions. Although estimates vary, 500,000-750,000 people are believed to have participated. The National Peace and Equality Coalition united disparate organizations and individuals with a call to "Say No! to the Bush Agenda." The organizers hoped to (1) communicate to the Bush administration and the world that the American people did not support the administration or its policies, particularly the war in Iraq, and (2) to advocate for economic and social justice and environmental responsibility.

The National Peace and Equality Coalition coordinated activists and organizations from all over the city, as well as those who had traveled from afar. It undertook strenuous permitting efforts,[1] engaged in extensive coalition building, coordinated nearly 20 feeder marches (arranging the meeting times and locations of the groups that called for sub-marches and eventually joined the main march), organized fund-raising, and facilitated training workshops (e.g., on nonviolent direct action, legal issues, street safety, and video witness skills). It also made child care available for those in the trainings, maintained a website, arranged the use of space for meetings, and managed countless logistical details, such as housing, sound and stage work, communication, transportation, and volunteer coordination. The National Peace and Equality Coalition successfully gathered a notable diversity of associations and individuals into a dense, peaceful march through midtown Manhattan from Seventh Avenue in Chelsea, past Madison Square Garden (the site of the RNC), back down Eighth Avenue, and ending in Union Square.

I began the day of the march with Jews for Justice, which organized a breakfast and feeder march with another progressive Jewish organization. After the breakfast, we waited on a side street for the National Peace and Equality Coalition march to approach. Young white women made up the majority of the crowd. Some carried large cardboard signs shaped like elephants, painted pink and reading, "Elephants Aren't Kosher!" Three women sat on the curb. One painted a "no-W" symbol on another's face. A young man, about 16 years old, did a handstand against the building, returned to his feet, jumped, clapped his hands together, and exclaimed, "Let's do this!" Others shared his eagerness, looking restless as we waited to join the march.

This anxiousness transformed into excitement as the noise gradually began to crescendo. If sound were visual, the swelling sounds of the approaching march would appear blurry—with undefined chanting, drums, and an undercurrent of whirring from the police and news helicopters overhead. Our feeder march worked its way down the street, making its own set of noises, and by the time we reached the main march, the volume had increased and become clearer. It sounded buoyant. This was not an angry crowd; instead the sound reminded me of being in a football stadium, standing shoulder to shoulder with fans of the winning team. I wondered if my memories of marches past are colored by the fact that my lasting impressions are of their ending, when the marchers are tired and ready for water and a break, but this one felt different, calling to mind Durkheim's collective effervescence.

Perhaps the difference was its sheer size. By the time our feeder march integrated into the main march, I could see neither its beginning nor its end, despite the linear route. Although I know that nearly 1,000 flag-draped cardboard caskets representing those who died in Iraq were part of the procession, I saw them only in the newspaper. The crowd was reflected in the glass windows of a building, which acted as a block-long mirror, providing better perspective on the march than any individual could have obtained while shoulder to shoulder with the other marchers.

The intergenerationality of the march was notable. Some people pushed strollers, while others held babies in front carriers, and the crowd was punctuated with a significant number of elderly marchers. The Radical Grandma Chorus stood on one corner, singing for the marchers, who applauded their efforts, but these "Grandmas" were younger than many of the white-haired women in the march. One marcher carried a sign that read, "I'm marching for their future," and featured photos of "not only my grandchildren, but my great grandchildren," she told me. She was 83 years old. We were still walking together when loud booing began as our section of the march neared the Fox News building. The crowd was fired up and someone started a staccato chant of "No more lies! No more lies!"

As we walked, the marchers offered various other chants, many short-lived and halfhearted, until we reached a cordoned-off cross-street lined with about a dozen counter-protesters who heckled the marchers. One of them shouted something about marchers supporting terrorists, another waved a sign that read, "Traitors," and a third held a sign with two small American flags taped to the top. The counter-protesters invigorated and irritated the crowd. Some marchers shouted back, a few laughed, and I watched two young women share an eye roll. Uniformed police crowded the nearby sidewalk corner. They waited in the wings, gathered in sizable groups of 20 to 40 officers at subway entrances and other points along the route, but it was actually representatives from the National Peace and Equality Coalition who

Figure 3.1. Having a presence in the street was a common strategy for attracting media attention. Here, activists participate in an immigrants' rights march in New York City during the 2004 RNC.

worked as "peacekeepers," encouraging the marchers to keep moving (lest violence erupt and create an unfavorable image). One said, "Just smile and keep walking—there are ten of them and a million of us!" Another repeated, "This is not a confrontational space. We are peaceful." A young man with an anti-Bush T-shirt, who was clearly irritated by the hecklers at the margins, said to his friend, "Not even worth my energy, dude. Not even worth it." As we gained distance from the counter-protesters, the crowd began to relax again, the mood lifted, and we continued in the August sun. I kept a decent pace, passing some of the more languorous marchers, but the march still took me several hours to complete. This dense and diverse march represented the National Peace and Equality Coalition's attempt to command media attention by being impossible to ignore. They succeeded in creating a massive, unified expression of resistance.[2]

While this mammoth, day-long march around the RNC was by far the largest street demonstration to emerge in response to the conventions and debates, it was certainly not the only one. Other groups urged people into the streets in both legal and illegal ways as a means of communicating with outsiders via the press. Disrupt, the organization introduced in chapter 1, called people into the streets in an unpermitted effort to disrupt the Philadelphia convention. As I show in the next chapter, journalists love large demonstrations, so efforts like these made sense. But sometimes the tactics were not so grand in scale; smaller marches, public rallies, and decentralized "days of action" (modest acts of civil disobedience or disruption, often geographically dispersed) were often used as secondary efforts, especially when association leaders were aware they could not generate a substantial turnout. For example, a subset of the activists from Stand Up St. Louis engaged in minor acts of civil disobedience at the end of the debate when the police attempted to disperse people on and around the Washington University campus. This action was part of the organization's master plan, but it was less rigorously organized and resource-intensive than their issues forum, which was held during the day, and the rally featuring Ralph Nader, which they organized prior to the debate.

Theatrics: Comedy and Drama

Street theater was also common, and organizations using it sought to impress the news media not with turnout but with creativity. In Philadelphia in 2000, the Land and Life Protection League used a comedic approach to capture attention. I arrived uncertain about what that approach might be, having been told only that something was going on at Seventeenth and Market at 10 a.m. When I arrived at 9:45, I was able to identify the event's precise location by the media presence. Multiple camera crews and approximately 15 credentialed journalists were gathered outside a downtown office building. The object of their gaze was a handful of people in their late 20s and early 30s who appeared to be setting up. There was a long folding table with a megaphone, a podium, and two people holding up a banner that read, "Citigroup—World's Most Destructive Bank."

A woman walked through the crowd distributing press releases to journalists, while a man wearing glasses created with green pipe cleaners as frames and play money as lenses offered duplicate pairs of these glasses to bystanders. He asked people if they wanted to see the world through the eyes of the rich and explained, "Everything they see is tainted by a desire for profit." The group members began to lay out literature on the table as a supporter walked up with a large bouquet of multicolored, helium-filled balloons. By 10 a.m., news workers outnumbered activists by a ratio of roughly four to one.

These smiling, lighthearted entertainers deviated from the stereotype of the angry, disruptive protester. One participant approached the podium and microphone, dramatically pulled out a large trophy with fake money attached to it, and announced that the Land and Life Protection League was there to present an award to Citigroup, whose offices were located in the building, for being the world's most destructive bank. He listed Citigroup's "achievements" in predatory lending in Third World countries, discrimination against African Americans, and environmental damage. He praised the savvy of the corporation for having the forethought to "buy" both presidential candidates by donating over $2 million to both the Democratic and Republican parties, and congratulated private finance for allowing neither ethics nor morality to intervene in the pursuit of greater profits. The reporter next to me smiled and exchanged a glance with a nearby photographer before returning to jotting down notes.

This opening speech was followed by speeches from representatives of community organizations. One speaker argued that Citigroup had denied African Americans mortgages four times as often as they denied mortgages to white people, even after controlling for income. He also provided information about harm Citigroup had inflicted through structural adjustment programs in Third World countries, supporting his claims with statistics and examples. Two additional speakers adopted a similar format; raising a social issue, implicating Citigroup, and providing supporting evidence for their claims.

The last two speakers incorporated elements of art and interaction into their presentations. The first read a poem comprising a series of statements, each beginning with, "In the name of greed, Citigroup has . . . ." Participants from the various organizations called out the "In the name of greed" portion, and the speaker responded to their call, finishing the statement with a different ending each time. The final speaker led a choir of activists in matching gay rights T-shirts as they sang two songs, one titled "Shut Down Citigroup." As the last song ended, the original speaker approached the podium and said that these issues led the Land and Life Protection League and the activists of Philadelphia to present Citigroup with this award. At that point, an activist tried to take the balloons and the trophy into the building, as the rest of the participants chanted, "Shame! Shame! Shame!" up toward the Citigroup offices on the 44th floor. They were stopped at the door by security guards and peacefully acquiesced. The event ended with an announcement that all the speakers would be available for interviews.

The intent of the mock award ceremony was to embarrass Citigroup by publicizing its practices and attempting to re-brand it via reverse advertising in the spirit of culture jamming. While the Land and Life Protection League was not attempting to disrupt the operations of the Citigroup offices, their intentions otherwise bore similarity to those of the National Peace and Equality Coalition, in that both organizations hoped to make an impression on outsiders via the mainstream news media. The two organizations' public displays differed in their size and tenor. The Land and Life Protection League put on an event with about 10 participants and half a dozen supporters, whereas the National Peace and Equality Coalition mobilized hundreds of thousands of participants for its march. Unlike the National Peace and Equality Coalition, which hoped to capture the attention of passersby and the media, the Land and Life Protection League never intended to reach bystanders, instead concentrating its efforts fully on the news media. Pedestrians passed, and a few lingered to see what was going on, but the "audience" was primarily made up of reporters, photographers, and stringers attempting to capture good video footage to sell to the networks. The Land and Life Protection League used satire to draw the media in and keep them "on message." Both groups worked to be media friendly by creating sound bites, photo opportunities, and, in the case of the Land and Life Protection League, written documentation for journalists and a professional public relations person on-site. The National Peace and Equality Coalition attempted to control their public image by containing conflict, while the Land and Life Protection League judiciously orchestrated a minor conflict with the police that they hoped would get them in the paper. Further, when security guards intervened to stop the award from being delivered, the Land and Life Protection League could point to its symbolic exclusion as a result of their contrived conflict.

The Land and Life Protection League was not the only organization that utilized humor in an effort to reach journalists during the campaign. In Los Angeles during the 2000 DNC, Rights Now, an international human rights organization, held a "people's beach party" on a beach adjacent to a party thrown for the conservative "blue dog" Democrats. In addition to throwing a loud, music-filled party, the group mimicked different politicians, used piggy banks covered with campaign finance reform slogans as noisemakers, carried "For Sale" signs covered with pictures of different politicians, and

listed human rights violations as "accomplishments" of corporations associated with the politicians through campaign contributions. The group used a
comedic approach to raise serious issues. Jake, a core member, described the
beach party as follows: "[It was] really the mood of the prankster. Here we
are throwing really what is an elaborate prank, with everything from weather
balloons to a soundstage, and so just as a prankster is very earnest in de-rob-
ing her target, the people out there were very earnest about getting money
out of politics." Inequality Forever also used comedy as a primary means to
raise serious issues. In their events, participants dressed as campy caricatures
of the excessively wealthy, with fake dollar bills falling out of their pockets,
top hats, canes, pearls, spats, and fake furs, as they carried tongue-in-cheek
signs with such slogans as "Free the Enron Seven."

Greg, from the Land and Life Protection League, explained why they
used a comedic approach:

> It invites people in. You know, drama, humor . . . the action we did out here
> on October seventeenth for the international day of action was, we did a
> New Orleans funeral march through the city. And we had all these people
> dressed in black, and we were carrying the coffin with a big globe in it, and
> the coffin said, "Murdered by Citibank." And we were all dressed in black,
> but we were walking with a loud sound system that was playing New Orleans
> funeral jazz music. You know, big brass band music. And it was so much fun,
> because, you know, it was a trip. The music was really good and it was like a
> spectacle and all these people were like, "What the hell is that?" You know,
> and it was inviting. It wasn't like, "One, two, three, four, we don't need these
> fucking corporations anymore!" You know, it's like—you know, people
> aren't like, "Oh my god, these people are crazy." It was rather, "Well, that's
> pretty cool, that's pretty funny." And it just takes down that barrier, which is
> so often there for mainstream America and the people doing this work.

Greg saw the anger common in a lot of political activism as unpalatable to outsiders, and understood that humor was welcoming. Even if bystanders are not
frightened by traditional street activism—though in the case of civil disobedience involving large numbers of activists and attracting the police, fear is not
an unreasonable response—they may be put off by it. Kara, a reporter with a
secondary newspaper in a major metropolitan area, shared her thoughts:

> I think that, you know, the "Joe Schmo" public would agree that some-
> times the cops are too brutal and overstep their bounds and stuff like

that. . . . But when you have a bunch of protesters, you know, blocking your car from getting home to a five o'clock dinner and stuff, I don't think, you know, the "Joe Schmo" public appreciates their message, you know, when they're personally inconvenienced or, you know, their taxes are raised because of police overtime during the protest or whatever.

Not only did Kara point to the distaste that the general public might have for activists' more disruptive efforts, she also described her own positive response to the comedic approach used by Inequality Forever:

By pretending to be [incredibly wealthy] and having funny slogans and dressing in velvet and pearls and stuff, I think they, you know, it wasn't anything . . . it wasn't what people were expecting to see at a protest march. So they got a lot of attention like that. Then, there were some other effective things, like they had some funny . . . funny . . . maybe that's the key—humor, because there was one group during the United for Change march who had a mud wrestling pit set up and had the fake Al Gore and George W. Bush candidates mud wrestling. I mean, that was hilarious. Maybe that was the point being made, dirty politics. So maybe humor is the key.

Compared to some more traditional forms of political action, comedic social commentary was a popular strategy that appeared to be fairly effective at drawing in journalists as well as people on the street.

Activists' theatrics weren't all funny; drama was also a prominent tactic. During the 2004 DNC, Boston Pacifists United staged a small but powerful walk through downtown. Seven or eight people marched with black hoods over their heads, evoking the disturbing photos from the Abu Ghraib prison scandal. Each person held a sign referencing Martin Niemöller's powerful "First They Came. . ." statement.[3] "First they came for the Native Americans," read one; the next read, "Then they came for the African Americans"; another read, "Then they came for the Japanese Americans." And so on until the sign, "Then they came for the protesters." On each person's back was a small, printed statement: "I am not a terrorist." The participants marched obediently in formation, following commands barked by an intimidating mock prison guard with a drill-sergeant-like demeanor. This dramatic commentary on the post-9/11 reduction of civil liberties highlights an alternative, more poignant, strategy for attracting attention that was used by several different organizations.

Figure 3.2. Many groups used drama in an effort to attract the attention of the news media. Here, activists from Boston Pacifists United symbolically link restrictions on activists' civil liberties with the treatment of prisoners revealed by the Abu Ghraib prison scandal (by having a "prison guard" bark orders at the activists and through the wearing of hoods) and the U.S. government with Nazism (by using a famous anti-Nazi statement that equates silence with complicity).

Motivational Speaking

The use of high-profile speakers was another common approach to attracting publicity. Veterans Opposing War coordinated a number of events at the time of the 2004 DNC in Boston, one of which was an all-star evening at one of the city's prominent historical venues to showcase antiwar efforts and arguments. The event title, "Veterans Speak to the Nation," made clear the evening's intent: to be heard by the public. This event was intended to reach far beyond those in the hall (the majority of whom were members), to communicate with the nation at large via the national media. Speakers included a veritable who's who of pacifist organization leaders, antiwar academics, activists, peace educators, survivors, antiwar politicians, and veterans. Featured guests offered commentary that ranged from movement-building talks in the style of motivational speakers, to music (e.g., a song titled "Who Would Jesus Bomb?"), to tearful personal accounts of lost sons and daughters, to compelling speeches from newly returned veterans explaining why they now opposed the war. The evening was presented as an opportunity for antiwar veterans to address the public, and in this spirit the event was open to all. I attended with a student active in the peace movement, and he practically climbed out of his seat with enthusiasm as he identified activist "celebrities" and political figures in the crowd. Filled to capacity with nearly 1,000 attendees of all ages, the crowd created a palpable energy and warmth in the room.

Unlike a massive street protest, a comedic wink, or a dramatic image, this event was information-rich. Part pep rally, part lecture, the myriad 15- to 20-minute presentations aimed to educate and motivate by critiquing the war from different angles. A Hiroshima survivor told gut-wrenching stories about his village and the lingering physical and emotional damage left in the wake of the atomic bomb. A historian offered a broader context

Figure 3.3. Veterans Opposing War's "Veterans Speak to the Nation" event in Faneuil Hall used a variety of public speakers (antiwar activists, academics, politicians, etc.) to try to bring attention to the diverse costs of war.

for the Iraq war and the steps leading up to it. An antiwar educator talked about his experiences teaching about the consequences of war in high schools and demonstrated one of his consciousness-raising techniques. A former soldier offered an alarming account of being raped by a fellow soldier and the unthinkable military-sanctioned aftermath. A group of 9/11 families passionately argued that the war should not be carried out in the name of their lost loved ones. The event organizers hoped that individuals confronted with these accounts of the damage engendered by war would be moved to rethink their positions. Those in attendance responded well, with cheers, whistles, and respectful silence, as appropriate.

Other groups created similar educational environments but executed them in different ways. Citizens' Campaign Watch and Envirolink, for example, held events that featured panels of high-profile speakers who addressed topics of concern to the organization. They hoped that political celebrities would attract the press and communicate the group's message to the general public.

These three cases illustrate the most common strategies for attracting the news media: taking to the streets en masse, using theatrics, and employing high-profile speakers. But even though the overwhelming majority of associations focused on luring the press, some organizations invested their energies in communal activities.

The Non-demonstrative Option:
Communal Activity and Community Building

Although it was very rare, two organizations I studied prioritized member-focused activities. Pro-Choice and Paying Attention (PCPA), a national organization that raises money to support pro-choice political candidates, saw the presence of the DNC in Los Angeles as an opportunity to draw on star power to motivate its members to make donations. Organizers did so by holding a $250-a-plate fund-raising luncheon in a lush Beverly Hills hotel at which several politicians, including Governor Gray Davis, Senator Barbara Boxer, and Senator Dianne Feinstein, mingled with the crowd. While the event was not restricted to members, it was certainly directed toward them, with the intention of building social cohesion and attachment to the group, in addition to increasing the funds available for the candidates supported by PCPA. As Daniel, a key organizer of the luncheon, explained:

We do our best to provide an ample amount of business combined with an ample amount of social time for people to—I don't want to say "network," but an opportunity to exchange information about what's up in their communities and their states. We want people to have a sense of place, a sense of the challenges that each other faces. . . .When they get together they have a lot to talk about, because we [feminist political activists] are always going to be the underdogs.

Unlike the cases described above, PCPA was not, at least at this gathering, concerned with recruiting new members or luring the news media. This event was about giving members an opportunity to spend time together, fostering their attachment to the association and building the organization's resources.

The luncheon drew approximately 1,000 attendees, who sat beneath ornate chandeliers in a two-tiered, gilded ballroom. Guests were seated by assignment at elaborately decorated round tables facing a large stage. Gazpacho and crème brûlée with fresh berries awaited guests at gold- and beige-colored place settings. The overwhelming majority of the guests were white women in their 40s and 50s, dressed in business and cocktail suits. Before lunch began there was a great deal of socializing, and it became apparent that many attendees knew one another. Even as lunch was being served, women walking by stopped to say, "Nice to see you," and "How are you?" to the women with whom I was seated.

It was impossible not to recognize this luncheon as an insider event. I was asked upon my arrival about my connection to the woman who was sponsoring the table. When I explained the circumstances of my attendance, the woman who asked physically turned her back to me and ended our discussion without any additional remark. Later, she commented about my researcher role to a new arrival, remarking, "I have no idea what she is doing here." I found this surprising because my race, gender, dress, and presentation of self sufficiently approximated those around me; I would have guessed I would be welcome, and if not welcome, certainly not treated as an outcast. But the only person at the table who spoke with me after the formal introductions was the woman to my immediate left, the wife of a governor. The rest of the women at the table avoided eye contact. The elegant ballroom felt like a middle-school cafeteria.

As the multicourse luncheon served by tuxedoed waiters drew to a close, a video began on two large screens at each side of a podium on the stage. Celebratory music played as images of people elected to office with

PCPA's help flashed across the screens. The video was about three minutes long, had excellent production values, and elicited a very good audience response; people clapped and cheered at key points throughout the presentation. The on-screen text highlighted PCPA as an important and effective political force. As the video wrapped up, the organization's president and founder took the microphone to a standing ovation. She delivered a compelling speech highlighting women's power at the voting booth, stressing the crucial importance of taking back seats in the House and the Senate from social conservatives. She received enthusiastic applause and was cheered at the conclusion of her talk, at which point she turned the microphone over to California's sitting governor, Gray Davis, who was followed by Senator Barbara Boxer, Senator Dianne Feinstein, and Representative Nancy Pelosi. The speakers emphasized the 2000 race as a "watershed election" and urged the audience to continue to "use their power" to support candidates willing to challenge the "right-wing agenda." The energy level remained high throughout the speeches, creating a boisterous, supportive, rally-like atmosphere.

When the event drew to a close, guests lingered in the ballroom. Some women exchanged embraces, others stood talking, and small clusters gathered around the politicians who remained. As the crowd spilled onto the sidewalk, groups of men and women in union T-shirts handed them flyers and asked them to wear yellow ribbons in support of their strike. Most of the fund-raiser attendees walked by without eye contact, but I watched Ann Richards, former governor of Texas, accept a ribbon and pin it to her lapel.

In comparison to the demonstrative activities designed to lure journalists, the luncheon's communal texture was punctuated with important differences that indicated an intra-group concern, including a more prominent focus on the organization's past accomplishments, spatial arrangements that promoted participant interaction, and a clear distinction between members and guests. The only other organization that chose exclusive communal mobilization of this sort was the Progressive Activists Coalition (PAC), which organized an elaborate three-day gathering with over 600 events—including plenaries, cultural activities, workshops, performances, and meetings—that were designed by the partnering organizations to address a broad array of topics, such as challenging corporate power, gay/lesbian/bisexual/transgender (GLBT) issues, health care, anti-poverty work, global justice, criminal justice issues, and immigration. This expansive conference was not designed with the public in mind. Instead, it was about building ties between organizations and individuals already working on progressive issues. The program defined the gathering as being "about spontaneous networking and relationship building. To facilitate this process . . . anyone can choose a space on the PAC site and list it as a meeting space for people who share their outlooks and/or identities and/or intellectual interests and/or geographies. Visit the directory to see spaces that others have created or to initiate one of your own." The organizers would have welcomed media attention; indeed, they hoped they might get some publicity and had even created press kits, but that was much less important than their goal of building a progressive movement and fostering ties that would aid the pursuit of left-leaning goals.

While these are the only two organizations in my sample that focused exclusively on communal mobilizations, the fund-raiser and the progressive conference offer a reminder that there are other viable mobilization styles. Nothing about a presidential campaign event mandates media-centrism, but that fact is easily forgotten amid voluntary associations clambering to be heard. How these outrageous, moving, and massive public displays fare in attracting the desired media attention is another story.

4

"Apparently They Don't Like Succinct and Articulate"

Journalists, Activists, and the Battle over News

PUBLIC SPHERE THEORISTS have long pointed to the centrality of the mass media for public discourse. Whether the mass media's ideal role is conceived as a marketplace of ideas, a force that facilitates political participation, an arena that promotes public deliberation and consensus building, or a tool to ferret out and represent marginalized interests,[1] theorists share a vision of the mass-mediated public sphere as central to expanding discussions of matters of common concern beyond their geographical and temporal boundaries.

While the mass media are crucial facilitators of public discourse in general, they are particularly salient for publics whose concerns or viewpoints fall outside the mainstream. When marginalized groups aspire to shift the center—to promote understanding, inclusion, or change—they face a special challenge. Unless they are to become enclaves, they need an opportunity to present their arguments to larger publics for consideration. While "sub-publics" or "counter-publics" may attempt to circulate their ideas by other means (e.g., holding public meetings and canvassing), ignoring or being ignored by the mainstream media dramatically limits their efforts to shape broader discourse. This is particularly true for groups that are less affluent or smaller in size, as they face sizable constraints in their attempts to reach the public via other mechanisms. This marginalization also affects mainstream society, because being open to new ideas and questions is critical for a healthy and legitimate democracy. As Young (2000, 172) articulates:

> Unless multiple public spheres are able to communicate with and influence one another, however, they are only separatist enclaves with little role to play in a process of solving problems that cross groups, or problems that concern relations among groups. Inclusiveness in democratic

processes, then, suggests that there must be a single public sphere, a process of interaction and exchange through which diverse sub-publics argue, influence one another, and influence policies and actions of state and economic institutions.

While Young resists the implication in Habermas's early work that a singular public sphere is the ideal, she argues that a communal space remains essential as an arena of exchange and cross-pollination. The mass media are the institutional spaces best able to provide this service, because other publics, such as religion, education, and public spaces in the physical sense, are more exclusionary. In this vein, Ferree et al. (2002) depict the public sphere as comprising many discursive fora (e.g., scientific communities, religious communities, social movements), but present the mass media as a "master forum," a useful metaphor for envisioning an arena that groups and individuals can enter not only as claims makers but also as listeners and critical discussants.[2]

Alongside the abundant and often well-founded critiques of the mass media in general, and the news media in particular, lie a set of heavily normative and ultimately hopeful visions of what the mass media can and should be in democratic societies.[3] In this literature, even when the mass media's shortcomings are presented along with the counterfactual ideals, optimism triumphs. In fact, it must—in order to conceive of a democratically viable public or a set of overlapping publics, communication among community members is necessary. This is hard to envision without the mass media, except in the smallest of communities.

Optimism about the media is often pinned to a belief that specific circumstances, such as crises, elections, times of elite conflict, or periods of mobilization, create moments when the media have the potential to transform and begin to skew toward inclusion, access, or dialogue.[4] A U.S. presidential campaign is precisely this type of occasion; this one moment encompasses an election, elite discord, and, as I have shown, a moment of popular mobilization. During the two campaigns I studied we find associations clamoring for inclusion, but to what extent do the media serve as a master forum in the context of a mobilized civil society during these pinnacles of political engagement?

Empirical research offers some ideas. Gitlin's (1980) landmark book, *The Whole World Is Watching*, paints a powerful picture of the inextricability of the mass media and social movements. Gitlin shows how Students for a Democratic Society withered under the media spotlight as the news media reported about anointed figureheads, narrowed the organization's focus, and exposed its vulnerabilities. Nonetheless, Gitlin argues that while the news media restrict and distort movements, they also provide a space in which issues are amplified. He writes, "Some of what the movement wanted to broadcast, about the world and about its own purposes, *got broadcast*. . . . The media spread the news that alternative opinions exist on virtually every issue. They create the impression that society is full of political vitality" (242, 285). It is clear that most members of the associations I studied would agree with him. Much like their scholarly counterparts, many activists proffered vitriolic critiques of the mainstream news media but still focused extensive energies on attracting that very media's attention. To use Gitlin's language, their hope was that some of what they wanted to be broadcast would be broadcast. If they didn't believe this might happen, it seems reasonable to assume that they would have behaved differently.

Does the news create an image of political vitality? Does it amplify at least some of the issues activists hope will be amplified? I found that although political activity flourished in the host cities' streets, parks, and community centers, the ideas and opinions expressed in these venues rarely circulated through mainstream news outlets. This chapter will show that despite their media-centrism, few organizations succeeded in their quest for news coverage. For those organizations that did receive coverage, we will see that familiar barriers to meaningful inclusion plagued the accounts, which were often characterized by trivialization and an emphasis on violence and disorder.

This is puzzling. Unlike national nominating conventions of the past, in which delegates gathered, battled it out, and ultimately anointed a presidential nominee, contemporary conventions are relentlessly scripted and choreographed infomercials for the major political parties, offering little in the way of substantive political news.[5] The nominees are predetermined. The speeches are crafted, vetted, and circulated in advance. And delegates serve a symbolic rather than political role as extras on set, micromanaged by staff who ensure that perfectly coordinated signs are waved at the appropriate moments. Quadrennial objections come from journalists who decry them as pseudo-events amounting to free advertising for the major parties. This was most infamously expressed in 1996 when Ted Koppel and his crew walked out on the grounds that there was simply no news to cover.

Presidential debates seem more open to spontaneity, but they are only incrementally less controlled, as illustrated by the 32-page "Memorandum of Understanding" created in anticipation of the 2004 debates.[6] This document, a product of extensive negotiation between the Bush-Cheney and Kerry-Edwards campaigns, painstakingly details the exact specifications for each debate, from the height (50 inches), distance apart (10 feet), and décor (none on the front) of the podiums, to camera rules[7] and the candidates' "freedom" to use the pens or pencils of their preference for taking notes. The debates themselves are so premeditated that in 2004 the *Arizona Republic*'s Laurie Roberts quipped, "We didn't have a debate. We had a dual press conference." Similarly, the *Los Angeles Times* opinion writer John Sexton (2004) wrote, "Not one of these events deserves to be called a debate. The organizers have appropriated the word—debate—and they have applied it to these performances in service of an illusion." The debates of recent elections have become so wooden that journalists, pundits, and the public increasingly look to clothing, body language, and other forms of nonverbal communication for insight. There were Al Gore's exasperated sighs in 2000 (neither the sighs nor the much-parodied "lockbox" made an appearance at the next debate). There was speculation about George W. Bush's mysterious hump in 2004, leaving analysts and bloggers wondering if Karl Rove was playing Cyrano de Bergerac. And there was George H. W. Bush's unfortunate glance at his watch in 1992, undoubtedly causing his campaign manager to cringe.

In light of this, if we imagine a split screen with this well-coiffed pageantry on one side and a cacophony of rather dramatic and often creative political expression from outsiders on the other, it seems entirely plausible that the press would *prefer* to cover the activists, gravitating toward the less predictable, more colorful set of events and organizations clamoring for attention in the wings. Yet this is not the case. Why is there such little news about these groups and their activism, and why is the news that does circulate so prone to exclude political content? I argue that this dismal showing in the news is a product of a set of unwritten expectations that govern the coverage of political "outsiders," which is diametrically opposed to the professional norms and work routines involved in the creation of most political news stories.[8] I begin with an analysis of the coverage received by the associations and then explore where things went wrong, focusing on the complex relationship between news workers and association affiliates as their respective organizational and cultural practices came into conflict. I then turn to consider the implications of this dynamic for the public sphere.

Reading the Papers

The diverse, colorful, and sometimes dramatic events described in the previous chapter were created to woo the press, yet most efforts—be they spectacular or mundane—proved ineffective. This is revealed in both the coverage itself and in the interviews and conversations I had with journalists and activists about their work around campaign events. I analyzed a news archive comprising newspaper articles referencing the voluntary organizations in my sample that appeared in the nation's papers of record,[9] the *New York Times* and the *Washington Post,* as well as the major local papers[10] published in the host city of each campaign event (*Philadelphia Daily News, Philadelphia Inquirer, Los Angeles Times, Los Angeles Daily News, Boston Globe, Boston Herald, Winston-Salem Journal, St. Louis Post-Dispatch, New York Daily News*). This archive reflects both the local and national print coverage of these events and organizations.[11] I include articles published on the days of the official campaign events, as well those that appeared two days before and two days after. The articles were located using hard copies of the papers gathered while in the field, LexisNexis, and the Library of Congress. The completed archive includes 92 articles, which were analyzed both quantitatively and qualitatively.

Initial results regarding the coverage in major national and local newspapers for each of the seven key campaign event cities appear promising. Of the 45 associations that hoped to attract mainstream media coverage, 29 associations or their events appeared in some manner in at least one article. In this competitive media environment, a success rate of nearly two-thirds seems quite significant.

Probing a little deeper, however, it becomes clear how misguided such an interpretation would be. Almost half of these "success stories" involved only fleeting, often partial-line references, occasionally without mention of the organization's name, and with such scant description that I might not have recognized the events had I not been there myself. Only 13 of the 29 represented groups appeared in an article that included their goal and a participant's quote. And only 2 of the 29 organizations (Inequality Forever from the 2000 RNC and Veterans Opposing War from the 2004 DNC) were mentioned in more than two such stories. Taken together, 45 associations invested tremendous amounts of time and energy in attracting mainstream media coverage, but only 2 were covered in what might be considered a meaningful way. The National Peace and Equality Coalition, which coordinated the massive march

Figure 4.1. A journalist interviews an antiwar activist at End Contemporary Colonialism's "Democratic Bazaar" on Boston Common.

around the 2004 RNC, appeared in the most articles (n-14), as a result of media interest in the group's struggles with the city over permitting. Even with all these articles, only two described the group's motives for the march and included a quote from a participant or group representative. It is important to note that this analysis does not included televised news. Yet, in light of research suggesting that network news covers activism less often than does print news, it is possible that this print-based analysis actually overstates the presence of activism in the news as a whole (Smith et al., 2001).

Beyond the Numbers

These quantitative barometers of representation in the news overstate the activists' success, because counting references and even quotes fails to account for the substance of the coverage. For example, many groups that get into the papers appear in "local color"–type accounts. These stories generally begin by suggesting that the convention or debate drew a particularly diverse collection of activists, proceed to list three or four groups either by name or by issue of concern (e.g., "antiwar groups" or "death penalty opponents"), and then offer a few interesting snapshot descriptions from the scene. Sometimes the organizations seem to be included in an attempt to capture the diversity of voices; at other times their inclusion highlights the most unusual elements on the scene. In both approaches, the stories most frequently depict the activists and the associations as spectacle rather than as legitimate political actors, much as Gitlin (1980) vividly showed thirty years ago. The associations and their members lack what Ferree et al. refer to as "standing"; when a group has standing, they are "treated as an actor with a voice, not merely as an object being discussed by others" (2002, 13). This lack of standing is illustrated well in the following (abridged) story from the *New York Times* (Belluck and Santora 2004):

> Tiny the Terrible had a point to make to the Democratic National Convention, so he headed for the designated protest site, a decrepit stretch of asphalt sandwiched under defunct train tracks and walled off with barbed wire coils and thick steel-mesh barriers. "There hasn't been a platform yet that has gone for the midget vote," Tiny, 36, wearing a red blazer, cowboy hat and basketball-sized gold medallion, barked to anyone who would listen, which was hardly anyone. He pledged that any candidate who promised to give people under 5 feet tall $1,200 a month

would capture the dwarf demographic on Election Day. Also in the "free speech zone" was Bob Kunst, 62, who came from Miami Beach to condemn Senator John Kerry, the presumptive Democratic presidential nominee, and his running mate, Senator John Edwards, with a sign that called them "Girlie Men." Mr. Kunst said he was "building a new American revolution right here in the concentration camp." And Randall Terry, the founder of Operation Rescue who once mobilized thousands of people to protest clinics that performed abortions, was perched in the protest zone, too, looking a bit as if he were doing a bitter stand-up routine at an after-hours dive. . . . What had been expected to be rowdy crowds of rallying protesters fizzled into a showcase for the political fringe. Convention organizers, obsessed with security, have relegated demonstrators to a backwater that most protest groups have shunned, and the scene on Monday quickly turned into a carnival sideshow, where most people ended up protesting against the location they were supposed to be protesting in. . . . It appeared that many of the larger and more organized protest groups had decided to take a vacation, too. The largest group to demonstrate inside the free speech zone was made up of about 100 opponents of the Israeli occupation of the West Bank. They decided that the prison-yard-like atmosphere was just the effect they were looking for. "We are doing this here because this is what Palestine looks like," said Hilda Silverman, 65, of the Boston Coalition for Palestinian Rights. Outside the zone, self-described anarchists managed to organize a rally and march of about 200 demonstrators, led by a group called the Bl(A)ck Tea Society, which may be against government but is apparently pro-parentheses. . . . "Wouldn't it be great if everyone rode a bike?" yelled one protester, asserting that a less car-dependent society would save "the blood of Iraqi children." Finally, the bikeless crowd made its way to the high metal fences enclosing the FleetCenter. Some pounded on the barrier, while some pacifist anarchists kissed it. Elsewhere in the city, stray demonstrators included the "weeping widows," women carrying dolls symbolizing dead babies to protest the killing of civilians in Iraq; two people wearing giant flip-flop sandals, symbols of their view that Mr. Kerry changed his positions too often; and a walking corn on the cob and two carrots, carrying a sign that said, "Eat Me." They were trying to stir up the vegetarian vote. . . . Everywhere, the protesters were vastly outnumbered by police officers, some equipped with riot gear. Prepared for much larger and more boisterous demonstrations, the police officers mostly watched the spectacle with quizzical expressions.

At several points in this story, the activists and associations are overtly cast as buffoons. The authors write, "Self-described anarchists managed to organize a rally and march of about 200 demonstrators, led by a group called the Bl(A)ck Tea Society, which may be against government but is apparently pro-parentheses." This disparagement is interesting, not only because it appears in a news article rather than an editorial, but also because it is describing a march of 200 demonstrators—not the largest of political protests, but certainly not an isolated jokester on a soapbox. These 200 demonstrators are not treated as legitimate actors participating in the political process, but rather are equated through narrative structure to "Tiny," the eccentric with whom the authors chose to open the story. The 200 demonstrators are portrayed as ridiculous—from the name of their organization to their political statements. Certainly the Bl(A)ck Tea Society was not the first to suggest a connection between fuel use and the war in Iraq, yet their proposition is presented as outlandish. Even where the authors are not explicitly mocking the activists, those who are included in the story are presented as part of a "carnival sideshow," chosen for their outrageousness rather than their contributions to political discourse. And this is the *New York Times*.

The local color story isn't the only recurring trend in reporting on voluntary associations. Activists and organizations are often taken quite seriously in stories that draw on a crime reporting model, presenting the activity as a threat to routine (e.g., traffic disruption or increased security measures) or as a heated standoff (e.g., between police and protesters, or between demonstrators and counterdemonstrators).[12] This thirst for conflict is something one can intuit by reading the papers, though it is also something journalists discuss at length. Amber, a reporter with a primary newspaper in a small city, reflected on her experience at the RNC in 2000:

> I think, even people who were hostile to the media, they see that [breaking the law] as a way to get the media's—maybe the only way to get the media's attention. I think people even said to me, "Well, if there's not violence or some sort of action like this, you don't get people's attention."

> *Do you think that's fair?*

> I do think that's fair in a way. . . . For every protester there [at Disrupt's direct action], there were two journalists. They're following them every step of the way. It felt kind of ridiculous. I feel like part of it is that, yeah, everyone's just waiting, "Are they gonna do something or not?" I remember the

second day when this [welfare rights] group marched through Philly, and they didn't have a permit. The police were pretty good about that, I'd have to say, the first two days . . . but it was sort of like you were just waiting for the bomb to go off, you know. Like the journalists were just like waiting. People almost felt, like, disappointed, "God, it didn't happen today."

What didn't happen?

The conflict, you know. I mean, I guess people like—you know, that's part of stories, to write conflict.

Dustin, a reporter with a primary newspaper for a major metropolitan area, shared the following:

I have never understood why people say that any kind of political violence doesn't work. If the goal is to get attention, it always works. 'Cause the media is never not going to cover violence or destruction or vandalism. You know, they just aren't going to ignore that. So, I suppose one option, although I'm not saying this is a good way to do things, is to just go break stuff. You know, go riot. If people riot, we'll pay attention. We'll wanna know why they're so damn upset.

The newspaper articles, however, suggest this is *not* the case, that there actually is minimal interest in "why they're so damn upset." In the conflict/ crime model stories, associations usually receive more extended attention than in local color stories, but they are still largely unsuccessful at injecting their issues and perspectives into the mainstream discourse. These conflict-oriented articles are primarily logistical in nature, emphasizing form over content. They tend to contain extensive details about who was there, how they looked, what they did, and whether there were arrests. Often *why* the activists were motivated to act goes unmentioned. The following excerpt from the *New York Times* (Clines 2000) on protests surrounding the RNC in 2000 is one example:

Scores of protesters were arrested in a running cat-and-mouse contest with the police across downtown thoroughfares today as they sought to disrupt the Republican National Convention with illegal hit-and-run demonstrations. . . . With the city intent on maintaining an upbeat convention gleam, the police clearly worked to avoid the sort of full-scale, baton-wielding clashes with street demonstrators that occurred last winter at the World Trade Organization conference and damaged Seattle's reputation. Demonstrators, on the other hand, clearly worked to steal the media spotlight and create street scenes of nonstop political protest as the focus for the 15,000 news workers here covering the Republican convention. . . . The Associated Press reported that at least 280 people had been taken into custody last night. The police said that four officers were injured and 20 patrol car windows smashed across the day of increasing disruption. A score of demonstrators, chanting denunciations of capital punishment, were arrested after blocking the westbound entrance to the interstate Vine Street Expressway north of City Hall. "The whole world is watching!" they screamed, echoing the protest of the 1968 anti-war demonstrators on the chaotic streets around the Democratic convention in Chicago. . . . Protesters representing a score of causes seemed energized by the day, the most tense and chaotic thus far in the convention week. They vowed to deploy their darting street tactics further over the next two days.

The only suggestion in the unabridged article that might give a reader insight into what prompted these protests is the passing reference in this excerpt to capital punishment, which actually *mis*represents the concerns of those active during these protests; some were focused primarily on the death penalty, but the vast majority of participants I had an opportunity to engage during my fieldwork saw themselves as global justice activists. Later in this chapter, I return to the absence of reporting on motives, the missing "why," but for now, it suffices to say that even those stories that give the activist groups more than a fleeting reference often omit the politically relevant content.

The quantitative data also inflate the associations' impact because they include a number of articles in which an activist group is referenced or a member quoted, but the story is not about political issues. For example, among the 92 articles in the archive are stories about lawsuits over the use of public space, reflections on police behavior, and even stories on campaign fashion.[13] This story from the *Boston Globe* (Russell 2004) provides an illustration:

When animal rights activists dressed as farm animals at the Democratic National Convention in Los Angeles four years ago, the police patrolling their protests barely cracked a smile. But in Boston, officers chuckled appreciatively at one protester, dressed like a 7-foot carrot. "Hands down, [the Boston police] are the most good-natured of any of the five conventions I've attended as an activist," said Bruce Friedrich of People for the Ethical Treatment for Animals, the "campaign manager" for presidential candidate Chris P. Carrot. "Police directing traffic are giving us a thumbs-up, police guarding places where we're standing are being sweethearts. . . . This is the first time the police, to a person, have gotten the joke." After several days of peaceful demonstrations, protest leaders and police once bracing for conflict have begun cautiously acknowledging one another's good points. Police Commissioner Kathleen O'Toole, who expects the largest protests today, said most demonstrations up to now have been orderly, in part because police and protesters have shared information about plans and procedures. Other protesters, some of whom spent months preparing for confrontations with police, gave them mixed reviews. Several complained about the noise from police helicopters; at a festival on Boston Common yesterday, the sound sometimes drowned out bands onstage. Protesters responded by lying on the ground to spell out an obscenity. But other protest leaders praised police. At a demonstration against prison abuse yesterday in Copley Square, tensions rose when two prowar demonstrators showed up. Police "helped defuse the situation, not escalate it," said United for Justice with Peace spokeswoman Jennifer Horan. Gael Murphy of Code Pink, a women's peace group, said police have been mostly respectful. "Some have said 'I'm with you,' or 'What can we say? It's a job.' Some are willing to explain their perspective." Boston police Sergeant Bill Fogerty, stationed at the FleetCenter, has seen all manner of protests and has been asked his opinions on world issues. "It's been a very interesting couple of days," he said.

In this story, activists are quoted but have no political voice. No group in this study was organized around bringing attention to the congeniality of the Boston Police Department or the orderliness of the protesters. Representation, then, should not be mistaken for political inclusion.[14] This is a story about the police, and though three voluntary associations are incorporated into the story, it certainly does little to communicate their focal issues to readers, convey what prompted them to become active around the election, address how readers might respond to these efforts, or indicate why readers may wish to consider their views in deciding how to vote.

The newspaper data suggest that a fair number of activist groups are given a nod, but that beneath the numbers there is remarkably little substance. Readers are left with a sense that some activity is going on outside the convention or debate, but are told little about why and only rarely hear participants' voices. Further, articles that mention the associations most often depict them as threats to law and order, as bizarre outposts of the culture, or as passersby commenting on the scene. Virtually no articles present activists as legitimate political actors or include their perspectives as part of an exploration of substantive issues. When the stories do treat activists as thoughtful contributors,[15] it is almost always in a context of contention (especially litigation) over the use of public space and free speech, rather than in the context of debates about political issues of concern to the activist groups or the candidates.

What Shapes Coverage?

Could it be possible that despite its magnitude, vibrancy, and drama, campaign-related activism simply was not seen as newsworthy? Sociologists have long called attention to the idea that newsworthiness is not an objective quality somewhere "out there" to be identified; rather, it emerges through a social process (Molotch and Lester 1974; Tuchman 1978; Lester 1980; Schudson 1978, 2000; Gitlin 1980). Research points to several factors that contribute to the likelihood that a story will be covered, including the organization of news production, the routines of news work, the characteristics or "news value" of an event itself, and journalists' ability to transform events into meaningful narratives.

The organization of news production leaves fingerprints on what emerges as news. Research repeatedly demonstrates that newsmaking is state-centered: beats are designed to cover the routine and nonroutine actions and statements of public officials, who are deemed ideal and fully legitimate sources by virtue of their positions (Bennett 2007; Bennett and Paletz 1994; Entman 1989; Fishman 1980; Gamson and Wolfsfeld 1993; Gans 1979; Patterson 1993; Tuchman 1978). The very absence of a "civil society beat" or a "community-organizing beat" suggests that those operating in these arenas must cross a threshold in order to command editors' and reporters' attention.[16] As Gamson and Wolfsfeld (1993, 122) describe, "Members of the club enter the media forum through the front door when they choose. . . . Challengers must contend with other would-be claimants for attention at the backdoor, finding some gimmick or act of disorder to force their way in." Political outsiders must earn entry, while the state is presumed newsworthy and this newsworthiness is institutionalized in the form of beats.

News is also shaped by the mundane routines of news work, such as deadline structures, which affect the depth of reporting and openness to unconventional sources, and the presence or absence of "news holes," which shape how many stories will be written on which topics and how long they will be. Regarding the latter point, if there are 18 column inches or 90 seconds available, the story will generally be 18 column inches or 90 seconds long. Oliver and Maney's (2000) study of Madison, Wisconsin, for example, shows that when the legislature is in session, protests are less likely to be covered. This is not to say that editors and producers are inflexible; on the contrary, they juggle to create room for breaking news and adjust story length to accommodate developing stories (Fishman 1980; Ryan 1991; Salzman 2003; Tuchman 1973). But the space for news, except in highly extraordinary circumstances, is finite and the play is limited.[17]

There is also research that locates the roots of coverage in event characteristics. For example, objective characteristics of protest activities and "civil disorders," such as size, police involvement, location, and the presence of counterdemonstrators, have been linked to coverage outcomes (Oliver and Maney 2000; Oliver and Myers 1999; Myers and Caniglia 2004). But findings on event characteristics as predictors of coverage have been inconsistent; characteristics other than event size have not always proved significant (e.g., McCarthy, McPhail, and Smith 1996).

Many attribute coverage patterns to more subjective characteristics, such as Galtung and Ruge's (1965) classic listing of news values, which includes uniqueness, size, negativity, and so forth. Far from seeing these criteria as objective qualities that demand coverage, most sociological accounts attribute coverage to compatibility between event characteristics and the journalists' assessment of what is newsworthy, and therefore the question is embedded in a larger field of professional assumptions, expectations, and standards (Benson 2006; Rohlinger 2007; Tuchman 1972, 1978, Schudson 2003). Good "news judgment" is not as much an individual attribute as it is a reflection of the degree to which a journalist (or editor/producer) has adopted widely shared professional standards as communicated via journalism schools, professional organizations, awards, and commendation or criticism within the workplace. Newsworthiness is a subjective, fluid, and contestable cultural construct. The key question is not whether an event *is* newsworthy, but whether an event is *interpreted* as newsworthy. Some of the interpretive work is conscious—as news workers assess the attributes of an event against well-known criteria for inclusion—and others more subtly linked to news workers' ability to transform events into compelling narratives (Darnton 1975; Jacobs 1996; Manoff 1986).

Researchers share differing opinions about which factors are most influential in shaping news content, but few conceive of one particular force (e.g., event characteristics or news routines) as the sole determinant. Instead, it is most useful to understand these varied forces as working together and interacting with broader political-economic, historical, and cultural circumstances to shape what ultimately emerges as news (Gitlin 1980; Schudson 2003).

This literature sheds light on the complex exchanges I found transpiring between journalists and activists. Both sides treat coverage of activist events as nonroutine, approaching it as episodic and contingent on activist groups doing something that is perceived as newsworthy. Because of this shared understanding, the associations I studied work diligently to win journalists' attention, while reporters approach those efforts with skepticism, attuned to the fact that they will need to use their "news judgment" to determine whether the activists' actions warrant attention.

Following the Rules Breaks Them

Gitlin (1980, 3) suggests that movements "become 'newsworthy' only by submitting to the implicit rules of newsmaking, by conforming to journalistic notions (themselves embedded in a history) of what a 'story' is, what an 'event' is, what a 'protest' is." I find that these implicit rules are misrecognized, mistakenly perceived as the same rules in place for routine political reporting, when in fact they are not. Goldenberg (1975) urges resource-poor organizations seeking news coverage to become more like established businesses and government agencies in their dealings with the press. Salzman (2003) advises groups to adopt such practices as creating sound bites, rehearsing answers, and writing quality press releases in an effort to communicate effectively with reporters. In general, the message seems to be that the path to inclusion requires: (1) activist groups doing something that qualifies as newsworthy, and (2) then demonstrating their credibility and reliability through the use of professional-caliber media work in keeping with that done by public relations agencies, communications departments, and spokespeople.

This is exactly what the groups I studied attempted to do. Taking their cues from the news-gathering and dissemination procedures that go on daily between journalists, parajournalists, and subjects, the organizations held elaborate media trainings during which members could practice techniques to prepare themselves to work effectively with the news media. These media trainings varied, but they generally involved some subset of the following elements: holding mock interviews and scrutinizing members' performances, creating and using sound bites, strategizing about ways to stay "on message" when imaginary reporters attempt to divert the speaker's focus, designating media spokespeople, and discussing how to steer inquiries to spokespeople without losing journalists' attention. Many associations also sent out press releases and worked to cultivate contacts in the press prior to their campaign-related activities.[18] They worked carefully to guide their members' behavior and construct events they believed would be newsworthy. Most organizers were aware of the allure of compelling visuals, for example, and strived to create what they interpreted as good photo opportunities. Yet, contrary to what one might initially expect, these careful media trainings aimed at engaging reporters and photographers often failed to produce tangible results. In fact, it appears that they undermined those goals.

I watched, time and time again, as reporters gave the cold shoulder to voluntary associations following standard industry practices. In many respects, those organizations that followed the rules most judiciously were the least attractive to the news workers they were courting. Journalists accept press releases, press conferences, and spokespeople in their routine political reporting, but their coverage of activism was governed by a very different set of rules and practices, which in many ways was diametrically opposed to those employed in routine newsgathering. When activists attempted to conform to journalists' model for routine newsgathering, they failed, not because they didn't conform to the "implicit rules of newsmaking," but because they were following the wrong rules.

Rules for Radicals (and Anyone Who Might Be Mistaken for One)

When journalists looked at activists they weren't looking for talking points, they were looking for *authenticity*. The concept of authenticity has been used in analyses of other cultural arenas. Examples include Grazian's (2003) work on the search for authenticity in the Chicago blues scene, Peterson's (1997) exploration of the construction and performance of authenticity in country music, Fine's (2004) research on the ways in which self-taught artists are deemed authentic and imposters weeded out, and MacCannell's (1999) interrogation of tourists' attempts to find the authentic and the tourism industry's attempt to construct it. Each work renders visible the construction and assessment of the authentic. But what is authenticity? Grazian (2003, 10–11) argues that authenticity refers to two phenomena. First, it is the ability of a place or an event to conform to an idealized representation of reality, a set of expectations regarding how a thing should look, sound, or feel. Second, discussions of authenticity refer to a performance's credibility or sincerity and its ability to come off as natural and effortless to observers. Peterson includes an additional component: originality.

Much like newsworthiness itself, authenticity is a construct that emerges out of our presumptions, beliefs, and imaginings in the absence of direct knowledge or lived experience. MacCannell illustrates this, arguing that we may disparage "touristy" attractions when traveling, and instead seek out authentic experiences, which may themselves be constructs that have been carefully built to conform to our expectations. In the case of country music, Peterson demonstrates that authenticity is fabricated; artists and their labels work to ensure that markers of authenticity are presented to the audience (e.g., use of rural Southern accents, playing specific instruments, such as the Dobro or fiddle, frequent mentioning of band members' hometowns, and being "down to earth"). Taken together, this body of research demonstrates that authenticity is actively sought and deliberately constructed in a variety of cultural arenas. It is negotiated between those seeking to present someone or something as authentic and those searching for this "realness."

As I listened to journalists, it became apparent that authenticity figured prominently in distinguishing the newsworthy from the unworthy in the realm of outsider politics, but it has gone unrecognized as a critical element in constructing this type of news. It is invisible in lists of news values that are generated via news *story* analysis, such as the Galtung and Ruge (1965) assessment. Looking only at the news, we are unable to see what goes unreported, what is unnoticed, and what is dismissed. The hunt for authenticity is visible in the news-making process, if not in the news itself.

Authentic Activist Events

Most journalists I encountered spoke more of the *in*authentic than the authentic. For them, inauthenticity was viewed as a form of manipulation, and they prided themselves on being able to identify it, as suggested by Jerry, a reporter with a secondary newspaper for a midsized city:

You ask somebody in the street why they just put their arm in a lockbox and they'll give a very pat sound bite—"I'm here to put my body on the line and face damage because the environment can't stand up for itself" or some kind of sound bite like that that will be nice on TV or as a pullout quote in the paper. . . . There is a conscious effort of the part of organizers, telling people how to do this. They have workshops on how to deal with the corporate media and what to say and how to not get off message. . . . It's pretty savvy. They teach them how to dodge issues of violence and vandalism. They had whole workshops on this. So, I think they even train these people to sort of keep an eye out for the cameras and to almost perform. Sometimes, they'd be just sort of standing 'cause they'd all be pooped and the police would be all nice behind the barricades. . . . If a news camera pulls up, they get out their little buckets and drum things and they start dancing around and chanting and trying to make it look as if there is all action, all the time.

This reporter "saw" and rejected the sound bites not because of their substantive content, but because they were created to attract news workers and fit with the templates of reportage. Embedded in his recognition of this as a performance was the assumption that it was also a charade. It was the activists' very savvy-ness that frustrated him. The media work— the workshops, the trainings, the organizers' "conscious effort"—undermined their success by violating the authenticity imperative. By following the commonly understood norms of newsmaking (e.g., condensing arguments into sound bites), the activists unknowingly breached the alternative norms that journalists use when reporting on political outsiders.

The antithesis of the event described by Jerry is the authentic event, which journalists witness as intrepid voyeurs rather than as audience members. Authentic association events are interpreted as "real" rather than as disingenuous performances consciously designed to lure journalists. Aiden, a reporter with a primary newspaper for a major metropolitan area, describes one such event as follows:

I saw a helicopter in the air, and I followed the beam and . . . I got to St. Mark's Church and there were thousands of bicyclists there and hundreds of cops, and the cops were making many, many arrests, and seizing bicycles, and it was a very tense standoff type of thing. I thought it was real news, it was real opposition and real conflict that wasn't some cooked-up press stunt. They didn't even pay attention to me.

Aiden, like Jerry, juxtaposed real news with press stunts. Real news happens and skillful reporters root it out, the implication being that a press event by its very nature is inauthentic and thus without news value. Voluntary associations that openly sought media attention or attempted to shape news coverage were interpreted as inauthentic and therefore, when possible, discounted.

At some level this is counterintuitive, because public relations personnel, "spin doctors," and media consultants are an established part of routine news production (Schudson 1982). In fact, most news comes from planned, intentional events, such as press releases, press conferences, and scheduled interviews. These reporters would be unlikely to dismiss a press statement issued by the Justice Department or an invitation to the White House Easter Egg Roll as inauthentic because it had been designed for the media. And they would be unlikely to ignore a pithy statement made by an elected official because it felt like a sound bite. This should not be mistaken for irony; the dominance of this micromanagement media culture in routine news work may be the very foundation of the journalists' skepticism regarding organizations outside that realm. Journalists are used to being relatively powerless in the face of information gatekeepers, so they may use their greater leeway in covering political outsiders to apply their own standardrs to activists and their behavior.

The burden of proof required to establish authenticity may be higher than normal in the context of political campaigns because these "outside events" were spaces where reporters believed they could escape the scripted, painstakingly engineered, and ceremonial nature of the conventions themselves. Some journalists addressed this directly. Again, according to Aiden:

> The real story is gonna be in the streets. I mean, really, the convention is, it's only important 'cause it's the president and the presidential election. I mean, it's totally stage-managed, there's nothing spontaneous in these things anymore, there's nothing newsworthy, there's no brokered convention. . . . It's his [George W. Bush's] second term, so the vice president's already known, the cabinet's in place. So, I've been saying, look, the real story is gonna be in the streets.

The stifling lack of spontaneity in electoral politics emerged in other interviews in less direct ways. In one revealing conversation, Dustin, a journalist who reported from both the convention hall and from the streets, described his reaction when Al Sharpton broke from the script onstage during the 2004 DNC: "I actually wrote some stuff about the Al Sharpton thing 'cause I kind of said, you know, 'Holy shit, this is big stuff, this is actually sort of substantive—it's not—hasn't been vetted. This is real, authentic [sic] reactions he's getting!'" Dustin was excited by Sharpton's transgression, recognizing that the politician was speaking freely and that the audience, which is implicated in these political spectacles as an essential element of the performance, had broken script as well, clapping and cheering in earnest enthusiasm, outside the scheduled applause breaks.

Fed up with the slick PR of electoral politics, many journalists approached their reporting outside the conventions and debates as an opportunity to tell an unscripted story. As a consequence, they often found the associations' diligent impression management tedious. Lucy, a reporter with a secondary newspaper for a major metropolitan area, provided an example:

> [Choice] always has, like, a spokesperson and they always speak like they've been told exactly what to say. . . . And a lot of times in politicians you get that. But, like, you'd hope that in something that's supposed to be more real and human and an expression of outrage or whatever that they'd be expressing something from the heart rather than something they downloaded from the official website. . . . You don't have to be a journalist to know when someone's giving you the company lines.

The convention was covered regardless of its scriptedness, but many outside organizations staged events that were not covered because they did not reach the journalists' threshold of authenticity. News organizations are bureaucratically oriented to take press statements from public officials—this is one of the pillars of political reporting—but these norms are not in place when the political actors are outsiders.

In order for an activist event to be authentic, it also needs to be outside. The Northeast Union of Part-Time Professionals organized two events during the presidential debate in Boston in 2000. Their primary event was a moderately sized, mildly disruptive rally in downtown Boston, for which they received some light news coverage, namely, a short news radio piece. Their second event was a teach-in series cosponsored by Students for Change, which received no coverage. Harry, a core member of the union, commented:

The *Globe* almost covered us [at the teach-ins], but decided not to. The *Globe* said, "When there's some conflict, call us." Typical journalist kind of thing. We did have press releases, but they didn't cover it. They don't want to cover political education, right? That's not a story! But, they [the teach-ins] were all of very, very high quality. . . . It wasn't just a bunch of people who wanted to be idiots and run out into the street and make noise, or a ruckus, you know? We had a large group of students, and others, sitting around and talking seriously about how to confront these pressing social issues. The media doesn't want that. It's very sad really, that in order for the disenfranchised to get press they have to break the law. The story could have been, you know, "Youth not apathetic after all," or "Progressive social issues still matter," or a dozen other things. I could come up with a list of angles.

When voluntary organizations held "indoor events"—teach-ins, speaker panels, forums, debate viewing parties, and the like—they routinely became what Fishman (1982) calls "nonevents." Fishman sees nonevents as those occurrences that are not part of the routine functioning of the institutions that reporters are assigned to cover, but the nonevent concept is useful for understanding the political outsiders' experiences as well. Editors' and reporters' expectations of newsworthy political activities draw heavily on images of protest and rarely encompass community meetings or intellectual discussions.[19] When I asked journalists questions about voluntary associations, indoor activism was never mentioned. Listening to the reporters, it is as if every association activity around the debates and conventions was a protest or a march; all the others were nonevents. In fact, many reporters were literally assigned to cover "protest," "action in the streets," or "outside events," narrowing the boundary of what counts as a newsworthy activism. This suggests that the scheme of interpretation is defined by the editor and by newsroom routines, such as the ways in which staff are used, as much as it is by a more micro-level sense of what counts as relevant.

One might argue that indoor events are simply less visible than outdoor ones and therefore lose out in the competition for news coverage. I don't think this is necessarily the case. In fact, some reporters who were assigned to cover extra-convention happenings wrote incredibly esoteric stories. One journalist I spoke with in 2004, for example, wrote a feature about "where Republicans could find sand in New York." The news environment is competitive, but the fact remains that association events lacking dramatic flair do not interest most news workers. When asked about the process of determining which events to check out, Shane, a national news-magazine reporter, explained:

> It's a tough call, but generally for me, and most journalists, they look for events that are going to involve a lot of people and that are going to have some sort of controversial edge to them or, sort of sadly, some sort of sex appeal to them. So, if you have a bunch of Hollywood stars at a Ralph Nader rally, that's going to draw folks, but also if you've got a thousand angry ironworkers who are protesting, that is going to draw me more than a thoughtful symposium on whether to open the Alaskan wilderness [to oil drilling]. I mean, I look for action, energy, and I think most people are looking for something where real people are involved where there is some sort of real folks out making some noise, doing something.

"Action" in this sense means physical action; debating public issues such as the Alaskan wilderness is not compelling to journalists. Despite the very different types of organizations in my sample, most of the reporters' quotes here have been about protesters. This is not an oversight or coincidence, but rather a reflection of their assignments and perceptions of what group political action looks like.

Because journalists mentioned indoor activities so rarely, I asked about them. Predictably, the reporters indicated little interest in such events. Here, Kris, a reporter with a primary newspaper for a midsized city, struggles to offer advice for associations trying to capture media attention:

> Shut down a highway, I don't know. I think getting angry won't help. Maybe having a forum and generally handing out information that is educational and really says this is why we are here, this is why this is a concern, this is why it should be your concern. That would maybe be effective at drawing media, but on the other hand, we didn't cover that type of stuff tonight and if someone shuts down a highway, that would definitely get your attention. The problem is then you are going to tick off a lot more people. I don't know if the media would so much go for a forum, but it would be effective. I don't know. It's sort of a catch-22.

In an effort to attract media attention, many organizations held substantial indoor events, including a debate viewing party in a movie theater to promote youth political engagement, a concert featuring pop stars to benefit pro-choice candidates, and informative panels featuring elected officials, community organizers, and researchers discussing a wide range of topics. But these events fared poorly with journalists. The directive to association leaders is unclear. While the disruptive events are more likely to be covered, journalists write about the disruption itself—the element of the activity they interpret as newsworthy—and rarely cover the issues that prompted the event in the first place.

Disrupt, United for Change, Boston Resistance, and the National Peace and Equality Coalition—two organizations holding large permitted marches and two engaging in civil disobedience—all achieved significant quantitative representation in the news archive articles. Each organization appeared in at least 10 different stories. Even so, these stories very rarely included the motives behind the groups' activities or quoted their members. United for Change, for example, appeared in 11 articles, but not a single one included a motive and a quote, and 9 of them never even mentioned the reason for the march. While reporters determined that the events held by these four associations were newsworthy despite their staged nature, there was a catch-22. Naomi, a reporter for national newsmagazine, described the dilemma as follows:

> I did try quite hard to get the issues out that people were protesting, but there definitely—I felt like there was a double message because a lot of the protesters would say that they really wanted the press to cover these issues, but then they were also very clear that they were precipitating these events that were "newsworthy." So, I do need to write about the news they create, you know, and I do worry that what I write gets read. So, you sort of try to balance between the arrests and things like that which people really seek out and then the issues that people were getting arrested for and they chose to get arrested, so it's wasn't—they knew that that was newsworthy and got themselves into that bind. . . . They staged the event to get publicity and then they don't want you to write about the event that they designed. I don't know. They tie my hands and then blame me for it. It's frustrating.

Naomi described a zero-sum game in which conflict or disruption pushes information about activists' motives out of the story. Yet in all but the shortest articles, it is difficult to make a convincing case that such pertinent information could not also be included. She imagined her readers as interested in arrests, but it is equally plausible that readers might want to know *why* so many people felt compelled to close down a street.

Further, the absence of violence or conflict does not then magically free space that journalists use to address the event's political substance. On the contrary, the press has such a powerful interest in reporting conflict and violence that when activists are peaceful, the story often becomes about the *absence* of violence or conflict, the logistics of protest, or both. Conflict does not steal the spotlight; it owns it. Juan, a reporter with a primary newspaper for a major metropolitan area, echoes this point:

> I contributed to a lot of stories, but one story that I played a bigger role in was how the protesters tried to police themselves and control divisions and tensions within a group so that their message didn't get kidnapped by sort of tension with police. . . . Because anytime there was a flare-up between protesters and police, that became the story, and secondary was exactly what these people were protesting. . . . It diminished all the thought and time they had put into what they were protesting as soon as there was a confrontation with police because that became the story. So, I worked on a story, and it got in, about how protesters control themselves and police themselves.

He shared this experience without so much as a hint of irony. What exactly *was* this group protesting? Didn't Juan's readers wonder? Omitting the "why" is the standard practice of reporters, but this omission has more to do with a history of journalistic apprehensiveness around objectivity than it does with word count.[20]

Authentic Activists

Journalists evaluate *events* as authentic or inauthentic, and they also evaluate *sources* in these terms. As journalists consider informants, they interpret anything that seems too tightly controlled as manipulative. Wanting to avoid being tricked by people who aren't being "real," they generally disregard these perceived imposters. Liam, a reporter with a secondary newspaper for a major metropolitan area, made the following comment about an anarchist collective that was active during the 2004 DNC in Boston:

> They had some sort of spokesman. Some of the other people were kind of reticent to speak with us. . . . I find it a little heavy-handed. I think it's—I think the protesters are like any other organization in the sense that they want to centralize and streamline their message. And I'm really conscious

of not wanting to get spun, of wanting honesty and spontaneity and to um, I guess characterize an organization as I see it. . . . They see the media more as a tool that they can use as they want.

Liam perceived the group's official statements as deceptive. He was wary of the spokesperson whose message he interpreted as a staged performance designed to mislead him.

In sum, prepared statements are welcome from those in positions of power, be that power political, economic, or celebrity, but rejected when they come from those in more marginalized positions. If the district attorney gives a statement that a reporter feels is contrived, he or she may attempt to find additional sources, but the journalist is unlikely to exclude the district attorney's statement or opt not to cover the event. This power dynamic is reversed when a story is more amorphous, such as when a reporter is assigned to cover "action in the streets" on the eve of a debate, or when potential sources are abundant, eager to be interviewed, and seen as interchangeable. Journalistic autonomy is far greater when covering political outsiders, particularly if many of them are available.[21] In fact, what is unusual here is not that journalists are skeptical of association representatives, their statements, and their activities, but that they are able to exercise less discretion when covering public officials' activities.[22]

This poses an interesting problem for both activists and reporters. For activist groups, the problem is that by shaping their public appearances to conform to prevailing journalistic norms, such as the use of sound bites, they jeopardize their groups' legitimacy as activists and leave reporters cold. Jessie, a reporter with a secondary newspaper for a midsized city, shared:

> There was one young woman who had clearly gotten some press. I think she was with the Young Communist Party or something like that and she was . . . very polished, and I think she mentioned she had been in some other articles. You do kind of try to stay away from folks like that who are used to the attention and very polished . . . but then you had this guy who lost his son. I don't think he even spoke much English. So there, not very polished at all, but obviously very eloquent and heartfelt in his comments . . . and you want to get what his story is.

Jessie defined "polished" not as informed but as inauthentic, and subsequently rejected the well-prepared woman as a potential source. This was complicated by the fact that the young woman was the spokesperson for her organization. As part of her association's media strategy, other group members, fearful of being misrepresented, were unwilling to talk with journalists and repeatedly directed reporters to the spokeswoman. As a result of the interplay between the association's media strategy and the reporter's skepticism, the voices of association members and ultimately the organization's message were excluded from the story.

Although the subject came up infrequently, a few activists I spoke with had become sensitized to the media's distaste for association efforts at spin control. I had one impromptu but revealing discussion with an activist in Boston whose organization recognized that journalists were not responding well to its approach and attempted to adapt:

> He [Kevin] also told me that now [his group] is training protesters to try to sound less polished in response to media complaints that the answers are too pat and practiced. Now they teach them to try to be more spontaneously articulate and to be well versed on the issues, but not to give the impression that they have thought of these answers in advance. He joked, "Apparently they don't like succinct and articulate." (Field notes, October 2, 2000)

Kevin's group began rehearsing spontaneity in an effort to ensure that participants remained on message while also satisfying those who sought to interview them.

The authenticity imperative also creates a problem for journalists. Several reporters, including Molly, who works for a wire service, described a process of shopping for informants based on their expectation that activist statements should be natural, sincere, and authentic:

> Well, I was pretty focused on just trying to get a few quotes to send in [to the writer] and, seriously, the first four or five people I spoke with gave me these crappy, memorized sound bites. It was like a bad telemarketer, you know [laughs], where you can practically hear the typed script through the phone [laughs]. I could completely envision them going over these things at their meetings, again and again. I mean, I totally understand, you know. They are trying to get their concern out, but I just want something real, not a walking press release. So, fine, whatever, get it off your chest, but I'm not sending that in. . . . I just stuck with it and kept working the crowd.

This impasse proved consequential. In effect, sensing inauthenticity often propelled journalists to keep foraging for a source until they found someone they interpreted as genuine. The paradox is that most of the organizations had been so diligent about media training that the respondents the journalists eventually determined to be authentic were often quite marginal to the association, or they would be "on message," too.

While it may seem as though journalists were finding the exact opposite of what they were seeking, many had a preconceived story in mind and were looking to place people in the character positions they had envisioned. They filled gaps in their story almost by audition, waiting for someone to give the type of quote they were looking for, rather than attempting to develop a deep understanding of the organizations, their issues, or their activities. Bennett (2007) describes the prevalence of formulas in newsmaking; Schudson (1982), Zelizer (1993), and Tuchman (1978) describe journalists as encountering the world as a series of stories; and Jacobs (1996) demonstrates the way narrative emplotment of an event helps determine the story's perceived newsworthiness and its eventual form. My analysis supports these assessments and suggests that journalists make sense of unfolding events by placing them into templates; the writers seek to populate their stories with the characters they have deemed essential to the story, even when their drive to typecast is thwarted. In other words, perhaps the fact that journalists' evaluations take them from center to margin does not undercut their objectives at all; rather, quite the opposite, these evaluations meet the journalists' objectives, enabling them to write a story that reinscribes their preexisting expectations. They create a story that they perceive as capturing the authenticity of a moment, and it does; it captures those idealized expectations and representations of reality so aptly outlined in earlier work on authenticity.

One of these expectations is that "real" activists are politically driven as a result of personal connection to an issue. Reporters preferred sources who discuss issues as individuals with stories to share, rather than as publicly minded advocates. This is primarily because the journalists were not looking to write about issues or about associations, they were looking to tell stories about individuals. When I asked Nick, a reporter for a prominent public radio news program, if he had initiated contact with any groups as he prepared to cover the protests surrounding the Boston debate in 2000, he curtly corrected me, "Not with groups. With individuals. I wanted to do portraits of protesters." His correction and our discussion that followed pointed to the journalists' preference for sources who speak not as representatives of a group but as individuals sharing personal stories.

Publicly minded speech—whether it involved expressing concern for the common good or sharing a collectively held perspective on a public issue—was routinely devalued and often discarded by reporters covering voluntary associations and their activities. In fact, journalists described public-spirited talk as the veneer they needed to peel away in order to get the story they wanted to write. Juan described this distinction:

> Most of the groups had organizers. As soon as they identified us as re-porters they would hand us literature, would ask us if we understood what the protest was about—really tried to make sure that we knew what they stood for and why it mattered. . . . Other people seemed to have interest-ing takes. I found most interesting was why somebody individually would be involved. I know, let's say, corporate influence is a problem in Ameri-can politics or environmental destruction is a problem in a lot of places—but why do you care about that and why did you decide to sort of steer your life toward that cause? . . . I thought that was interesting . . . talking to people about sort of what got them fired up. You don't meet a lot of people in your day-to-day life that are really sort of living a cause.

Juan's story *may* ultimately mention the issues his subjects want to publi-cize, but for him the issues do not merit a story on their own, at least not when activists raise them. This is linked to authenticity in important ways, as the activists who are perceived as truthful, forthright, and open are those who speak in ways that link more explicitly to their own self-interest. Shar-ing a story he found particularly meaningful, Juan later explained: "There was a march to Rampart [police] Station. A lot of people in that area have had problems with the police department. . . . So, I thought that was in-teresting. I talked to people that actually had to sort of confront the issues that they were protesting. It wasn't abstract, but it was very concrete what they were living with." These preferred victim-activists exist in opposition to their foil, disconnected do-gooders who advocate for causes that do not affect them directly or who address concerns that do affect their lives but speak about them solely as public issues.

Eliasoph (1998) details a fascinating transformation from activists who speak in publicly minded ways in private settings to activists who speak in private, self-interested ways in public settings. This would be hard to understand if not for her observation, further supported by my data, that journalists ignore attempts at more publicly minded types of speech. I found that some activist groups deployed the power of personal narratives as a strategy to engage others, but far more often I found groups resolutely determined to keep the big picture at the forefront.[23] These organizations worked diligently to help their members articulate their concerns in publicly minded ways. This turned off some reporters and propelled them toward those groups, or, more accurately, those individuals, more apt to offer the type of accounts they hoped to include.

The very best sources are those willing to share their emotions in addition to their experiences. Aiden shared his approach to covering the massive march in New York coordinated by the National Peace and Equality Coalition: "I know from experience with these types of things, what really makes it into the paper, and what we're looking for, and what we want, is a description of activities, actions, and behavior, mixed in with quotes too to get some sense of what the *individuals* within the crowd are *feeling*" (emphasis added). He could as easily have been interested in what motivated the participants, what they organized around or planned for the future, but it is "feelings," those intimacies of human experience, that take precedence. This preference for access to activists' inner lives focuses the story on the personal rather than on the public elements of activism, and stands at odds with the way associations have worked to professionalize their media work. Fearing they will be perceived as irrational, ill-informed, or extremist, media teams and spokespeople often deliberately bury their emotions under a carefully erected architecture of cool, reasoned analysis. Journalists interpret this professionalism as the antithesis of authenticity. It is a fine line to walk, because fervor simultaneously attracts and repels the news media. Too little passion and the associations are inauthentic, too much and they are zealots.

The Parameters of Political Acceptability

Authenticity is not the only filter journalists use when deciding what to cover. Associations must also be interpreted as politically *reasonable* if they wish to appear in print without being ridiculed. What does it mean to be politically reasonable? Journalists prefer organizations that tackle one issue at a time and present "plausible" solutions to "reasonable" concerns (taking issue with capitalism, for example, relegates an organization to an eye roll). Because these preferences often prove a poor fit for association concerns and objectives, they can create a communicative impasse between journalists, whose work to obtain good stories is repeatedly thwarted by association efforts, and association members, who are befuddled by the news media's unwillingness to give them the kind of coverage they want.

Part of being reasonable is providing simple, clearly articulated messages. Coalitions of diverse organizations and individual organizations raising multiple issues often troubled reporters' templates because they did not appear to have a clear message. The coexistence of multiple messages was usually interpreted as the *absence* of any message, as Dick, a reporter with a primary newspaper for a major metropolitan area, illustrates:

> What was difficult for people to grasp was walking out onto the parkway that day [before the RNC in 2000] and seeing every issue under the sun being shouted about. Everything from Say No to Breast Feeding to Free Mumia to, there was even a group in support of Americans who died defending the old dictatorial South Vietnamese government. There was just weird stuff and in a situation like that, the message that they are trying to put across comes across as just garbled. It becomes hard to report coherently, readers—most of the e-mails I got after those protests—were saying, "Well, what do they want?" "Why didn't you tell us what they were after?" Well, I would tell you if they would have told me. They just, they were all over the map.

In the presence of multiple organizations working together in these two marches, many reporters saw fragmentation and discord rather than commonality.

In other cases, confusion emerged as a by-product of geographic proximity, with the simultaneous use of designated "free speech zones" or public spaces giving reporters the erroneous impression that unrelated groups were collaborating. Brenda from Stand Up St. Louis felt this happened to their organization at the St. Louis debate in 2000:

> They [the local paper] just kind of talked about all the groups who were out there for anything and they didn't really make a distinction between those and Stand Up St. Louis—they just started describing protesters who they ran into. There were some across the way in the pen . . . with all kinds of signs and they started talking about those protesters and didn't distinguish them from our group and so they made it sound like people were just out there doing anything.

Similarly, United Trades organized a mass leafleting of downtown Philadelphia at the 2000 RNC, with clusters of representatives in yellow T-shirts stationed on more than 25 corners within a one-mile radius. Even with their distinctive dress, the union members were lumped in with others who were also out on the busy city streets. Franklin from United Trades blamed the press for not taking more initiative:

> Many of the reports wrote that there were so many issues that nothing was defined. I mean, that is not correct. You could have taken an interview with me or some other labor person and understood the labor reasons for being there. You could have taken the Buddhist monks and Free Tibet folks and interviewed someone there, but what they did was they took the whole thing and said that there wasn't one consolidated issue, but there are many issues in this country.

Franklin and Brenda both described their frustration with journalists who depicted their efforts as disorganized or confused, feeling that they did not take time to understand the situation adequately before writing their stories. It is difficult to know how much responsibility for this miscommunication falls on organizations that fail to streamline their messages and how much falls on journalists who do not probe deeply enough to uncover the distinctions among groups, but the outcome frustrates both sides.

Some associations communicated their concerns clearly but found that broad, social-structural critiques fell on deaf ears. Loren from Disrupt expressed his intense frustration with the coverage his organization received after their efforts at the 2000 Republican National Convention:

> So much of the coverage just said things like, "Protesters gathered for a range of causes" or "protesting every issue under the sun." Things like that give the impression that we are all out there talking about different things. They don't get it—that these are all the same thing. It's not fractured, you know, these problems are interrelated and so yes, some people mention the prison-industrial complex, and others are talking about corporate welfare, and then there are people talking about the death penalty and poverty and health care and everything else, but they are all tied together and that's what the media can't take the time to get. It's like it's just easier for them just to say it makes no sense, what we're saying, than it is to explain or figure out why it makes sense. . . .We don't just want some proposition

passed; we are trying to show that something is seriously, seriously wrong here. Is it capitalism or a two-party system or globalization? I don't know, but what we are pissed off about is the fact that there is a ridiculous imbalance in economic resources in this country that is basically leading to injustice at every corner. How do you fit that into a sound bite? We have no message? . . . I don't want to say it's like laziness on the part of the mainstream media, but it seems that way from here. . . . It's like they ask questions and don't bother to listen to the answer, they just look for the one line that they can use and trash the rest.

Jerry, a reporter for a secondary newspaper in a midsized city, who covered Disrupt, said he did not feel that the protesters successfully communicated their concerns, yet later, when I asked if he knew what their goals were, he mimicked the activists in a deep, mock-serious voice:

"To bring attention to the abuses of global capitalism . . . " I mean, I could be their spokesman; I know all this stuff after hearing it so much. To bring attention to the—what they say is the corrupting influence of corporate money on domestic politics and globalization in the global economy, and I think there is a million other issues. The criminal injustice system, which is also the fault of the corporations running the criminal injustice system and you know, which is also a racist system, which is how freeing Mumia fits in.

This is a respectable synopsis of Disrupt's concerns, yet his article describes their efforts as fractured and confused.

Journalists may hear broad, social-structural critiques, but they have difficulty incorporating them into their stories because they are anticipating opposition groups with more focused complaints. Ed, a wire service reporter who covered the protests surrounding the debate in Boston in 2000, contrasted the disorderly approach with the one he preferred:

What seemed to be sort of lost is sort of the message. . . . Like they knew how to protest, but it was unclear, sort of, why. Outside of something clear, like a clear message. Like, Nader should get in to the debate and it's unfair he's being kept out. That's a fairly clear message, whether you agree with it or not you can say, "OK, this is an argument. This is maybe a reason to protest." Some of the other stuff is just kind of so fuzzy that it just looks like the kids out there getting themselves arrested.

And another reporter, Juan, offers the following:

> "We're upset about corporate greed. We're upset about monotony in American politics. We're upset about people having too much money." When you start having like this sort of smorgasbord of issues, it gets confusing what you're standing for. So, I would have had like really issue-focused demonstrations, and I covered a few. Like, there's a Puerto Rican parade where people were really upset about the U.S. Navy in that island, Vieques, and that was very clear exactly what they were protesting. They were protesting the presence of the U.S. Navy on an island 'cause they didn't think that was a good sort of example of American sovereignty.

The "closed debates" critique is straightforward, as is the concern about Puerto Rican sovereignty. The economic consequences of globalization are more difficult to parse, but are "corporate greed" or "economic inequality" less clear-cut complaints or are they simply more difficult to address?

Throughout the interviews it also became clear that journalists expect groups to present realistic solutions to the problems they identify. The following remarks, from Amber and Dustin, respectively, are illustrative:

> What would they do in place of what's going on? That's the only thing . . . they could say what's wrong . . . what they don't like . . . but what sort of vision do you have, you know, for an alternative government?

> I tend to take seriously a protester who says, "Look, there's a better way to do this and here's the better way.". . . I have to know why they're there and what it is they wanted. Umm, and I didn't feel like I got that.

Reporters often dismissed groups that offered critiques without solutions. But solutions for seemingly intractable social problems are not easy to pinpoint, so in some cases when associations did offer solutions, journalists panned them as unrealistic. Rather than acknowledge the complexity of these problems, journalists blamed the associations and their members for doing things incorrectly.

Getting In and Getting the Message Out

Veterans Opposing War succeeded in a way that other groups did not: its substantive message appeared in the news. At first blush, this veterans organization seems an unlikely success story. It was not particularly photogenic, had no particularly new things to say, and was not particularly clever or charismatic. Its members weren't innovative or funny, and their gatherings were not the largest on the scene. Yes, the war in Iraq was a pivotal issue in 2004, but this antiwar group succeeded while many others floundered because it followed the unwritten rules, even if it did so inadvertently. Journalists perceived the organization as authentic. And although Veterans Opposing War held a successful and emotionally powerful indoor event that was primarily an effort to attract publicity, they also planned and held activities for their members (a convention) and a small protest outside a veterans caucus aimed at pushing key Democrats toward an antiwar position. Perhaps not unexpectedly, the news stories that included the voices of group members were not about the "media event," but about events that were interpreted as "real." In addition, Veterans Opposing War had members who spoke like "good activists," offering personal narratives to illuminate a concrete problem while proffering a reasonable solution.

Inequality Forever staged events that were transparently oriented toward the media but still managed to attract coverage, because it established its authenticity through its originality, as Peterson (1997) describes. The group used satirical street theater, dressing as caricatures of the wealthy in top hats, ascots, monocles, tiaras, superfluous "jewels," and velvet gloves, and publicly championing the rights of the affluent. These Wealth Warriors highlighted the benefits of economic inequality to underscore policies that had exacerbated poverty and social divisions in the United States. In the process, they became the most successful outsider organization in terms of gaining media access in the presidential campaign context.

This success was the result of the near-mandatory double take that their performance required, which was reinforced by the Wealth Warriors' cheeky unwillingness to break character. From bumper stickers and picket signs to witty pro-wealth folk songs, the activists put on a good show with a clear message. They were a walking political cartoon. In return, the group was rewarded with press coverage and even compliments from reporters. Journalists liked them because they "got" the joke; the Wealth Warriors did not pit members against journalists in a struggle to control meaning, but rather pulled the journalists into the performance. If the journalists understood the joke, which they did, then they implicitly accepted the critique embedded in the humor. This is the foundation of satire. If the audience doesn't see the "truth" in the parody, then it simply fails to be funny.

Inequality Forever received coverage and also succeeded at catapulting its political message into the stories. Two of the three articles that included both the motive for their events and a quote from a member were stories quite similar to the one that Juan wrote, behind-the-scenes accounts of protest. This is exactly the kind of story that usually omits the "why." In this case, however, the why *had* to be included. For journalists to share the joke with their readers, they needed to include either quotes from participants or slogans from their signs, such as "Save the Tax Loopholes." The journalists transmitted Inequality Forever's critique in the process of describing its performance. Even including the organization's name conveyed an element of the critique that the group hoped to offer. As Rich from Inequality Forever shared, all of this was intentional:

> I mean, we designed it just knowing how the media hacks into pieces and misses things and fucks up everything, you know? I mean that's just the nature of things; if I was a journalist, I'm sure I'd do it, too, because I'm whizzing around trying to cover things I don't understand in a short amount of time. . . . We took care that our sound bites said a lot and then that these things would stand alone if they were sort of chopped and fragmented and misrepresented, and then we had deeper content if someone was willing to cover us more responsibly. . . . Anyway, they mostly just covered our name, they got some of our sound bites. It was decent.

Decent?

> Well, once they got a photograph—that was good. We knew we'd be photo-worthy and we planned it so that if we were photographed we'd have a clear, easy-to-read sign in our possession, because then that can't be screwed up. The *Washington Post* ran a photograph of a briefcase that had a bumper sticker on it, so that was really good. We got pretty good press for our thing, but I don't think they covered the whole scene very well, but in terms of our piece, we were good. They liked us personally. . . . You know, we're making them laugh, we're giving them good stuff. We understand what they want and what they want to feed to their readership and then we give that to them, inserting the stuff that we want in it, so they've got a good visual with a concept that can be captioned and thrown in. As a little virus interlaced in there is our message and that's the idea and it worked out OK. We assumed we would get very little from them time-wise, space-wise, blah, blah, blah, so we packed up our stuff in bite-sized pieces and fed it to them.

Other associations that used similar tactics had far less success. Inequality Forever succeeded because its members knew that almost all coverage of outsider activities is descriptive, and they used that knowledge to its advantage.[24] In the case of Inequality Forever, the description *was* the message. For journalists to convey the joke to their readers, they had no alternative but to pass the message along with it.

Damned If They Do, Damned If They Don't

Looking at the divergence between the well-documented practices of routine political reporting and reporting on voluntary associations in the presidential campaign context, several striking contrasts emerge. Table 4.1 summarizes these differences. Many protocols, such as the norm of balanced reporting and the importance of sourcing legitimate representatives, are shelved when activist voluntary associations become the subject of the story. Further, not only are insiders and outsiders treated differently, the norms applied to each are also often contradictory. While these two sets of rules are ideal types, and exceptions exist, they prove remarkably consistent across the data in this sample.

Activists were attuned to the first norm of association reporting: they know that they cannot take news coverage for granted. But the rest of their choices and behaviors suggest they were attempting to follow norms for reporting on political insiders, with deleterious consequences. Most groups were focused on demonstrating to the press that they were newsworthy, but they did so by actively working to construct the appearance of *legitimacy* by showcasing their professionalism, and this ran counter to the image of *authenticity* that is so critical to reporters. In short, voluntary associations fail when they act like organizations instead of like clumps of individuals. Candidates raise issues, point to problems, and talk about the need for change, but activists must have all the answers, and the proposed solutions need to be concrete and easy to implement.

The table reveals how challenging it is for associations with political concerns to amplify them via the media. If they follow the unwritten rules that journalists use, and thereby successfully attract coverage, the coverage is apt to be limited to emotional, individualistic expressions of concern or outrage about straightforward problems that are easily solved. But if they violate the journalists' norms for covering political outsiders, they become, as Fishman (1982) would say, irrelevant to the reporters' scheme of interpretation and remain invisible in news accounts.

TABLE 4.1.

Norms for Reporting on Political Insiders and Political Outsiders

Norms for Political Insiders	Norms for Activists
CONDITIONS OF INCLUSION	
Structured into routine journalistic work through the assignment of beats, etc.	Nonroutine, conditional, no "community organizing," "civil society," or "activist" beat
Players are actively pursued by the news media	Players must actively pursue the press
ACCEPTABLE EVENTS	
Good events are reporter-friendly:	Good events are authentic:
Often overtly constructed for the media (e.g., press conferences), and guide reporters to the official story	Do not appear to be soliciting the press, as real activism is about political zeal not calculated media work
Predictable, routine	Original, innovative, unexpected
Can be held where organization / office sees fit	Should be held in public, preferably outdoors
ACCEPTABLE SOURCES	
Good sources are legitimate as established through:	Good sources are authentic as established through:
Professional status	Amateur status
Institutional authority or credentials	Moral authority or personal proximity to issue raised
Providing rational reasoned evidence	
Preparing remarks, even reading scripts is acceptable	Sharing emotions and feelings
Speaking on behalf of organization /office	Providing natural remarks, scripts / hints of scripting unacceptable
Discussing common good / vision	Speaking as individuals, share personal narratives
	Avoiding publicly-minded speech
ACCEPTABLE POLITICS	
Acceptable politics may be visionary:	Acceptable politics are reasonable:
May address individual issues or broad concerns	Address one concrete issue, avoid broad concerns
Issues are reasonable, not radical	Issues are reasonable, not radical
Raising issues in need of address is acceptable	Should present plausible solutions to problems
NATURE OF THE ARTICLES	
Generally treat subjects and sources with respect	Often belittle subjects and sources
Articles generally include a quote from a key, informed source	Articles often do not quote group representatives or participants
Balance is essential to the article, journalists seek comment from subjects of criticism	Balance is unnecessary, journalists rarely seek comment from subject of criticism

In sum, news stories about activism are the product of elaborate, mutually dependent, and often adversarial relationships between journalists and group members. This is significant, because the attention of mainstream news organizations is not simply a trophy to be won, but rather an opening to participate, to enter the "master forum" in which matters of common concern are raised for discussion, exploration, and contestation. Coverage is a prize that is both symbolic and instrumental—symbolic in that outside groups who enter the forum become visible, and instrumental in that social and political challenges to existing arrangements cannot be waged in isolation. Indeed, there are other mechanisms that activists can employ to try to shape public discourse, but none that offer this type of amplification. It is not surprising, then, that the associations tether their ambitions to the press, even if doing so proves a poor investment.

At the beginning of the chapter I asked if the news creates an image of political vitality; in Gitlin's (1980) words, does some of what the movement wants to have broadcast actually get broadcast? The answer is, not really. What is particularly noteworthy is that this is probably about as good as it gets. Presidential elections pique political interest, draw audiences to the news, bring news workers to campaign event cities, and are the preeminent ritual of political participation in the United States. Theory suggests that elections are potentially transformative moments for the mass media, an opening for these fora to become more inclusive and promote dialogue. Perhaps sometimes this actually happens, but the organizations I observed were rarely included, and when they were, they were most often presented either as amusing outposts of the culture or as criminals. These associations often substituted media strategy for political strategy, leaving them empty-handed when their efforts failed. Failure was so common that activists proceeded to define even the most meager coverage as an accomplishment; a one-line reference in which the group's name was incorrect and their political concerns avoided was sometimes viewed as cause for celebration. For their part, journalists adhered so rigidly to industry norms as to reify them. They touted their autonomy but rigidly self-censored what they wrote. I'm reminded here of Naomi's statement: "So, they [the protesters] staged the event to get publicity and then they don't want you to write about the event that they designed. I don't know. They tie my hands and then blame me for it. It's frustrating." Her hands are indeed tied, but not by the associations. These are socially constructed norms of the journalistic field, institutionalized through education, professional associations, and decisions made in news organizations. They are cultural practices, not legal ones.

Voluntary associations, as publics, are valued because they provide communal spaces for marginalized groups to safely articulate their needs and goals, but also because they allow participants to develop strategies to amplify their voices when they enter mainstream public arenas. The experiences of the groups in this study demonstrate that while such strategizing abounds, attempts to expand mainstream dialogue via the news media are profoundly limited. When meaningful news coverage fails to materialize, the associations are left involuntarily enclaved, unable to engage mainstream audiences. This disempowers activist groups, but it also diminishes the quality of political discourse more broadly by narrowing the range of perspectives and priorities that circulate through mainstream channels.

To the extent that Castells (1997) is correct that political debates are increasingly forced to be waged in the "media space," voluntary associations' struggle for coverage reveals the exceptionally limited opportunities these groups have to participate in political discourse. In the end, this struggle reveals that the tremendous resources invested in pursuit of mainstream media attention are not only ineffective, they may even be detrimental. In the next two chapters I turn to the hidden costs of courting the press.

5

Wait, Isn't That a Bird in Your Hand?

*Pushing Bystanders out of the Way in
an Effort to Reach "the Public"*

ONE MORNING DURING the 2004 Democratic National Convention in Boston, I walked out of the Park Street subway station and did a double take. A barefoot woman in white, blood-spattered clothing sat stiffly in a straight-backed wooden chair, her arms tied down with rope. Two men wearing dark sunglasses, dressed from head to toe in black, stood at her side. One held a funnel high in the air, raising the end of the attached hose to her mouth, simulating force-feeding.

All three people were completely still, posed like mannequins. Immediately adjacent to this disconcerting trio, a woman in similar white, blood-splattered clothing sat in another chair. A man stood at her side in a threatening pose, with one hand on her head and his opposing arm pulled back high into the air, club in hand. He was frozen in mid-swing, the club's trajectory headed toward the woman's knee. Where the weapon would make contact, her pant leg was ripped open and the skin appeared bloody, conveying that the man was already well into the beating. Grisly still lifes continued along Boston Common. Accompanying each silent, visual representation of brutality was a large poster, propped on a wooden easel, that contained detailed descriptions about the form of torture represented by the particular group of human statues. Examining these displays was like walking through a museum, studying the works of art, and reading about the artists. Pedestrians drifted reverently from display to display. Some took photographs. Along the pedestrian pathways adjacent to these exhibits, people in matching T-shirts carrying literature waited respectfully. An elderly Asian woman and a young white man approached me after I had lingered at five or six stations. The man softly asked, "Do you have any questions?" I did.

All the organizations that chose these demonstrative activities hoped to get news coverage, but some, like the Chinese Cultural Freedom Collective, an international organization promoting religious tolerance in China,

Figure 5.1. The Chinese Cultural Freedom Collective encouraged pedestrians in Boston Common to learn about religious persecution in China by positioning activists like mannequins frozen in silent scenes of abuse, providing information alongside each scene, and making representatives available to answer questions.

had a dual focus and gave serious thought to promoting meaningful, face-to-face encounters with bystanders. The exhibit dramatizing religious persecution in China and the guides that mingled to answer questions and share their concerns with pedestrians could have been created as a media stunt, but instead the organizers directed their efforts toward people on the street. Representatives from the organization told me that they hoped to educate people one at a time and believed this education would eventually lead to a swelling of resistance. Reaching out to new people does not require the news media as an intermediary, but strikingly few organizations active in the campaign context took the alternatives seriously.

Face-to-face communication necessarily targets smaller audiences than do attempts to speak through the mass media, but groups engaging directly with outsiders were able to control the way they presented themselves, as well as the issues they brought to the fore. Despite these advantages, very few associations designed mobilizations in which success was conceptualized as connecting face-to-face with new people. The previous chapter demonstrated that relying on the news media rarely pays off. In this chapter, I show that in addition to failing to produce substantive news coverage, attempts to reach the public via the media also had the deleterious side effect of corrupting such direct communication with outsiders.

It took me a while to recognize that the organizations were neglecting unmediated communication. I initially noted a couple of revealing glimpses of the activist/layperson relationship, which sent me scouring my field notes for more, only to come up frustrated. The colorful scenes in the streets depicted in chapter 2 and the troubled relationships between journalists and activists visible in chapter 4 are red flags, revealing the disconnect between associations' efforts and news workers' desires. The chasm between activists and laypeople, on the other hand, must be excavated from the gaps. The silences are the data—meetings that did not transpire, conversations that failed to take place, pedestrian strategy workshops that no one organized. These gaps and silences suggest that intensive media work distracted groups from direct outreach, while the face-to-face encounters I witnessed reveal that group practices honed during media trainings translated poorly in conversations with laypeople, creating communicative hurdles.

Conceptualizing the Public

Associations were drawn to public spaces because they wanted to command the public's eyes and ears, but this public was implicitly conceptualized as remote: reading newspapers over morning coffee, tuned into NPR as they commuted, or watching the evening news from an armchair. As a result, the organizations invested copious amounts of energy in reaching out to these distant audiences. This emphasis was visible in their meetings and planning sessions. Activist groups designated subcommittees, affinity groups, or staff people to work on everything from permitting and legal issues to housing, but there was a dearth of subcommittees, agenda items, and e-mail list threads devoted to strategizing in preparation for one-on-one communication. Media trainings were ubiquitous, but there were no analogous sessions focused on improving direct outreach. This is not to say that the activists ignored it completely. Some groups leafleted in dense areas and a few set up literature tables. But although associations wrangled torturously over what "works" with journalists and photographers, they did not discuss how best to approach strangers, how to explain complex issues in an accessible way for bystanders, or how to encourage inquisitive onlookers to become more involved.

The Chinese Cultural Freedom Collective torture exhibit worked because of the association's concerted effort to foster effective communication with pedestrians. Most associations behaved more like Network for Peace. Elise, a member, explained what they wanted out of their mobilization:

> We wanted the [50-foot inflatable] missile to come to Boston on the day of the debate because we really feel it's a crucial issue for the presidential race—this issue of the Star Wars missile defense. And George Bush is in favor of it and Al Gore is in favor of it and they are not being asked to defend their position on it. No journalists, very few journalists, and certainly on television, certainly in the debates as we've seen, they weren't even asked about it. So, in that case we felt that it was our responsibility as a grassroots advocacy group to bring it up and so what we were trying to do in Boston was through a very big visual statement to make the journalists aware that this is an issue that they should be covering and to make the public aware, if they didn't hear it through other media, that at least they can see it with their own eyes and hear about it.

Paying close attention to Elise reveals a great deal. This was a mobilization about communicating with journalists. She said that the missile was there for the (immediate) public as well, but the secondary nature of this concern is apparent in the thrust of her explanation of the group's objectives, as well as in its preparation for and execution of the event. Here is another member's partial recounting of the media work that they did around this mobilization. Charles explained:

> We used similar strategies [for their convention and debate mobilizations] and it's not like rocket science. We had a press release made up and we got it out to the national media. We also tried to get it out to Philadelphia media there in advance of the event, and then while we were at the event, we had people assigned who were media liaisons who helped to focus the media attention on the few people who were going to do interviews, which was the director and myself. We also have a media sign-up list so we make sure that we get their names and can contact them later for other events. And we kind of had the same strategy there as we did in Boston,

and, you know, we had the release that we worked on before I went up there that was sent out by the Boston affiliate, and they did follow-up phone calls to the media there. And then at the event we had a sign-up list again, and, you know, tried to work with the media who came out and to see what they wanted and to help them get their picture, what have you. So, it's not terribly complicated stuff. It's just that we have a general strategy. The norm is that you send out your press advisory to your daybook so you get on the list. Then, you send out your release the day before or the day of [the event]. Then you have to do phone calls to make sure that people are actually coming out.

The "people" they were working to get out were journalists. The organization did no advance work at all to publicize their event to laypeople in an effort to bring them out. The plan for making "the public aware," in Elise's words, was limited to setting up a table with some literature and a petition on it for pedestrians interested enough to approach.

In this chapter, I will show that because most associations did not plan ways to engage the immediate public, they rarely did so. Activists lost opportunities to connect meaningfully with nonmembers by treating bystanders as passive audience members and offering pedestrians symbolic *acts* rather than *interactions*. Their public performances were often compelling but rarely engaging. In most cases, onlookers had no structured opportunity to ask questions, share insights, or probe behind the chants, comedic skits, or dramatic displays of emotion. Speech about politics was central to association activities around the conventions and debates, but talk about issues—two-way exchange—was exceedingly rare. The same flamboyant techniques that groups concocted to draw the media often captured pedestrians' attention, but the activists did not know what to do with that attention once they had it.

I will also show that when activists did attempt to create openings for dialogue or when outsiders took the initiative and approached group members, the interactions were often stilted and awkward. Activists were often so deeply embedded in a media-hungry marketing mentality that they were unable to converse with real people, substituting affected sound bites and forced slogans for comprehensible answers, attentive listening, and productive conversation. At other times, activists' ability to converse was hobbled by the media-oriented events that the associations orchestrated. This was particularly true for groups using illegal tactics whose members came to distrust nonmembers. Concerns about government infiltration and ill-intentioned journalists left these activists leery of those who asked questions or attempted to talk with them. Wielding a "you're either with us or against us" shield left little room for potential supporters to feel comfortable. It is not pleasant to be treated like an enemy.

Unexpectedly, it was the oft-vilified large national membership associations, with their professional staff and top-down management style, that appeared to expand participation and dialogue most fully. These organizations reached out to nonmembers with collaborative discursive environments more often associated with the activities of grassroots community groups—the very organizations from which they seem most distant. While Skocpol (2003), Putnam (2000), and others see contemporary national citizen groups as feeble substitutes for classic American voluntary associations (e.g., the Elks), association activity around the conventions and debates highlight the meaningful contributions that contemporary citizen groups can make to civic life as a result of their emphasis on working with laypeople.

Face-to-face efforts can promote discussion about association issues, but this chapter reveals that bystanders were so low on activists' priority lists that when opportunities for personal conversations with outsiders presented themselves, association members were often unprepared, directed people elsewhere, fell back on ineffective public relations gimmicks, or shied away from the conversation. Ultimately, media-centrism failed with journalists, distracted associations from focusing on one-on-one interactions, and corrupted those personal conversations when they managed to sprout on their own.

Quiet, the Show Is Starting! Public Displays of Activism

A few organizations used the Chinese Cultural Freedom Collective model, working to thoughtfully engage pedestrians, but most offered people in the streets of New York or Los Angeles or Boston an opportunity to watch a show and little more. Demonstrative activity as performance dominated the landscape. Sometimes performances were staged to look like something else, such as a protest, a rally, or a march, but these were symbolic events rather than instrumental efforts. Choice's march across the Brooklyn Bridge was not a march to the courthouse to intervene in a hearing or a trial. Nor was it a march to an abortion clinic to shepherd clients in and out of buildings safely. It was a march to visually demonstrate support for reproductive rights to the public, elected officials, and the RNC platform committee. Similarly, organizers of the huge march before the 2004 RNC never set their sights on disrupting the convention. Instead, they sought to demonstrate to the world that the Bush agenda was not without opposition in the United States.

At times, symbolic events were quite literally performances for the public. Members of the Radical Grandma Chorus dressed like matronly older women, singing subversive political lyrics set to classic patriotic melodies. Alternacheer members donned torn fuchsia fishnets and black vinyl skirts and performed choreographed cheers that indicted capitalism and cheekily promoted masturbation as an alternative to war. Conservatives for Reproductive Rights gathered musicians, comedians, and actors for a live concert. These politically loaded performances were often wonderful, but it is significant that they were oriented around being watched and heard rather than engaging in dialogue. Most groups created no substantive participatory opportunities during their performances, nor did they circulate members to welcome people or answer questions; in most cases, groups did not even have literature available for pedestrians (although some had "press kits" ready). To the extent that most groups strategized at all about how to draw pedestrians, they did so because they conceptualized them as necessary pieces of the show for the media, as critical elements of their photo opportunity.

This absence of effort is significant. Some laypeople were out and about precisely because the cities were politically charged. I met one such young man on the MIT campus before the first presidential debate in 2000. He was sitting at the perimeter of the quad in the fall sun, watching a group of activists set up a table. I mistakenly assumed he was a student between classes, but he was on campus because he had heard that there were going to be some activist groups there. "I'm here to get informed," he told me. "I know what happens in the debate will just be one point of view." Regardless of whether they planned to be in the area, pedestrians were clearly curious about the colorful performances. Many stopped to watch, particularly if others had already begun to gather. Some smiled at activists and a few clapped, their body language indicating openness to or approval of the ideas expressed through the performances, but pedestrians almost never attempted to engage the activists in conversation. This absence of bystander-initiated dialogue should not be interpreted as a lack of interest or the absence of questions. On the contrary, I regularly observed conversations between peers who approached together, as well as inquiries made by one bystander of another. As an observer, I was often approached by pedestrians asking what was going on or if it had to do with the convention or debate. Over time, I realized that almost all discussion in the performance context transpired among observers.

It was as if an invisible barrier existed between activists and bystanders. This boundary was most likely an outgrowth of existing norms surrounding performers and audiences, which association members failed to deconstruct. In most familiar settings, the respective roles of the audience and the performer are distinct: lecture halls, sports arenas, churches, recital halls, and theaters have established a priori assumptions about the role of the audience. In each of these situations, there are moments when the audience is expected to participate, such as class discussions or responsorial prayers in a Catholic church, but it is always those in the performer role who initiate this audience participation. These well-established norms about audience involvement undoubtedly shape bystanders' expectations of appropriate behavior in performance spaces. Since audiences do not usually participate unless prompted, it is unsurprising that the pedestrians would act as witnesses instead of participants in the absence of overt association efforts to disrupt this norm. Professors who lecture often ask if there are questions at the end of a class session, but most of the time activists did not even offer this nod to dialogue. Instead, I observed group members finish their songs, cheers, speeches, and skits only to retreat into private conversations with other insiders or make an announcement that such and such person was "available for interviews."

Following the performances, I watched adrenaline-filled group members begin chatting with one another, dismantling props, preparing for their next performance, or anxiously combing the crowd for journalists, none of which created openings for bystanders interested in asking questions, having a discussion, or obtaining additional information about the group. It is intimidating to approach strangers, particularly when they know one another. In addition to this routine social awkwardness, onlookers might have felt reluctant to extend themselves to a group of politically vocal strangers whose viewpoints they may not yet have fully unraveled, concerned that they could be perceived as a supporter or participant by other pedestrians. Such social anxiety was likely amplified when adherents were loud, outrageously dressed, appeared angry, looked different from witnesses, or had racial or ethnic backgrounds that differed from those of the observers. As a result, I noticed that the few onlookers who were assertive enough to approach association members were usually those with great ideological compatibility, wishing to share their similar views, insights, or relevant experiences. For example, in Winston-Salem, one young man was eager to tell civil disobedience leaders about his protest experiences from the Boston debate. For the less enthusiastic, activist events served as *potential* catalysts for political conversations that rarely ensued, most often as a result of associations' tacit acceptance of the social barriers between performers and audience members. Had the organizations devoted time to planning for direct outreach, they likely would have strategized about how to facilitate communication across this divide.

Inside Jokes and Abstract Art: Symbols and Political Communication

The one-way communication in the performances amounted to talking at rather than engaging with attendees, but some groups skipped talking altogether. Some attempted to broadcast their messages with symbols rather than with symbolic acts. Two associations arranged to have members scale city buildings to do banner drops (the Land and Life Protection League and Women Against War). Other groups deployed roving eye-catchers: a 12-foot cigarette dressed as Uncle Sam (Business Watch), a 50-foot inflatable missile (Network for Peace), a 70-foot puppet resembling a human spine (Guts Initiative), and a person in a furry shark costume (NC Citizens for Smaller Government). They were intriguing and sometimes impressive—a 70-foot spine is sight to behold—but symbols need to draw on a common stock of knowledge in order to communicate intended meanings effectively to outsiders. Could nonmembers possibly intuit that the shark costume was a commentary on the need for tort reform? Because members and nonmembers rarely interacted, the significance of these symbolic efforts, the *meaning* of the 50-foot missile or the patriotic cigarette, was likely lost on most observers. One enormous banner illegally draped from a high-rise in New York City visually implied that "Bush" and "truth" were mutually exclusive. The lettering of the words "Bush" and "truth" was easy to read, but would most onlookers truly understand the critique without additional information? Whom did he lie to? About what? What were the consequences? What do you suggest that I do?

This approach requires an intermediary—an activist or journalist—to translate in order to be effective. If a newspaper had included a photo of the 12-foot-tall cigarette (none in the archive did), a caption would provide background information or some other sort of interpretive frame to help readers contextualize the image, but what of those people who were present? The use of such symbols would have been far more meaningful if association members had worked to engage bystanders, if they had used the costume or float as a social lubricant to begin a conversation about the issues they found so important. Indeed, it's easy to imagine a scenario in which the 70-foot spine used by Guts Initiative was not stationed as an irresistible photo opportunity to bait news workers, but rather as fodder for a conversation with the immediate public about vital issues the progressive organization felt were being ignored by the Democratic Party.

Without question, activist groups have a right to express their concerns or to dissent without the obligation to provide a complete education for those in the vicinity. In fact, such expression in and of itself is valuable, particularly when it unites group members or allows activists to give voice to issues normally shrouded in silence. But in cases where the primary goal is to reach outsiders, to bring dialogue from the margins to the center and push these issues into the mainstream, this type of closed communication does little to further the organizations' own objectives for their mobilizations.

Crossing the Divide: When Bystanders Take the Risk

Periodically, bystanders would go out on a limb and attempt to engage association members, even when members offered little in the way of incentive or were firmly in "performer mode." Because I recognized these moments as aberrations, I was particularly interested in how they unfolded. What I watched repeatedly were activists who floundered in their interactions with pedestrians.

Why Don't You Visit Our Website?

If associations seeking to influence mainstream political discourse had not defined the public as an abstract mass, they would have welcomed conversations with bystanders as expressions of potential interest and consequently prepared to answer their questions, introduced them to other members, and perhaps invited them to become involved. Instead, the activists faltered, dismissing interested bystanders by offhandedly directing them to their website, giving them a brochure, or claiming they weren't

Figure 5.2. Republican Freakshow hoped to attract the attention of the news media with an eye-catching dance performance titled "Republicans Gone Wild," but the political message was difficult for onlookers to understand.

the "right person" to answer, as if every inquiry required a spokesperson's official reply. I was among a group of approximately 20 people clustered around Republican Freakshow's bizarrely comedic "Republicans Gone Wild" performance in Union Square during the 2004 RNC. The group gave onlookers reason to pause. One member shook his hips while wearing a giant Dick Cheney mask and a button-down shirt opened wide, exposing his hairy stomach and a set of plastic breasts, which he rubbed suggestively as he danced to music blaring from a portable stereo. Collaborators dressed as Donald Rumsfeld, George W. Bush, and Condoleezza Rice also danced, though their moves were restrained and awkward.

The music and dancing dwindled to an anticlimactic ending. A few bystanders clapped asynchronously, but most simply moved along. One young man seemed to want to strike up a conversation with the performers. He lingered a bit and eventually asked where they were from (San Francisco), although no one asked him in return. "Dick Cheney" fumbled

with the batteries in the portable radio, while his cronies, who had removed their masks, stood nearby sharing a hushed chuckle and passing a
Nalgene water bottle. Still lingering, now a bit closer to Cheney and the
radio, the young man asked if they were "promoters from a political show
or something." "Nope, just voters," said Cheney, still attending to the radio. Smiling, the young man asked, "All the way from SF? Is this, like, for
work—your job or something?" "Hang on," said Cheney. The performer
exhaled audibly as he set down the troublesome radio and, appearing
slightly inconvenienced, rummaged through a duffle bag. He fished out
a small pile of glossy three-by-five cards and handed one to the young
man and one to me, and said, "You can check out our website if you're
interested." The card had an image of the Bush administration officials on
it, depicting them as circus sideshow characters, and their URL in yellow
letters.

I empathized with the young man, because I also wanted more information. Was this a group of friends? Were they affiliated with an organization? Were they starving artists? It was difficult to tell who they were and
what they were attempting to say. A dancing, transgendered Dick Cheney
implies some sort of critique, but what? I stuck around and probed further,
eventually finding out that the dancers were part of a small antiwar organization called Republican Freakshow. They wanted people to know that
the Bush administration's decisions around Iraq were based on corrupt
relationships among oil companies, defense contractors, and high-ranking
officials. The performance did not communicate this clearly, and this problem was exacerbated by the fact that association members failed to take
advantage of the opportunity for clarification, explanation, and discussion.
Cheney's real name was Eli. When I later asked Eli why they didn't "work
the crowd" a little more, he explained that they were mostly focused on
being available to journalists. When I pressed him, commenting that there
were no journalists around, he indicated that he just wanted to get ready to
do the routine again in hopes that some would come by.

Republican Freakshow did variations of this performance at approximately a dozen points around the city over the course of several days. Despite being interviewed by reporters from three New York newspapers (in
one case by the same reporter on two different days), the group received no
coverage in the mainstream news media. Republican Freakshow failed at
three levels: they were unable to obtain news coverage, their performance
was so vague that it was meaningless to those watching, and, when pressed
by an inquisitive bystander seeking information to help him interpret their

actions, they snubbed him. In its dogged pursuit of journalists, the group lost an opportunity to connect with bystanders by failing to contextualize their performance, offer literature, or provide ideas for action that observers might take if they shared the association's concerns.

Most activists were more responsive to pedestrians than were Eli and his colleagues, but they often deferred interested parties to websites or handed them a pamphlet. They were usually prepared to direct bystanders to resources, but they seemed noticeably unprepared or unwilling to actually *talk* with them.

Selling Used Cars: Media Work Backfires Again

In the rare instances when activists talked with pedestrians, the interactions were plagued by the same disciplined speech that proved problematic in reporter-activist communications. Overly practiced sound bites, use of organization slogans, and publicly minded speech often served to distance activists from bystanders. My field notes from the Land and Life Protection League award ceremony in Philadelphia provide an illustration:

> A red headed woman . . . is handing out materials [to bystanders] when two women who are professionally dressed [appearing to work in the area] approach her. One of them asks what she is protesting. The young woman says that they are concerned about "private finance destroying the environment, hurting Third World nations, and discriminating against African Americans." One woman is now smiling; the other says [sarcastically], "OK, well that's good to know." (August 2, 2000)

This answer was technically accurate and "on message," but it did absolutely nothing to promote an understanding of the issues or to encourage the bystanders to ask additional questions. The professionals walked away exchanging smirks. This would have been less significant if the event had not been explicitly designed to promote public awareness. "Private finance destroying the environment, hurting Third World nations, and discriminating against African Americans" was, of course, the answer that the organization hoped would land in the news. This was what they practiced, but it was not the appropriate script for the interaction at hand.

It makes sense that the media script would fail. The language is exclusionary—the activist should not have assumed that a stranger would know what she meant by "private finance" or even "Third World nations"—and real people don't converse in sound bites. Better answers would prompt conversation, enable the activist to assess the pedestrian's background and level of interest, and help the bystander connect the group's issues to his or her life. Gauging interest, knowledge, and experience requires the respondent to listen as well as talk. And listening was a remarkably rare occurrence.

The activist's tone, cadence, and demeanor also discouraged the curious women from pressing for more information. The spokesperson did not pause, give them her full attention, or offer a reply in a measured attempt to explain a complex situation. Instead, she was curt and dismissive. The nonverbal message was that her brusque retort was *the* answer. The member could have offered a more accessible and detailed explanation—her deep commitment to and knowledge about the group's issues was apparent in our interview—but she was limited by her media-centrism. She had practiced a reply for a different audience.

Having rehearsed shallow sound bites, some organization members were less informed about their groups' focal issues than they should have been, and this also limited the exchanges that transpired between members and outsiders. After working with Inequality Forever in Philadelphia, I was pleased to run into a group of Wealth Warriors in Los Angeles. I saw three young men in top hats and suit jackets on a park bench before the start of a small women's rights march. I introduced myself to a young man named Matt, and we began to discuss different events happening during the week. As we talked, more Wealth Warriors approached and a handful of them started to heckle the women's rights activists, pretending to oppose their proposals (on equal pay and immigrant rights). They were rewarded with wide smiles, cheers, and many playful rejoinders from the marchers. Two people asked to take their photo. Their point, that existing political arrangements benefit the wealthy, was well received.

The Wealth Warriors and I joined the march, and as we walked a telling exchange transpired. A young woman from a welfare rights organization said she thought it would be fun to start a spontaneous mock debate between the Wealth Warriors and some members of her group. She and Matt began scheming, but it soon became apparent that Matt was unprepared, with little more than his rehearsed sound bites to draw on. For example, the woman from the welfare rights organization suggested health care as a topic, because the Wealth Warriors had a poster with a heath-related slogan on it. They tossed this idea around, but then Matt hedged a bit and said, "It's really not my area." Then, taking a cue from another Inequality Forever poster, she suggested they debate the estate tax. Matt loved the idea but lamented not having Internet access, so that he could "look some stuff up." Her proposal to debate required a thicker knowledge than Matt needed to chant, heckle, or charm journalists, and thus put him in an awkward position. He had practiced his lines and was skilled in witty repartee, but he was less informed about the subtleties of the issues behind the slogans. After batting a few more ideas around, they scaled back and decided to chant back and forth, taunting each other. The welfare rights contingent started to chant "Whose streets?," and the Wealth Warriors retorted "Our streets!," allowing their faux-luxury garb to imbue the familiar activist refrain with new meaning. Then they reversed the chant so that the Wealth Warriors would ask, "Whose streets?," and the welfare rights group would grumble quietly, "Their streets." Other marchers seemed to enjoy the joke, but the opportunity to say something more was lost and the struggle revealed how ill-informed Matt was beyond his repertoire of clever slogans.

Media Events

In some exceptional cases, activists actually feared outsiders and worked to insulate themselves from nonmembers. Distrust led some groups to establish and reinforce a boundary between insiders and outsiders that surpassed normal levels of social cohesion that might be expected among group members. In these cases, the link between insiders and outsiders was conceptualized as an "us versus them" dichotomy that left no room for supporters or friends. Obviously, this narrowed the potential for dialogue between group members and the immediate public.

When I arrived in Philadelphia in 2000, I was interested in the planned direct action, but found it incredibly difficult to locate concrete information about planning meetings, the time and location of the planned events, or where to go for more information. I approached activists twice with questions, only to be asked if I was an undercover police officer and then given the cold shoulder. Explaining my role as a researcher, dragging out business cards and the Internal Review Board documentation sanctioning my research, and offering earnest claims of sincerity proved futile. The third time this happened, exasperation led me to argue with a group of 18- to 20-year-olds, asking what I could possibly do to convince them that I did not intend to sabotage their work. Out of frustration, I eventually pulled out my cell phone and half yelled, "What do you want to do—call my mother?," before I threw my arms in the air and walked off. One young man, whom I later came to know as Loren from Disrupt, jogged after me and said, "OK, look, if you want people to trust you, go buy a black T-shirt and participate."

Loren was helpful, but he relented only after I pleaded with him and his peers, and the first two clusters of activists I approached absolutely refused to share any information with me. It is unlikely that an interested or supportive bystander with less at stake than me would have persisted in the face of repeated rejections. Enclaves of distrust do not facilitate communication. Like so many other mobilizing organizations, Disrupt was not concerned with laypeople in the vicinity; it was fixated on viewers and readers at home, and the journalists who could carry news of their efforts to this abstract public and further build the burgeoning global justice movement. Toward this end, they planned a dramatic set of illegal events intended to disrupt the convention, provoke the public into critically examining existing political and economic arrangements, and to raise the profile of the increasing number of people who find those arrangements unacceptable.

The reality of organizing illegal activities meant that activists were vulnerable and therefore needed secrecy. This extreme guardedness was understandable for groups that feared police intervention and arrest. Members of Disrupt believed they had been under surveillance for weeks. There was evidence that group meetings had been videotaped and photographed, although there had been no confirmation whether this surveillance had been the work of local police or the FBI. Law enforcement had also allegedly infiltrated their meetings, and while I was there, the police raided one of their workspaces and confiscated the elaborate political puppets the group had created for the subsequent day's mobilization. This backstory explains members' reluctance to share information with outsiders, but the legitimacy of their fears does not alter the consequences of their guarded responses.

Disrupt was a large, well-organized umbrella organization for many affinity groups and coalition partners, and after the initial resistance that I faced, it proved to be the most accessible of the groups I encountered that were coordinating illegal activities. I found others much less approachable, and sometimes this remained true even after the possibility for sabotage was largely over. In 2004, Boston Resistance held an unpermitted march through the city. A large pirate ship constructed from cardboard figured prominently in the procession, and many participants wore makeshift pirate costumes. I marched with them and spoke with other marchers as we walked. Most people I spoke with turned out to be from other organizations, participating to support the group's efforts. This was quite common; the activist community shared an understanding of the importance of turnout at mass mobilizations, and members of different groups made a point to support one another's events. What surprised me, though, was how little these supporters knew about Boston Resistance or the event. While there was a general awareness that the group was an anarchist collective, no one I spoke with was clear about what motivated the march or what the pirate theme was intended to communicate. The march continued with a police escort and no sign of impending arrests, and eventually, when I felt it would not be overly intrusive or disruptive, I approached a couple of people who were clearly focal decision makers for more information. That I had marched with them and was part of the scene made no difference; they were so leery of outsiders that they rebuffed my innocuous questions.

These two groups demanded to be heard but were willing to speak only on their terms, dismissing outsiders interested enough to approach their members. This is deeply problematic for organizations hoping to expand their base of support, because it alienates the very people they need in order to succeed—potential advocates and members. Loren said that if I wanted to be trusted, I would need to "buy a black T-shirt and participate." Essentially requiring an outsider to commit to the group in order to be granted basic information is an unreasonably high threshold for most people. Regardless of whether this distrust was warranted, the outcome was the same: a rigid distinction between insiders and outsiders and the active narrowing of space for meaningful exchange. This lack of face-to-face communication between members and nonmembers yields the most extreme type of reliance on the mass media, as they become the sole vehicle for disseminating the associations' issues and perspectives.

The Exceptions: Rethinking National Mailing List Organizations

National mailing list citizen groups emerged as unlikely exceptions, focusing significant energy on unmediated communication. While not all national citizen groups emphasized face-to-face work, the activities oriented around the immediate public were disproportionately organized by such organizations. Of the nearly 100 events organized by the associations I studied, 12 focused primarily on face-to-face interactions (with most still perceiving the media as a secondary target), and 8 of these 12 events were facilitated by national mailing list organizations, even though they made up less than a third of the organizations in the sample. Skocpol (2003), Putnam (1995, 2000), and others depict these professionally managed groups as anathema to "join in and lend a hand" community organizations, such as the Elks chapters or the Moose lodges, whose halcyon days have passed. By these accounts, contemporary citizen groups pale in comparison, depicted as shallow bureaucratic shells with disconnected members who do little more than send checks and receive newsletters that often go unread. Those concerned with civic engagement wonder how such organizations can possibly provide opportunities to develop civic skills, cultivate social solidarity, and enhance the legitimacy of representative democracy.[1]

National citizen groups' activities around the conventions and debates suggest that the hand-wringing may very well be justified, at least with respect to members' civic development. These associations' events were far removed from the lives of their members. The American Adult Network called on a few local chapters for volunteer support, but in most cases lay members had nothing to do with their organizations' campaign mobilizations. Instead, the national citizen groups' mobilizations were organized and implemented primarily by professionals. Lay members were unlikely to participate in the event-planning process and often were unaware that the events even transpired. Invitations were generally extended to members as announcements in newsletters, but there was no earnest outreach intended to generate member interest or attendance. In fact, when asked if members attended their events, some organizers were uncertain and others described seeing members at events as surprising or coincidental. I asked Jake, an organizer for Rights Now, if he could direct me to a member who attended one of their events. He replied: "Umm . . . I'll send out a staff e-mail. I just have no idea if any of the people who were there [at the party or march] were members, but, I mean, we get the word out, so in all likelihood there were some members who [went]. Let me see where the e-mail gets us. If you don't hear back from me, that's because I couldn't find someone. OK?" Putnam, Skocpol, and their contemporaries seem to be correct: citizen groups did not provide meaningful opportunities for face-to-face connections between most members, at least in this context. These citizen groups approached the conventions and debates as opportunities to spread their messages in new directions, rather than to cultivate social cohesion among members or to help members develop their civic skills.

But national citizen groups' approach to demonstrative activity was robust in fostering civic engagement, even if the engagement they fostered was not among their members.

National mailing list citizen groups created fertile arenas for pedestrian involvement. To return to the American Adult Network as an illustration, the organization used a red, white, and blue tour bus to drive from campaign event to campaign event during the general election (stopping in several additional cities en route). It used the bus tour to incorporate more people into a discussion about election issues relevant to senior citizens, most notably social security and health care. The American Adult Network sought to promote dialogue by holding free, interactive sessions for the public during each stop on the tour. For each session, organizers worked to recruit participants, provided seating, facilitated issue-oriented games, and offered refreshments to engage onlookers. These accessible meetings were information-rich and participatory. Organizers hoped for publicity and prepared carefully for the possibility that they might attract journalists, but they invested the bulk of their thought and planning into communicating directly with people in the streets.

Citizens' Campaign Watch facilitated face-to-face political discussion by convening two large, multiday conferences coinciding with the national nominating conventions in 2000. These free, nonpartisan, public events focused on domestic issues that were not represented in mainstream campaign discourse (economic inequality, campaign finance reform, and drug policy). Each conference offered entertainment and speakers—both high-profile public figures and "ordinary" individuals whose lives had been affected by the issues on the agenda—but also incorporated breakout sessions designed to encourage attendees to share their views and discuss paths toward change in their communities.

Citizens' Campaign Watch webcast the conferences and established conference chat rooms so that the events would be accessible to those unable to attend. On its website, the conferences were described as "engaged in the politics of ideas" and as attempting to "revitalize what has become a superficial political debate in America." In other words, in intent and form, these conferences explicitly sought to foster public discourse about matters of common concern. They attempted to be inclusive, circulate the information exchanged at the conference, and elicit feedback from those not physically present. Rather than advocating for a particular ideological position, the conferences included speakers with different political perspectives and fostered open discussion on these issues.

The efforts undertaken by national citizen groups, so often referred to in pejorative terms, were among the most robust in fostering meaningful communication with outsiders. The organizations were not focused exclusively on lobbying during the campaign events, but rather invested significant energy into promoting participatory discursive environments more often associated with the activities of grassroots community groups.

Local Organizations and Real Live People

National prominence and vast resources are not necessary to perform this type of public outreach. Bootstraps, a tiny local organization in Boston, organized what they referred to as an "ethics hour." The event involved a core member of Bootstraps dividing attendees into small groups to discuss issues that had figured prominently during the campaign season. The groups were given background information on their particular issue (e.g., social security) and information about the respective positions of both presidential candidates (presented in some depth without editorializing, and accompanied by quotes from the candidates). Each small group read through the information and then a moderator facilitated discussion on the policy issue. The goal was to help participants gather adequate information to guide their political choices, rather than to persuade them to support a particular set of policy preferences. Ken, a core member from Bootstraps, explained their goals: "Civic participation is exactly the type of thing we like to promote and increasing awareness around that, and trying to get people excited about dialogue and discussing issues and diversity of perspective is exactly the type of thing that we aspire to, so it [the ethics hour prior to the debate] was a natural thing." Ken even used the language that we associate with the public sphere. One of Bootstraps' primary organizational motives is to generate public mindedness and rational, egalitarian debate, which they worked to create in their mobilization.

Bootstraps was one of a few local groups that worked to engage people directly, but the national mailing list citizen groups stood out as the unsung heroes of face-to-face political communication. These professionally run citizen groups might not facilitate social solidarity among members like the classic American voluntary associations preferred by Skocpol and Putnam, but they make new, noteworthy contributions to the public sphere. In the campaign context, citizen groups created discursive opportunities and politicized public spaces in which participants had occasion to recognize shared interests, learn about the perspectives of others, and practice public mindedness. This type of political discussion is recognized as both increasingly rare and vitally important.[2]

Talk to Me

The media obsession is particularly interesting since the associations had many different motives for participating. As discussed in chapter 2, some were explicitly interested in capturing the moment of heightened political interest prompted by the presidential election. Others sought to take advantage of the energy and interest the campaign events sparked in the host cities. These motives both suggest reaching out to people in the vicinity, and yet this was eclipsed by media-centrism. Not all goals are best served by media coverage, and yet the media loom large, seeming to hover over the public sphere as the only (or at least the best) route to communication, even when unmediated interactions are possible.

That these ambitious groups fared so poorly with the mainstream news media is disconcerting, though not entirely surprising. But it is somewhat counterintuitive that groups of people bending over backward training to communicate a message would be unwilling or unable to communicate with regular people. If the activists had approached public outreach as a more local and gradual process, as an opportunity to organize, their preparations would have been dramatically different. Imagine trainings designed to break down the barrier between activists and pedestrians. What set of circumstances would most likely prompt a commuter on his or her way into the office or a parent pushing a stroller to stop and think seriously about their issues? How might group members raise awareness and encourage outsiders to support their efforts, or even participate in them? How might they move from eye-catching stunt to meaningful communication?

The Chinese Cultural Freedom Collective's compelling exhibit of torture and the gentle inquiry of their guides offer some insight. There are diverse paths to face-to-face outreach, but leaving a pile of newsletters on a table or passing out fliers as pedestrians whisk past does not take seriously the challenge and importance of reaching regular people. In a cluttered urban landscape littered with canvassers, panhandlers, solicitous survey researchers, and vulture-like sales people at kiosks wanting to "ask you a question," pedestrians are leery of being approached. A political flier is at best a curiosity, at worst immediate trash—a symbol of a conversation thankfully averted—not a call to learn or understand or become involved. Given this context, it's possible that activists felt intimidated by pedestrians, afraid of being rebuffed. If that were the case, then all the more reason associations might be well served to invest time strategizing about how best to reach busy, skeptical people. But activist groups simply did not invest resources in face-to-face communication.

The activists practiced their scripts, but the lines they rehearsed proved unsuccessful with laypeople, who were put off by their dogmatism and exclusionary language. Perhaps reaching 5 or 20 or even 100 people just didn't feel visionary enough, when the news media offered the hope of reaching a mass audience. But in their fervor to engage that remote public—which we have seen is rarely reached—associations missed an opportunity for more modest success. An exclusionary news media, then, is not a sufficient explanation for associations' inability to transmit their cares and concerns to outsiders. And direct outreach is not the only cost of the media chase, as I show in the next chapter.

6

What About Us?

Bittersweet Residues of Mobilization

IN LOS ANGELES, a coalition of voluntary associations, including Christians for Families and Rights Now, organized a march for immigrant rights. The late afternoon event was poignant. Large white crosses, each one carried to symbolize the life of someone who had died as a result of U.S. immigration policies, punctuated the sizable, intergenerational, multiethnic crowd. On a flatbed truck, a young woman of color holding a microphone shared her experience working at a Gap factory outside the United States. She described being beaten and fired when the supervisor learned that she was pregnant. Meanwhile, the march wound its way through the garment district, and workers wearing hairnets peered out the windows overhead. Some opened the windows and cheered, while a few waved T-shirts over their heads in support of the marchers. The event was unusually riveting, with its sea of white crosses, the diverse crowd, the garment workers in the windows, and the disturbing testimony.

Despite this arresting mise-en-scène, news cameras were clustered to the side of the street, camera operators turned away from the march with their cameras angled slightly downward. As I got closer, I recognized an on-air personality from a Los Angeles news program, holding a microphone. She looked out of place; her meticulously colored and styled hair, fresh makeup, and well-pressed suit seemed impossible in the unrelenting August sun. The cameras were not pointed at her; instead, they pointed toward a person sitting on the curb, whom I could barely make out through the forest of media personnel. The newscaster shook her head in frustration, complaining to a camera operator, "He isn't saying anything." I strained to peer around the cameras and discovered that the "he" in question was a 14- or 15-year-old boy sitting on the curb, dressed as many black-bloc anarchists dress: black pants and a black T-shirt, with a red bandana covering his nose and mouth. His pale white skin was brightly flushed from the heat, and his wavy blond hair was matted with sweat. He did not look well. Although the boy wasn't saying anything, I stood and watched the news workers stare at him.

Figure 6.1. Much like the media's intense focus on the under-the-weather anarchist at the immigrants' rights march in Los Angeles, here photographers come running when a mild verbal altercation erupts between pro-life and pro-choice demonstrators. The activists are not visible in the photo, as they are engulfed by the horde of photographers with cameras poised to capture the conflict.

The cameras stayed on the boy, and the anchorwoman lingered. After a few minutes, there was a tightening of the already clustered cameras; something was happening. The huddle released fairly quickly, and the on-air personality worked her way out of the circle as she exasperatedly griped to her camera crew that the boy was just tired and wanted some water. "Isn't that ridiculous?!" she blurted as she hustled away.

There it was: the ultimate reporting cliché, almost a caricature of the critiques levied against the news media. Here, amid what, at least to me, appeared to be an incredible story of immigrant pain, loss, and determination in Los Angeles, was a cluster of news workers with blinders on, hungry for conflict.

These media members were so desperate for conflict that they laid in wait, hoping this boy would behave like they thought an anarchist should behave—that he would do something defiant or angry or violent. Their expectations were rooted so firmly in place that at least a subset of the crew was irritated with him when he failed to live up to their expectations. How dare this kid be hot, tired, and thirsty? *Now* what were they supposed to do? It should not be surprising to learn that the coordinating coalition did not get the press they were after. Yet we should not focus exclusively on external communication, even if that's what most associations seem to do.

The immigrants' rights coalition, with its palpable solidarity, clearly articulated shared injuries and outrage, and unexpected onlookers cheering from the windows overhead, presses us to ask the following: Even if failing to obtain media attention means that most associations haven't met their objectives, doesn't mobilization generate other by-products? Doesn't this community count for something? While the voluntary associations I describe placed disproportionate emphasis on attempting to shape mainstream political discourse, it is also important to explore how the act of mobilizing shapes the associations themselves. Leaving questions of political impact aside, what are the consequences of this swelling of participation for group life?

The answers are complex and contradictory, and marked by significant variation across the organizations, but listening to activists suggests at least two things. First, the notion that "the worst thing that can happen to activists is to be ignored" (Davis, Pre-born Protectors) is incorrect. Although the injuries vary from group to group, it is clear that being "just" invisible is somewhat of a neutral outcome—nothing ventured, nothing gained. But most organizations do venture something for mobilizations of this magnitude, and as a result, for many groups the pursuit of the media gaze is not neutral in its effect on their organizations, but rather yields tangible and intangible losses. The second thing the data reveal about association outcomes is that while an outsider may see doom and gloom, feeling the sting of disappointment for their modest accomplishments, many organizations and their members feel fully satisfied, even elated, by their efforts. This sense of achievement—as improbable as it seems given their stated goals and objectives—matters a great deal.

The Costs We Expect to Find:
Major Association Efforts Require Major Effort

By definition, heightened activity involves an increased organizational commitment. Activist groups allocated significant time, funding, and

energy to their campaign efforts, often at the expense of other priorities. Similarly, the mobilizations often required staff, leaders, members,
and participants to contribute more of themselves, frequently drawing
energy away from other priorities within and even outside the organization (e.g., work, family, personal interests). This was particularly true for
leaders. Most activists reported that the efforts were "worth it," but there
were dissenting voices. Greg, from the Land and Life Protection League,
quite candidly described the ambivalence he felt about his organization's
investment in campaign work:

> We put a big chunk of money into the convergence space and just sort of
> the overall organizing. In Philly, in particular, the resource-intensiveness
> was, you know, three or four of us [paid staff] there for a good solid at
> least a week and a half, focusing predominantly on Philly. So, that's quite
> a lot for an organization like ours to have three or four campaigners and
> organizers focused on one thing for a week and a half, almost two weeks.
> And it was just a lot of strategic kind of thoughts about—is it worth our
> time, is it worth our energy, you know, short-term, long-term, building
> relationships in the movement, supporting these kind of efforts, and so
> on.

> *Was it?*

> The jury is still out, I think. There were definitely benefits for us and for
> others, no doubt, but there were a lot of costs for sure. We sort of haven't
> sat down and sort of really debriefed to the extent that we need to about,
> you know, what role would we play in this similar situation. I know it
> would be different. Let me put it that way.

> *Oh really?*

> Yes. You know, it totally destroyed us. I mean, the folks who went to
> Philly, man, we worked eighteen-, nineteen-hour days. We put our other
> work aside and you know, what were the real benefits of it? To what extent
> was it necessary for us as an organization?

In a similar vein, Dagan from Jews for Justice described the stress on her
organization as it grappled with "trying to balance the different parts of
what we were trying to do. . . . I think it was a little too much for what we

have the capacity for, but once we were into it, it was sort of hard to think about cutting anything."

Most groups strained themselves rather than "cutting anything," and sometimes organizations were sufficiently overtaxed that they could not carry out their plans effectively. Paul from Pre-born Protectors described a challenge his organization faced as a result of not having more help on location:

> We did have one or two events there that were some follow-up marches to the [John] Kerry condo [protest], which did have, unfortunately, people showing up—people showed up when there was no event. You know, because we were not able to get "approval" for actually going down to the condo itself. So we dropped two [scheduled events] and we just couldn't get somebody there to kind of ward off the ones who were gonna show up, which is always a very negative thing. As an organizer, you don't want to have something and then have people just, you know, show up for nothing. Or at least with somebody there to say, "We're sorry, this was canceled."

Paul described feeling concerned about how members would react, and he saw the problem as linked both to the group being understaffed and to the "fatigue factor" he and the other organizer experienced.

It was not easy to manage these efforts, and the leaders I spoke with, such as Aaron from Veterans Opposing War, were far more likely than lay members to describe themselves as depleted:

> I felt burned out. I was working on the thing. The average [member] who comes there, they participate. I was one of the people who was helping produce it, so I was in a little different position. . . . I was just glad it was over when it was over and it came off well. That's because I was in the core of organizing. I don't mean alone, there was a lot of us, but it's like—that's an emotional and an energy commitment.

Other leaders described feeling exhausted and run down from keeping up a frenetic pace: one mentioned a physical toll on his back, another described what he called the "psychological toll," and several described feeling guilty about time they had taken away from other responsibilities. For example, when asked about the future of Stand Up St. Louis, Brenda commented: "I plan to stay involved and to support the events, but probably to be less active than I was in this mobilization. I really put my life on hold to do this. My family, my work, my community efforts, they just really were neglected."

Rochelle, from Disrupt, expressed the deepest frustration with her leadership role. She felt that she and the other local organizers did a tremendous amount of work but were unappreciated by the people who came from out of town to participate. As a result, Rochelle expressed uncertainty about whether she would be willing to extend herself in the future. The responsibility placed on leaders was not something that affected them solely as individuals; it also affected the larger organizations when feelings of physical or emotional burnout prompted attrition.

These organizational costs were to be expected, and robust groups most likely absorbed them gracefully over time. But the cost of mobilization that I found most striking went without remark by most individuals involved: the toll on internal communication.

Hidden Costs: How the Culture of Mobilization Sabotages Discourse Among Association Members

Communication is the lifeblood of voluntary associations. Warren (2001, 39) argues, "In contrast to markets and bureaucracies, association is the form of social organization that thrives on talk, normative agreement, cultural similarity, and shared ambitions—that is, forms of communication that are rooted in speech, gesture, self-presentation, and related forms of social interaction." And Lichterman (2006) revisits Tocqueville, reminding us that while civic health has been assessed largely by counting group memberships, it is the interaction that transpires within these groups, the meaningful relationships among group members, that Tocqueville valued, seeing these connections as vital to helping participants think and work in public-spirited ways.

Perrin (2006) draws on this Tocquevillian tradition, asserting that group talk about politics is an important form of political activity in its own right. He argues that thinking and talking about politics are important citizenship activities that shape the democratic imagination, which we draw on when we consider our political options and ultimately choose our political behaviors.[1] Polletta (2002) also highlights the value of talk, arguing that meaningful deliberation in social movement organizations benefits the group as well as its individual members. Specifically, she argues that extended, egalitarian dialogue fosters tactical innovation by drawing on multiple input streams, builds solidarity by connecting members to one another in meaningful ways, and produces developmental benefits (e.g., learning how to negotiate) for those who partake. Polletta also points to such outcomes as tolerance, which emerges as participants listen to the ideas of others with whom they may not agree, and commitment to the group, which stems from the belief that their contributions are valuable and have been taken seriously.

Some of the best recent sociological work on voluntary associations has explored the variation in discourse in different group settings, demonstrating the differing character, quantity, and quality of talk across groups. Perrin (2005, 2006) points to "political microcultures"—social environments with distinct discourse contexts, which serve as resources for political thinking and behavior—as central to understanding the ways people think about citizenship and engagement. Hart (2001) compares groups that are more expansive with those that are more constrained in their political talk. Eliasoph and Lichterman (2003) show how "group style" or context, of which speech norms are a prominent characteristic, shape behavior. Lichterman (2006) further demonstrates not only that talk varies in different associations, but also that the *meaning* of talk is constructed in different ways in different group contexts. There are, for example, some settings in which talk is valued and seen as an end in itself, and others in which talk is merely tolerated, seen as the unwanted stepchild of "real" action.

Media-centric Activism and Internal Talk

Activists' efforts at external communication in the campaign context were thwarted by their inability to circulate their ideas via the news, and by the absence of effort on the part of most organizations to cultivate face-to-face communication with laypeople. Nonetheless, it remained possible—even probable—that these external setbacks could be accompanied by the kind of internal group enrichment that Perrin, Polletta, and others identify as emerging through talk. Members' heightened involvement during a mobilization coupled with the increase in time spent working together seem to create an environment ripe for enhanced communication.

Because my unit of analysis is the group, I am not equipped to assess whether group members developed tolerance or negotiation skills by talking through difficult issues with those from whom they differed. Nor do I have a means to assess whether participants expanded the vitality of their democratic imaginations. But I can address the degree to which talk was nurtured in the associations I studied. The answer is, not very well. In fact, I found that in the process of mobilizing, most groups actively worked to restrict and control their internal communication.

I identified three distinct ways in which political talk was stifled within the associations as a by-product of media-centered activism. First, with organizers focused intently on ensuring that their mobilizations would be successful in terms of public relations, they often approached participants as potential liabilities in need of management, rather than as trusted peers able to make valuable contributions. Second, association discourse was suppressed through norms of confluence that privileged consensus so highly that discussing issues on which participants disagreed was deemed inappropriate, lest the group appear divided to outsiders or muddle the take-home message for the media. Finally, association culture became relentlessly focused on logistics, marginalizing broader political or philosophical discussions, which were perceived as inefficient. Taken as a whole, not only did the activist groups fail to promote *external* public discourse, many also suppressed *internal* dialogue. This emerged from the relentless concentration on impression management that accompanied the pursuit of media attention.

Member Management

Leaders were so intent on ensuring that their mobilizations were effective media events that many worked to monitor and regulate the speech of the general members, whom they perceived as potential liabilities. When I asked Charles from Network for Peace why they trained activists to bring journalists to designated spokespeople instead of answering questions themselves, he replied that it was a "lesson learned the hard way":

> If you let your members talk to the media, they may have all the best intentions and just really not be well-informed, which would make the organization look terrible or, even if the media folks come up to someone who is well-informed, that person might freeze up on camera. A video camera is a permanent record. You can't go back and proofread it before it goes out there to the world. That is why we don't just let anyone talk, you know; it's just too big a risk.

It was fairly common for leaders to describe participants in this way, as good-hearted incompetents, people who would intend to represent the group well but would likely be unable to do so. Network for Peace has a small staff and there is a clear distinction between lay members and leaders, so perhaps it is unsurprising that this would be their approach, but such member management was not limited to hierarchical or professionally run organizations. For example, Disrupt, which used a participatory democracy model with an affinity group/spokes-council structure to disperse power, was also intent on disciplining the speech of participants. Instead of insisting that members funnel reporters to authorized spokespeople, Disrupt implemented extensive media trainings designed to shape what participants would say if approached by a journalist. Rochelle, a core member, explained why they needed to be so thorough: "I think that it's scary to have a camera in your face, so I think that that is a major factor—people getting scared, and you always worry that someone is going to say something stupid and that's going to be the thing that makes it onto the news." Rochelle sympathized with those who felt unsettled by the prospect of being interviewed, but her overriding concern was that this discomfort might lead a member to "say something stupid." This worry transferred to those who participated in the training. In the first moments of my fieldwork with Disrupt's Loren, I thanked him for being willing to speak with me and described the stonewalling I had received from other activists working in the group (discussed in chapter 4)[2]. He explained somewhat apologetically, "Everyone is trained to shut up," and went on to say that all they had been "taught" was "to have a sound bite ready to give away." They were not prepared to speak as themselves, in a non-spokesperson capacity; in fact, they had been cautioned against doing so.

Implicit in these strategies was a recognition that while the groups hoped to garner media attention, the color and the character of the publicity remained outside their control. Unlike paid advertisements, organizations relying on news coverage relinquished the right to edit or to choose the context in which their group or issues would be discussed. Since they were unable to control journalists, editors, and producers, the groups strived to control their participants.

Some activists described feeling ready for their media work and expressed interest in being approached by journalists, but many were anxious. They seemed to distrust their ability to handle the situation, adopting this view of themselves as potential liabilities. Sid, an outgoing and loquacious volunteer with the American Adult Network, transitioned away from his warm and open demeanor when I asked a question about working with journalists. He was edgy and awkward as he explained to me that he was prepared and could handle himself:

They teach us how to look on camera and how to look off camera and how to answer the questions. They talked to us about how to be comfortable, how to, you know, think of reporters as human, just like I am, and that I shouldn't have anxiety because I'm speaking to a person who is knowledgeable as a journalist. I need to not worry about entrapment, because I don't think—if I thought a reporter was trying to do some entrapment, I'd walk away. They want us to stick in with the interviews you know, but to say what we're supposed to say. If we say what we're supposed to say, if we're on message, you can't get entrapped at all.

Sid was apprehensive and concerned that if he did not stick to that script the press would use his words against him, and this fear seems to have emerged from the media training he received. He alluded to three distinct components of this training: an effort to demystify the experience of communicating with journalists in order to calm members and prevent them from freezing up on camera (several leaders expressed this concern); a contradictory message that journalists may, in fact, try to make them say something inappropriate; and finally, rhetorical techniques to help prevent their statements from being misconstrued (i.e., staying "on message"). Sid's repeated references to saying what he is "supposed to say" indicates the presence of a party line to which he had been instructed to adhere.

While Sid's media training may sound extensive, it was common for associations to train their members in this way. Some went even further. Liza, a United Trades union member, provided an example of how elaborate these trainings could become:

They talked to us about how to do a good job if we get approached on the street by a reporter, you know, making sure we had accurate information and making sure we could get it in a little sound bite. Just to make it sound OK. They showed us tapes of news shows and we talked about what the reporters want to have. We were focused a lot on making the job easy for the news and also on making ourselves look good. Then after we had the talk, we each got to practice getting interviewed and then we watched ourselves on TV so we could see how we did, you know, what we could do better. That was really fun. They asked us different questions and we could see how we did under pressure. We were laughing a lot, but we also learned a lot. I never thought so much about the news in my life.

The union sought to help members understand the objectives and constraints of the news production process so that they could give accounts that would fit into the model. This training sounds more collaborative and less hierarchical than the trainings referenced by Sid and Loren. Yet a key element of this workshop involved practice interviews on camera, which were subsequently reviewed and critiqued. The goal of both the "predatory journalist" training received by Sid and the behind-the-scenes news production training that Liza received was the same: to shape members' speech. The associations presumed that members' candid responses were too risky. And yet, Sid was an active member of the organization and a longtime volunteer with a deep commitment to the group's political goals. Did he need media boot camp in order to represent the American Adult Network well? The irony is that candid responses would have been more desirable to the news workers, as demonstrated in chapter 4.

The emphasis on member management reveals a lopsided discourse. When participants are given information to recite or are trained to "shut up," the implicit message is that left to their own devices, members will make a mistake, and that what they think and feel without such coiffing is inaccurate or dangerous.

Having a series of talking points in and of itself does not indicate a stifling of dialogue. On the contrary, a clearly articulated set of priorities may very well be the product of open debate within a group. But as these interview excerpts reveal, the subtext of the media trainings that respondents described (and I witnessed) was one of infantilization and damage control, rather than a collaborative environment where participants worked together to develop messages and strategies. Indeed, at moments the extensive handling of lay activists by leaders (in some cases professional staff and in others unpaid leaders) evoked memories of an elementary school photographer working to set up the class group shot, disposable combs at the ready and detailed instruction on how to position each chin, shoulder, and hand.

Perhaps the most pronounced example of member management emerged at an event held by Moms for New Leadership, an organization that had formed in response to the 2004 election. Moms for New Leadership was an unusual organization in many respects. It was brand-new, made up almost exclusively of middle-aged women, and had developed many chapters across the country very quickly as a result of a good website and some early publicity stemming from the activists' clever and kitschy presentation of themselves as a wholesome "bunch of moms" calling for the ouster of the president. When the organizers came to New York for the convention, they reached out to their relatively new local chapters and invited members to come to the organization's big national event in their backyard—a publicity event for journalists that involved screening their new campaign advertisement, accompanied by commentary from the organization's founder, two prominent activists, and an A-list celebrity.

Melissa, a member, was excited to attend to support the organization, meet the leaders, and become more involved (she had already donated money, attended two meetings of the New York chapter, and helped with an art auction to raise funds for the group). She was disappointed to find that she was only invited, in her words, "for looks." She went to participate but felt she was ultimately ignored:

> Basically they had told me to come and wear one of their T-shirts. But then there was no clear instructions for what I was supposed to do. So I sort of hung out in the hall with some other people. Some people were actually kind of offended because they shuttled us into a different room when they were ushering the press people in. We were *persona non grata*. And—

> *Why did they do that?*

> To get us out of the way. We were just there for looks, so that it wouldn't look like the organizers were the whole group. But they didn't know what else to do with us I guess. I don't really know. I mean, I didn't get much of a sense from the people who organized sort of why they wanted me to be there. They could have cared less who I was or if I had anything to offer other than just to show that there was some membership in this organization. I felt a little used [laughs].

Here, the lay members of the group were handled like props, used to meet the organizers' needs without so much as a nod toward their ideas, interests, or experiences. Melissa went on to say that one of the other women from New York was so angry about the way they had been treated that she almost walked out before the screening even began.

This was not a moment when we would expect association members to be engaging in deliberative talk. It was an instrumental event that organizers wanted to execute properly. Yet there was an opportunity for the leaders, who are based in the mid-Atlantic, to connect with some of their most supportive members. Instead of capitalizing on this opportunity by creating some adjacent time for community building or member contributions, they deployed members strategically, without their input, and when they had served their purpose, they herded them away in an effort to restrict their contact with journalists. At the event's end, Melissa didn't bask in the afterglow of a hard-earned group victory; she felt exploited. Given these circumstances, it is not surprising that she decided to discontinue her involvement with the group. In contrast, Rose, the leader of the organization, perceived the event as a success.

Rose was pleased with the event because she had adopted a marketing mentality. Her goal for the organization was to attract media and showcase the group and its work. Because this was her central focus, member engagement and social cohesion were not her metrics for success. Instead, communication within the association in this context amounted to maneuvering participants to ensure that they helped construct the image of the group that the leaders wanted broadcast: one of a lively and large organization of reasonable people—"moms"—determined that George W. Bush not be reelected. The support of lay members was needed, but only to create a visual impression. This is why there were no clear instructions for Melissa. She wasn't told what to do because there was nothing for her to do, apart from showing up in the T-shirt and then getting out of the way. She was treated like a mannequin.

Listen to how differently the discussion of members sounds when described by representatives from Veterans Opposing War, whose mobilization was *not* focused primarily on obtaining media attention. Here is Aaron, one of national leaders of the organization:

> When we do conventions, we do a public event, but we sort of try to treat them as being—I don't want to use the word retreat, like a retreat, but it's a place where you get [members] together and you network, and you share information, and you make plans. A large piece of it is internal, the organization meeting.

And Case, a Veterans Opposing War member, had gotten the message that members mattered beyond their instrumental utility:

> Well, we have something; we have a unifying thing in our [former military] service . . . and part of it is the relationship with each other. . . . The relationship with each other is one of the most important things that we have and [we are] really putting a lot of energy into the relationship. And if we can relate to each other and become fond of each other, then once that happens, you know, there's cohesion there. There's a lot of cohesion from fondness.

The difference between the message that Aaron received from Veterans Opposing War and the message that Melissa received from Moms for New Leadership was dramatic. Veterans Opposing War carved out space for members to connect with one another and communicated that these relationships mattered, while Moms for New Leadership had indicated that the press was what mattered and that members were essentially disposable.

It is possible to imagine scenarios in which activist groups cultivate internal communication *and* seek the attention of outsiders, but organizations in this sample demonstrate that in the absence of media-centrism, space emerges for internal talk, which is much harder to uncover in organizations with an external focus. Member management practices create hierarchical and in some cases unidirectional internal communication, implicitly suggesting that member contributions are not valued. This fails to align with images of voluntary associations as free spaces in which ideas circulate, debates unfold, and deliberation among equals transpires. Interestingly, this hierarchy emerged even in organizations that viewed themselves as egalitarian and emphasized consensus-based decision-making processes.

Even without individual-level data to assess the outcome of this control culture, it is safe to assume that limiting members' ability to contribute freely thwarted organizations' ability to offer developmental benefits to participants and robbed leaders of the opportunity to learn from the members. Fisher's (2006) case study of the People's Project shows us what happens when member management is taken to the extreme. Her book depicts a climate in which enthusiastic activists are put through assembly-line training and asked to interact with potential supporters constantly, but only in the language of a script regurgitated verbatim. Long hours of canvassing with minimal opportunity to contribute (other than physically) leads to low member morale and high turnover, and ultimately drives some out of progressive politics altogether.

Agreeing to Agree

Some groups restricted dialogue by establishing parameters of permissible conversation. Many set up ground rules for respectful communication, and some went even further, explicitly urging participants to not discuss matters on which they disagreed. Presumably, activists shared the broad goals of the groups with which they were affiliated, yet variations in interests and priorities often were quashed in favor of maintaining consensus and support for existing philosophies. As a result, room for dialogue about sensitive or difficult issues was eliminated in some organizations for fear that it would erode social solidarity, give outsiders an impression that the organization was plagued by internal divisiveness, or render the organization's message murky.

Activists often expressed concern that talking about complicated or contentious political issues would be damaging to the relationships among members and affect their ability to work together. As a result, many described intentionally avoiding discussion of matters over which there was disagreement. Ajay talked about this happening in Students for Change:

> Some people were pro-Nader and others were about voting for Gore to avoid Bush, and others didn't see Nader as left enough and were in support of other candidates. We actually talked very little about voting—it was too sensitive, I guess. We could agree on all being left politically, though. That's how we kept our disagreement from being a problem; we talked about the things we did agree on, or the thing we agreed on, which was basically that the debates weren't democratic. We left our personal political views out of meetings and basically focused on talking about the problem, the fact that there wasn't real dialogue happening in the debate. The solution was what was messier, I mean, not the solution to the lack of dialogue, but the political solutions to the issues we were raising.

The participants limited talk to the issues that everyone could agree on, the least common denominator, rather than addressing the issues where they sensed conflict might arise. Ironically, Students for Change avoided difficult discussions yet hoped to call attention to the absence of "real dialogue" in the debate.

Other organizations avoided sensitive topics as well, hoping to prevent tension and group conflict. Nina from End Contemporary Colonialism alluded to problems that emerged in her organization around "political differences," but indicated that the group handled them by "just moving on," avoiding controversial subjects while focusing on the areas of agreement. This was also the strategy used by Jews for Justice, whose members had differing feelings about the Israeli-Palestinian conflict that were too sensitive to engage and were therefore officially off-limits.

This choice is not entirely surprising. Talking through difficult issues is stressful and time-consuming, and has been perceived as a shortcoming of some social movement groups of the late 1960s. The decision to float over the thorny patches allows groups to function in the instrumental sense, yet at the same time it eliminates the possibility of confronting difficult issues in what might be the ideal space to do so. Since group members have common ground, it is likely that participants would be more willing to listen to others' arguments and viewpoints, and would feel more comfortable sharing their own, than they might in other contexts. If there is no room to talk about difficult political issues in organizations of largely like-minded activists, then where is there room to do so? Yet, paralyzed by fear that conflict would interfere with goal attainment, many associations deemed this communicative work too risky.

Because of their fragility, coalitions worked unusually hard to establish and stick to uniting principles, but this was not necessarily easy. Prior to the first presidential debate in Boston, Students for Change and the Northeast Union of Professionals splintered away from a coalition they had joined to coordinate a response to the debate. The two subgroups left the coalition because they sensed an underlying tension among member organizations but also perceived that the key organizers were unwilling to work through the problems. The issues that most worried the splintering groups were: (1) a lack of consensus on the role of civil disobedience in the events they were planning; and (2) strenuous disagreement between groups who felt the debate was fatally flawed and should be condemned in its entirety (because it was not open to third-party candidates), and those organizations whose representatives wanted to come out in support of Al Gore (particularly labor unions).

Students for Change and the Northeast Union of Professionals were prescient; on the evening of the debate, the perimeter of the UMass–Boston campus erupted with heated conflicts between the tremendous labor presence (estimated at 5,000 people) and those critical of the debate altogether, who engaged in a largely unsuccessful effort to disrupt the event. In addition to the standard reports of police/protester conflict (or lack thereof), the Boston newspapers documented incidents of verbal altercations, physical skirmishes, and rock throwing between union members and other activists (Bombardieri 2000; Richardson and Hanchett 2000). The issues forum organized by Stand Up St. Louis simmered with similar tensions, though without the conflagrations experienced in Boston. Despite the dangers that might have emerged when substantive disagreements were ignored, avoidance seemed to be a common strategy.

While common, this was not something that appeared in all associations. In some groups, although members had points of disagreement, there was neither a formal prohibition on dialogue nor the sense that participants were walking on eggshells. And some organizations shared widespread consensus on salient issues, making that thickly shared worldview the very foundation of the group. I saw this kind of ideological camaraderie in Feminists for a Socialist Future and most groups that were religiously based, such as the Wrath of Christ, Christians for Families, and Pre-born Protectors. Not prohibiting the discussion of sensitive issues, however, is not the same thing as nurturing internal political talk, which I encountered only with the Progressive Activists Coalition, as I will describe below.

In addition to encountering an implicit and sometimes explicit[2] preference for avoiding disagreement, a more generalized norm of conformity permeated many organizations. Group members frequently made presumptions about my political beliefs and values based on nothing more than my presence. And although it was uncommon, there were moments where pressure to conform was overt. Because, in most groups, participants were ideologically compatible, norms of conformity usually became visible around relatively minor issues. For example, during my interview with Rochelle from Disrupt, two young group members abruptly interrupted us (an emergency was unfolding at one of Disrupt's workspaces), and my audio recorder captured the following interaction:

YOUNG MAN: [out of breath] Excuse me. Is there a local ordinance against infiltrating groups?

ROCHELLE: I don't know exactly what the story is.

ME: The police aren't allowed to do any intelligence gathering.

YOUNG MAN: Really? I just don't know what the jurisdiction is.

ROCHELLE: I don't know any of the legality of it, but there was a big thing when they admitted that they had been spying on us because previously they had said, "No, if we were doing that, it would be illegal."

YOUNG MAN: But I know there is a consent decree against some of the things they do, I'm just not sure exactly what the extent of it is. After they bombed the MOVE cult, they got an order, which they agreed to, so it's some kind of judicial order that prevents them from—

ROCHELLE: Are you talking about MOVE? *I don't really think it's appropriate to call them a cult.*

YOUNG MAN: Well, OK, that just the way I read them—

ROCHELLE: Well, I mean, yeah, that is the media depiction, but *I think that, especially if you are here working on this kind of thing, you should be a little more aware of things.*

YOUNG MAN: So what's the story on them?

ROCHELLE: They were just a radical group. They are still active in Philadelphia and they are still working. They do a lot of Mumia support; their organization is the center of it, and I think that they get a really bad rap and are misunderstood by the mainstream people. *So people who are here, working on something like the convention . . . I definitely think should not be referring to them as a cult.*

YOUNG MAN: OK. I didn't know anything about them.

This conversation revolved around the 1985 police bombing of a house in West Philadelphia occupied by MOVE, a predominantly African American antigovernment organization.³ Many have perceived MOVE as a cult over the years, because the members followed the teachings of its leader, John Africa, practiced a form of voluntary simplicity, and adopted the surname "Africa." The young man was sternly reprimanded not because he was misinformed, but because he failed to share an appropriately progressive understanding of MOVE.⁴ Norms were in place regarding what language and interpretations were acceptable, and this young man had violated them. The rapport between Rochelle and the young man recovered somewhat as he and his friend described the details of a raid happening elsewhere in the city, but the young man was visibly embarrassed to have been corrected.

As mentioned above, I found a noteworthy space where disagreement and dialogue, while not easy, were allowed to flourish. The Progressive Activists Coalition was one of the only organizations that mobilized communally, hoping to build relationships among different progressive organizations by creating a multiday conference on progressive issues. Organizers created physical spaces for exchange, and the culture of movement building that permeated the event produced markedly different results from the various participants' perspectives.

Alena was one of the lead organizers of the progressive coalition and a member of a subcommittee working on one of the most politically sensitive issues for progressives, the Israeli occupation of Palestine. One of the strategies she and her collaborators used in discussing this divisive issue with a group comprising participants with divergent views was to focus on the abstract principles that apply to the conflict. In particular, they framed the discussion around international humanitarian laws and the United

Nations resolutions that have been passed in response to the Israeli-Palestinian conflict. Organizers approached the sensitive topic by moving up one level of abstraction to principles on which participants could agree, but they did so as an appeal to reason, to avoid knee-jerk emotional responses, not to avoid talking about the controversial topic. In fact, although they entered the topic from the vantage point of humanitarian law, Alena and her collaborators repeatedly linked this back to the specific conditions and experiences of the Palestinian people. Alena stressed that they focused on treating other people with respect throughout the process. The outcome was not avoidance, but rather engagement:

> You know, there were a lot of disagreements and whatever, but the people that were there—even the people who disagree, you know—were willing to listen. See, that's a difficult thing with [this] position. Many times, you know, people will just immediately cut you off and they will not want to listen, but the good thing about the [opportunity to work with other organizations in this setting] is the caliber of the people that were there. I mean they may have strongly disagreed with you and in some cases even vehemently disagreed with you, but they would talk to you. They would talk to you.

It is no coincidence that this counterexample exists in one of the rare spaces where mainstream news coverage was not the primary objective. Groups that sought publicity via the mainstream news media felt compelled to quash difficult conversations, lest the logistics get lost or the target audience be left with a potentially unflattering image of the group.

Political Discourse as Inefficient

Participants in some organizations attempted to rein in political discussions, because they were seen as inefficient—perceived as frivolous and less important than strategic or logistical matters. Brian from Inequality Forever shared his disdain for groups with a propensity to talk too much about such things: "I think that we've already, you know, ideology has already been agreed upon [in advance] . . . because I think most organizing groups nowadays don't like to discuss ideology because then you get into those stupid arguments—people that call themselves anarchists, people that call themselves communists. It's just a waste of time." He regarded such discussions as pointless, a sentiment that was not uncommon. Sometimes the message was less categorical and political conversations were acknowledged as useful, but even when this was the case, respondents expressed a shared belief that mobilization was not the appropriate time or place for such discussions.

This was particularly visible in e-mail lists and group meetings, where people raising larger questions were chastised for straying from "more important" logistical issues (e.g., coordinating volunteers or signage). Below is one example from the United for Change e-mail list. When talk turned briefly from logistics to a more substantive discussion about the long-term political goals of the group, one of the members whose contributions were particularly valued e-mailed the following:

> Date: Wednesday, July 12, 2000 6:50 PM
> To: July 30 in Philly
> Subject: Re: [July30] Our Goals
>
> Hello:
>   I think we should get the word out and not waste so much energy on political points amongst ourselves. Go download a poster, print copies and staple to phone poles. This will do more.
>
>   —Aaron

But these reprimands were rarely required. There was a conspicuous silence where one might expect to find political talk. Most group meetings and e-mail list exchanges were focused on planning, and more general political questions were rarely raised. Politics danced at the margins, with periodic expressions of mockery or anger directed at one of the candidates, multinational corporations, the rich, or the blasphemers—these groups were clearly not planning a bake sale—but dialogue was conspicuously absent.

Brye with Boston Resistance was a young man who was not reluctant to discuss politics. Here is one short excerpt of his commentary on why he opposed Kerry in 2004 despite the fact that many on the left were supporting him:

> I'm of the opinion that Kerry, and any Democrat, can do just as bad as him [President Bush] and because, you know, Democrats are seen as more liberal, they can sort of hide their policies. Like nobody ever

criticizes Clinton or Gore for, you know, the destructiveness of NAFTA, which they played a big part of. And that's something that's had a continuing legacy, not only in the form of NAFTA, but in the FTAA [Free Trade Area of the Americas] and other trade policies.

He shared this freely, without being asked his opinion on the candidates, but when I asked him if he had discussed this with anyone during his convention mobilization, he replied:

> I don't really remember conversing with anybody about opposing Kerry at the convention [mobilization]. Now after that, you know, especially now when the election's closer or whatever, I'm having a lot of discussions with people [outside the group], because I'm not voting for Kerry and I'm not voting for Bush. So now is really the time when I'm, you know, having those conversations with people and criticizing him.

I then asked Brye if he had had an opportunity to talk about politics in general with the people he organized with in Boston or with other participants at events. He answered:

> You know, I think the majority of the time that I talked about politics is more in terms of what we can do locally to support ourselves. . . . A lot of my discussions revolved around how we can sustain ourselves financially and organizationally when we're not at mass actions. . . . There's usually not a lot of [political] dialogue [at mass actions], in my experience.

Brye talked comfortably about politics with me and had a strong opinion on the election, which he shared frequently with people in his hometown, yet he reported *not having any conversations about his opinion on the election while mobilizing around the convention, even though he was on location with his group for a full week.* And when I pressed him further about political conversations, he described "political" discussions within Boston Resistance as being about sustaining the group, not about political views or priorities.

Without question, a major public outreach requires careful preparation and attention to detail. It may even require immersion in logistics and management at the expense of all else. This is precisely the point. Mobilizing in ways that place outsiders at the center—demonstrative work—is a mode of engagement that has important implications for the associations that choose such a path. Limiting internal talk about substantive issues emerges as one of these implications.

Even in organizations that valued open communication, there was a desire to avoid ideological and political debates. Interestingly, two of the groups that spent the most time in internal dialogue around political issues did so as a means to an end. As discussed in chapter 4, the issue-oriented discussions at the United for Change coalition meetings were plentiful, but they were understood as a necessary step to finding a path of mutual agreement down which the member organizations could proceed. Similarly, members of Stand Up St. Louis devoted time to deciding which topics they wanted to highlight in their issues forum. This was something that had to be discussed and renegotiated as new participants entered the group, but in Brenda's eyes these were logistical details to be addressed. She explained this constant need to revisit issues and reach consensus as her greatest frustration with the group, because she saw it as unfocused and inhibiting progress.

This sense that political dialogue is a distraction even inside politically oriented voluntary associations may seem unexpected, but it supports earlier findings by Lichterman (1999) and Eliasoph (1998), which indicate that people gathering in more public spaces value "real" action over "mere" discussion. This is intriguing, because it suggests that some voluntary associations operate with the same working theory of politics that they have criticized in journalists. Journalists, as we have seen, tend to focus on strategy, on form over substance, when covering activism, and many group members justifiably criticize them for not attending to concrete political issues. Yet most activist groups also placed a pronounced emphasis on strategic communication, at the expense of substantive dialogue. It seems contradictory that organizations so fervently focused on prompting others (e.g., the press, political figures, the general public) to discuss "real" issues preferred to avoid becoming mired in such messiness themselves.

What is the significance of all this "avoiding politics," to borrow from Eliasoph? Meaningful connections to others and to associations are a valuable social good, and political talk is vital to helping people think and work in publicly spirited ways. Without question, we need associations that can represent their members' collective interests in the political arena; efficacy should not be ignored. But group life in its richer forms is also meaningful, promoting social cohesion, norms of reciprocity, civic skills, a connection to political life, and a sense of responsibility to and for others.

Such arguments may be not be compelling for groups focused on closing down an intersection or flaunting celebrities to get into the headlines.

As we have seen, many groups had cultures in which political talk was understood as a waste of time, but even from a coarsely utilitarian stand-point, it is entirely likely that more talk—not less—is what the associations need in order to become stronger. Katherine Cramer Walsh's (2004) ethnographic work shows (among other things) that even informal political dialogue in voluntary associations works to clarify social identities and create a sense of inclusion and cohesion among participants. While some (e.g., Minkoff 1997; Warren 2001) rightly point to the value of loose ties in contemporary society, it's also important to acknowledge their fragility. The members of most associations implicitly attend to their vulner-ability, treating connections between activists and those between activists and the organizations with which they affiliate as frail. Embedded in the fear of sensitive political discussions is an unspoken concern that disagree-ment might create painful divides too deep for participants to overcome. If discovering the details about what others think or feel strongly about is enough to wrench the group apart, then these ties don't show much resil-ience. Many of the groups handled these links gingerly, doing legwork to keep them from fraying, but that legwork might have just as easily been invested in building internal relationships to fortify these connections. I suggest that these ties are asked to accomplish too little: associations satis-fied with respectable membership rosters, and individuals content with an ambient sense of connectedness to an organization whose members they know little about.

If activists had been immersed in more meaningful ways in their re-spective organizations, I suspect leaders would have worried less that par-ticipants' impromptu utterances would reflect badly on the association. If members could understand the organization, its work, and its priorities, their unrehearsed responses to journalists' questions would be "on mes-sage." In other words, talk is exactly the type of association activity that builds these relationships, and with stronger ties, activist groups could worry less about being derailed by their members and could begin to ben-efit from them. Promoting healthy dialogue, then, would likely yield both cultural and instrumental benefits.

But this is conjecture. Regardless of whether the nurturing of meaning-ful political talk can help rescue organizers from their roles as microman-agers, peacekeepers, and guardians of their associations' good names, and free them to attend more fully to their political goals, one thing is clear: the media-centered activism adopted by the majority of groups as they mobi-lize narrows the perceived space for substantive dialogue among members.

The experiences of these associations suggest that the pursuit of media attention is harmful, not because it saps organizational resources, but because of its impact on the health of group life.

Here, in this moment that so many activist groups approached as their most significant undertaking of the year, in this context that energized and increased member willingness to extend themselves, in what was for many groups a rare face-to-face gathering, the majority of associations missed the opportunity to strengthen their organizations. In lieu of this, they patrolled their members and allowed tensions to fester, mistaking a marathon for a sprint, behaving in many ways as if each demonstrative mobilization was the long-term goal, rather than a short-term tactic in the service of other goals.

Serendipity

Standing back and surveying the evidence, mobilization in the campaign context looks like a bit of a train wreck. Activist groups pull out all the stops to garner attention from the media, most reap little more than a published wink or an eye roll, and at the end of the day the organizations are left licking their wounds: budgets dented, leaders exhausted, other priorities neglected. The thing is, the activists aren't standing back. They are marching, listening to inspirational speeches from esteemed panelists, and basking in the righteous passion and energy that bubbles from crowds of like-minded peers. They are knee-deep in poster board, media trainings, and skit rehearsals. They are commiserating about the corporate media or the liberal media (politics depending), evaluating policing, and coping with people who dislike what they have to say. And most of them love it.

Although many opportunities are eclipsed by media-centrism, and all but the most modest goals remain unmet for most groups, mobilization around the conventions and debates bears some important, if serendipitous, fruit. Many groups see an increase in the membership rolls or mailing lists and a significant number of organizations—like those involved with the immigrants' rights march—report that they benefit from collaborating with other organizations in the campaign context. And, ultimately, these groups accrue significant gains in the development or revitalization of collective identity, renewed member commitment, and even feelings of efficacy.

Expanding Their Bases of Support

Some associations found that the campaign efforts helped to increase their bases of support. The most striking example is the runaway expansion of Inequality Forever, which spawned 40 new chapters in the months following their debate and convention appearances in 2000, giving them momentum as they headed into the 2004 election season, around which point the number of chapters again doubled. Although this dramatic growth was atypical—driven as it was by Inequality Forever's media success and the playful, inviting nature of its activities—many groups found that their campaign mobilizations helped with recruitment. Harry of the Northeast Union of Professionals expressed this sentiment, saying, "Absolutely. We have. We attracted new members, whatever membership means, new activists. We've done that. The debate mobilization got our name out [in activist circles]." This may seem counterintuitive in light of the lack of effort invested in face-to-face outreach and the dreary media coverage they received. If not bystanders and not the home viewers/readers, whom did these groups recruit? They recruited other activists. The Northeast Union of Professionals, like many organizations I studied, got their "name out" primarily through coalition work and by showing up to support other activist events. This reciprocity is one of the hallmarks of campaign mobilizations. Many organizations forged new connections by working in coalition or becoming acquainted through large clearinghouse meetings (where information is exchanged about policing, permitting, and other issues of common concern) or by virtue of proximity (sharing the same stages, public spaces, and "free speech zones"). Women Against War, for example, reported a significant membership increase as a result of their efforts around the conventions in New York City and Boston in 2004, which they attribute to the convergence of so many peace advocates and organizations.

Some organizations used these networks to garner support for specific initiatives. Network for Peace reported collecting approximately 5,000 new signatures on a missile defense petition during their activities around the RNC in Philadelphia and a significant number of signatures at campus demonstrations in the Boston area on the day of the first presidential debate. Art, from NC Citizens for Smaller Government, explained that his organization gathered far more petition signatures at the Winston-Salem debate viewing party and concert than they typically collected at other public appearances, even at large venues such as fairs and festivals. These signatures came from the general public who attended the concert and debate watch, but also from members of the many other groups present. Other organizations (e.g., Business Watch, Young Adult Voters Association, Abolish, and GenNext) also utilized these multi-organizational spaces and events as opportunities to solicit names for petitions and mailing lists to be used in subsequent recruitment.

Collaboration Among Voluntary Associations

As this reciprocity suggests, the major campaign events acted as dedifferentiating moments, in which activist groups frequently worked in unison. Approximately two-thirds of the organizations worked with other groups in coalitions or as cosponsors for at least one campaign event activity.[5] As Habermas and Tocqueville would expect, many of these alliances were logical groupings of organizations committed to similar social or political issues (e.g., women's rights groups, peace organizations, environmental groups), but they also formed between associations with quite different interests.

The most resilient connections formed when ideologically compatible groups collaborated on an event dealing with a shared core issue. For example, Abolish worked with a variety of other anti–death penalty organizations to organize a day of activities devoted to that cause during the Republican National Convention. Similarly, Shariece, with Boston Pacifists United and the Progressive Activists Coalition, described being part of the PAC's women's working group, a collaborative effort on the part of 29 women's organizations. When ideological compatibility, shared substantive interests, and a clearly defined objective existed among the groups, coalitions were efficient, supportive, and inclined to produce enduring ties.

George from Abolish explained that the chance to work together with groups active on similar issues created networks that would last:

> It [the rally] was a good event for us to connect with other anti–death penalty groups from outside of Pennsylvania. . . . They were really good groups to work with, really good staff people. . . . I worked very closely and got to know a number of people at LIFE [anti–death penalty group] who I hadn't known before and got to work with. They are focused on much more of a national level and that helps for us to be presented on more of a national level. Afterwards we were like, "We will definitely have to work on stuff in the future planning major events like that."

Suki, of the Young Adult Voter's Association, shared similar sentiments: "I got to meet a lot of people and that was great and I got to learn about a lot of organizations in the Boston area and statewide and that was also great, and that opened a lot of relationships for the future to possibly work together on different kinds of events and coordinate different things in the future." Enduring networks periodically emerged from less focused, multi-issue coalitions as well. Brenda from Stand Up St. Louis explained that many of the largely white, anticorporate groups had hoped to link up with groups working on racial issues to create a broader-based movement. She felt that goal was at least partially accomplished through their collaboration during the debate, and that the connections these groups established would endure beyond the debate activity:

> There was a big demonstration the weekend after ours [at the debate] on police brutality and a lot of [predominantly white] Stand Up St. Louis activists went to that and have started going to meetings of those folks and of the predominantly African American coalitions. I think this will, I hope this will continue.

The conventions and debates provided an opportunity for associations to attempt to reach the candidates, delegates, and the general public, but they also provided opportunities for groups to reach one another.

Without question, collaborative efforts also involved some challenges and disappointments, but activists frequently indicated that these new linkages were the greatest accomplishment of their mobilizations. While many shared this opinion, Greg from the Land and Life Protection League perhaps explained it the most clearly:

> This is where this stuff really happens with the networking and the allies and you know, like I said, you can't have fifty demonstrations around the country on a month's notice unless you have developed trust and relationships with the groups who are actually going to organize those demonstrations. So, that was worth its weight in gold for sure. Finding the—it's just sort of being in that kind of intense kind of crucible kind of situation where there is a lot going on and inevitably you are just deepening personal relationships with people, and then to sort of have that as a foundation makes it a lot easier to kind of talk about specific campaigns and issues. So, groups that I knew we would want to be allies with—it helps when I am sitting with the guy who is the director

for three days and you know we are leaning on each other's shoulders because we are exhausted. Once you have been through such a major effort and worked well together, you can call on that person. They trust you and you know that you are dealing with someone who will take you seriously and give you a listen because they now know you are a person of substance.

The Land and Life Protection League is based in San Francisco, but staff came to Philadelphia to participate in a variety of coalition-organized activities, as well as to coordinate their own event with the support of local activist organizations. Consequently, the convention provided an opportunity for meaningful collaboration with activists and organizations based on the East Coast, rather than just superficial networking.

Greg valued these ties because he felt they would help his organization in the future, but some representatives also appreciated these connections at the interpersonal level. Serena from Choice indicated that the "best part" about organizing around the RNC in New York City was "the relationships you build . . . working with people from other organizations, because working in a nonprofit inevitably becomes your life. People you work with become part of your everyday life as well and those relationships usually get stronger." Choice worked with other national and local reproductive health and rights organizations, and Serena described feeling at home with the organizers of other groups because they shared similar interests and a similar way of life.

The Amazing Intangibles

The communicative constraints that I described above—micromanaging members, devaluing and suffocating substantive political discourse, and demanding consensus—created a bleak picture of relations within the groups. But while these pressures worked to limit and discipline political talk, in most cases they did not dampen the esprit de corps. On the contrary, rather than decrying group life, many activists were giddy with it. Participants described feeling powerfully connected to their organizations and experiencing a renewed sense of efficacy engendered by the feeling that they were a part of something larger.

Activists frequently sounded invigorated by their involvement. Robert from the American Adult Network was a sedate man with a rather flat affect, yet he bubbled with enthusiasm as he described his favorite part of their event:

The whole thing. The whole day was a high point. Really, it's hard for me to say. I guess one best part were the speakers. There were a couple individuals who gave very personal accounts of their experiences and that was very powerful. Still, though, I hate to say that was the one highlight. Another big thing was simply seeing all of the AAN support and having such a great event. It felt good! People were smiling, talking, clapping, it was very alive, very, I don't know, maybe you had to be there. It was an event that we put together ourselves. We had support from people going by, there was a good energy that day. I felt energized when it was over, instead of let down like you might expect after all that planning and work.

References to energy and excitement also pervaded Brandy's assessment of the pre-rally scene as School Choice, Family Choice activists headed toward the Democratic National Convention site:

When we started getting closer to the location [Staples Center in Los Angeles], they [organization supporters] were looking out of the windows and they were saying, "Oh look! Look!"—that kind of thing. It was like taking kids to an amusement park or something. They could barely stay in their seats. They were excited just being a part of the process of voicing their concerns . . . they were actually doing it. They were excited about that. . . . The energy was very, very high. It also helped that we had a busload full of kids . . . [who were] hyped the whole time and you know, they were there holding up the signs and shouting, "It's all about the kids! It's all about the kids!"

The sense of belonging that emerged when association members found themselves surrounded by like-minded people made participating a powerful experience, as explained by Brye from Boston Resistance:

I think for one of the first times, I, you know, I didn't feel like an outsider, as far as my politics, you know. Regardless of whether, you know, I agreed with everyone on every point, which I'm sure I didn't, you know, I knew that I didn't have to explain, you know, why I believe in queer rights, or why I'm a feminist, or why I'm antiracist, or you know, anything like that. And that's just a really freeing thing for me. . . . I just don't feel like I'm part of a community where I live, because of those things.

This sense of community is one of the benefits of face-to-face meetings.

In addition to creating a diffuse sense of being part of something larger, action also served more specifically to foster the development of a collective identity. Rich, from Inequality Forever, described how their events brought his group together physically and symbolically:

> I don't think there is anything any more bonding than a collective challenge, you know? Especially when you meet it victoriously. Particularly, this is true when there is a lot of creativity involved and it's relatively democratic and participatory. It's like a team sport. We turned political expression into a team sport. There's confrontation, there's intensity, there's the magic moment of it all coming together, you know, when you are actually doing it and there's the whole idea brainstorming and planning and there's stress. . . . It was just so exciting in Philadelphia. We were all staying in the same place, so it was very socially bonding that way. We all sort of camped out in this huge house. . . . So there were thirty or forty of us sleeping in like four or five rooms. It was like a big campout kind of thing at night and then you'd go into battle every day. So, you never knew what was going to happen and it was very successful, so we had this great feeling of victory, just an incredible feeling and everyone had a hand in it. There was this strange identity that we all developed as Wealth Warriors, you know? The rest of the movement recognized us as Wealth Warriors. People loved us.

In Rich's narrative, we sense the electricity of his experience, and it becomes apparent that a "we-ness" emerged that came as much from the creation of a clear distinction between insiders and outsiders as from the development of relationships among insiders. Part of this likely stemmed from the constant re-articulation of group goals and values as representatives communicated with the media and nonmembers, but unlike other settings where goals and values of the membership were re-articulated (e.g., the process of revising a mission statement), the participants' campaign experiences were often intense and impassioned, calling to mind Durkheim's (1995) descriptions of collective effervescence, as well as what Fantasia (1988) refers to as "cultures of solidarity."

Similarly, Liza, from United Trades told me that the planning meetings for their activities around the Republican National Convention were "great." Planning meetings great? When asked what made them great, she replied:

The camaraderie, the camaraderie. We were all there in order to fight for the shop workers. The people who don't work in the shop were all there because they wanted to be and the people who are fighting for a contract were glad to see everyone out, so grateful. You can imagine how pumped up everyone was planning and realizing how big it was going to be. It was exciting. It may sound dumb, but it was a rush being with old friends who I worked with at my old job and meeting new people I had never worked with before. . . . We could relate to each other because we were both union and both out there doing the work on the same side of the issues. We were all in it together.

Liza pointed to the sense of group ("we were both union") that was present during the meetings in addition to the interactions among individual members.

Even if the substance of communication among participants is social and logistical and not particularly egalitarian, collective identity is constructed and maintained through campaign-related mobilizations because participants have an opportunity to work together and develop relationships with one another and the group itself.[6] Indeed, the setting heightens the sense of being a part of a group, though this is also achieved through symbolic cues such as matching T-shirts, costumes, or paraphernalia (e.g., buttons, signs, stickers) and through the performance of group songs, chants, and the like. Further, with so many organizations active, one of the first questions asked at clearinghouse meetings, coalition events, and in designated protest zones was "Who are you with?" People who in other contexts might identify themselves by occupation, place of study, or hometown foreground their associational affiliation in this milieu. The togetherness and sense of being part of a group is of course meaningful for all groups, but this is particularly important for those voluntary associations whose members have looser connections, such as national mailing list organizations and web-based grassroots groups.

The other intangible benefit of mobilization is a bit more unexpected. Many participants described leaving the mobilizations with an increased sense of efficacy, saying that the work demonstrated to them that they could really do something. Laurie from NC Parents Against Gun Violence expressed this sentiment as follows: "I think it [mobilizing for the Winston-Salem debate] . . . was just such a good experience and really shed so much light on why we are doing this. It kind of helped, I think, make us realize that we really can make a difference. . . . It kind of empowered me personally to continue on with the organization and try to achieve those goals." Laurie was a new member of the group, and her involvement with the presidential debate protest was her first active participation. This experience assured her that the organization was something with which she wanted to be involved, because she felt the group could make a difference. This is particularly interesting given that of all the locations studied, the Winston-Salem debate protests were the most limited both in participant turnout and protest conditions for permitted organizations.[7] What was it about the mobilization that demonstrated to Laurie that the group could make a difference?

There were many cases of what we might call efficacy without evidence, participants feeling that their organization could be effective even in cases where the lack of impact was apparent. The peace groups provide a good illustration, with activists reporting a sense of efficacy despite the resilience of the war effort. According to Marissa from Faith in Peace, "We all knew that we were part of something really incredible and that it was something big and something that was really gonna affect people." And Alena from the Progressive Activists Coalition said: "I think the best part of being active was . . . being involved in a larger community—and a larger community of people that care about different issues going on in the world. And that you know, you're not just a person alone somewhere you know, kinda saying, well this has gotta stop—'cause there's other people there and that you can work with them—and that you can basically make a difference, in however small a way." This sense of efficacy seems incredibly unlikely given the realities of the environment in which these organizations were working. Elaine from Women Against War described feeling "pretty high after the RNC" and achieving accomplishments "beyond our expectations . . . even though we haven't stopped the war and the occupation, even though Bush did win the election." With the core organizational objectives—to stop the war and ensure Bush not be reelected—unrealized, it becomes clear that the sense of efficacy came not from effecting social change but from the collective action itself.

Voluntary Associations, the News Media, and the Democratic Process

The glimpse I offer in this book is peculiar. In some ways it is fractured and broken. It lumps too many diverse associations together; the groups in the sample have disparate political concerns, organizational structures, histories, and tactics. It does not offer the rich cultural excavations of associational life that some of my predecessors have provided. But what casting this broad net does is offer a descriptive account of a largely hidden component of presidential elections, as well as an unsettling overview of the limits faced by associations interested in participating in pubic political debates (if not private ones).

And yet there is good news in this book. The campaign context high-lights the fact that there is a noteworthy subset of Americans who care deeply about political issues and work in concert with others in an effort to participate in the political process. I watched public space (and private spaces as well) bubble with political activity in a spirited and buoyant way that simply failed to sync with the narrative of apathy and disengage-ment so common in the popular media. Presidential campaigns inspired people and associations to take action, even before the energizing election of 2008. And for every group I encountered in my fieldwork, there were certainly many others that did not travel to the host cities and instead orga-nized activities in their local communities.

In the convention and debate cities, voluntary organizations held de-bate viewing parties, concerts, discussion circles, fund-raisers, and marches comprising anywhere from 5 to 500,000 people. They performed street theater, held "alternative conventions," leafleted on street corners, threw parties, and coordinated rallies in front of city hall. Their chants, signs, and literature addressed gun control, the environment, capitalism, and the two-party political system. They were passionate about stopping abortion, war, the death penalty, and unfair trade relations. They proffered pleas to promote a better social safety net, school vouchers, open debates, stronger corporate oversight, and tort reform. Some were angry. Some were som-ber. Some were celebratory. They clustered, usually visually marked as part of a group: thick contingents of union members in coordinated T-shirts, the Wealth Warriors in their over-the-top costumes, Women Against War decked out in pink, and the anarchists in their nonconformist uniforms. Taken together, the signage, chanting, leaflets, and ubiquitous groups of activists created quite an impression. Never before had I witnessed such images of political vitality.

The activists' demonstrative tactics served to politicize public space in a way rarely seen in the United States. While in theory Boston Common or Union Square are always places where people can come together and dis-cuss the issues of the day, in practice these spaces do not operate as politi-cal publics in the Habermasian sense. Instead, they serve as thoroughfares for commuters, resting places for the homeless, areas of respite for workers and students eating lunch or reading, and as points of interest for tourists. Yet in the shadow of the conventions and debates, these spaces, and others like them, became political amphitheaters. In the case of the debates, the political crescendo lasted only a day or two, but the national nominating conventions transformed host cities for a nearly a week. This exciting process created spaces where groups interacted, raised political issues, and modeled political engagement for city dwellers who may have been less attuned and involved.

The other heartening finding is that involvement engenders feelings of connectedness and efficacy that are deeply meaningful for most participants. As this chapter demonstrates, mobilization feels good for those involved. Most participants described feeling emboldened and reassured by the sense that they were part of something larger. This suggests that simply joining an organization does not offer the same benefits as being an active participant. Many of the activists I spoke with indicated that they were long-time members of their organizations—they already knew that they were not alone—but described their mobilization involvement as giving them a palpable sense of shared struggle. Whether this feeling was the product of the tangible face-to-face work, an outcome of having participated in a significant intervention by mobilizing, or some combination of both is difficult to ascertain. Regardless, the experience enhanced feelings of efficacy and fortified the connection between individuals and the groups with which they were affiliated.

These campaign events also offered an exciting opportunity for activist groups to work with one another. Coalitions and other less formal collaborations were abundant in this environment because such a broad array of organizations found their concerns salient to the presidential campaign and deemed the election significant enough to require a response. The pull of the conventions and debates pressed groups to work in unison to maximize resources and impact. These cooperative efforts took place between like-minded organizations, but also between groups with significant political differences. While Democratic and Republican reproductive rights advocates shared a concern with keeping abortion legal, working together as they did to sponsor a benefit concert required tolerance. Overall, coalition work came with distinct opportunities and challenges that the associations had to navigate. And while some associations parted ways uncomfortably, most were able to establish or reconfirm healthy interorganizational linkages, and some groups found meaningful alliances they felt would continue to bear fruit.

Mobilization offers some benefits at the individual and organizational levels, and the flurry of political activity reminds us that not all Americans are apathetic; however, the bigger picture of activism in the campaign context is deeply disconcerting. Civil society has no formal political power; rather, it relies on the ability to exert influence on decision makers. This influence can take many forms, such as shifting public opinion, accruing votes, or leveraging financial or political resources, but acquiring influence of any sort requires communication between those who wish to wield influence and those they hope to persuade. And ultimately, the media-centered campaign mobilizations reveal roadblocks between civil society and the public sphere that are difficult to deny and too consequential to ignore.

If we put the mainstream news media under a microscope, we find a set of unwritten yet culturally powerful professional practices that serve to marginalize the political viewpoints of activists. Many groups make their way into the news, but almost always as voiceless criminals, clowns, or intriguing curiosities, rather than as legitimate political actors. This is true across the associational spectrum. There is little difference in the treatment of a group of 20 people raising issues linked only very loosely to the election and a gathering of several hundred or even thousands attempting to weigh in on a focal campaign issue.

There is a catch-22 in place that makes it incredibly difficult for activist groups to participate in the "master forum." As I have shown, if associations follow the unwritten rules that journalists apply to political outsiders and do obtain coverage, the stories are likely to be limited to emotional, individualistic expressions of concern or outrage about relatively simple problems with easy-to-identify, "reasonable" solutions. Yet refusing to comply—by using publicly minded speech or tackling seemingly intractable social problems (e.g., global inequality or racism)—virtually guarantees that their political voice will go unheard.

But not all the blame belongs to the news media. In all but a few cases, the associations were so feverishly focused on wooing reporters that they were hobbled—unable or unwilling to do the slow, tedious work required to communicate directly with regular people, and seemingly uninterested in utilizing independent media as a venue to broadcast or in working to circulate information via user-generated content vehicles available online.[8] Media training and readiness dominated the agendas in most groups, and the focus on meeting the (inaccurately) perceived desires of news workers was so laser-like that opportunities for face-to-face advocacy were often ignored. Association members were ill-prepared to talk with actual people: I watched them repeatedly turn their backs on on-lookers, awkwardly deflect simple inquiries toward other group members, refer people to websites in lieu of answering their questions, or respond in stilted, made-for-TV slogans. In the worst cases, the associations were so media-centered that they even distorted communication within their own organizations, treating their peers as potential liabilities and placing them on a short leash.

Perhaps this is unfair. In light of existing arrangements, who can blame these organizations for pursuing the media spotlight? The associations were savvy enough to recognize that the public sphere is dominated by the mass media, and that this space is exclusionary. In response, the groups put forth herculean efforts to break through the clutter and get a foot (or a word) in the door. Associations would be well served to work toward media reform (we all would), but I also believe these groups should question the very premise of the media chase. The implicit (and sometimes explicit) theory at play in media work is that news coverage will effect change, but there are a tremendous number of contingencies at play that must pan out for this vision to be realized. The organization's events or activities must yield coverage, the coverage must contain the substantive information necessary to be convincing, this information must be widely read/watched/heard, those who read/watch/hear the story must be persuaded to think about the issue in a new way, this new thinking must generate some form of action, and this action must be effective. In other words, even if the groups had attracted coverage, I am not convinced it would have mattered in the political/instrumental sense that the activists presumed. And given the rate of failure for just the first contingency—getting covered—activist groups would be smart to reevaluate the costs and benefits of extensive media work.

To the extent that voluntary associations still feel the mainstream news media are essential to furthering their political goals, they would be wise to reconsider their media strategy. Given the impasse between journalists and activists in the negotiations over news, activists might try refocusing their media work away from training members to stay *on message* with sound bites, key statistics, and slogans, and toward finding compelling *stories* for members to share that may resonate better with news workers. Polletta (2006) makes a convincing case that the right stories can be strategically deployed by activists to bring about social change. The aversions and affinities of the journalists interviewed here suggest that if groups can embed publicly minded political content in an emotionally rich account of group/

community experiences, and this story can be told in an unscripted way by a variety of people who feel connected to it, this is likely to be more effective than the rational activist-as-educator model in use by most of the organizations I encountered.

In chapter 1, I told the stories of two different organizations. Disrupt held a major civil disobedience effort in Philadelphia for the Republican National Convention in 2000 to call attention to the injustices of unchecked global capitalism and the growing opposition to these problems. Despite the major disturbance to the city (blocking traffic at multiple points during rush hour) and hundreds of arrests, Disrupt's political issues went unexplored in the news. The other story was that of IATSE, the stagehands' union that successfully pressured the management of the Apollo Theater to settle their contract by threatening to strike on the evening of the Gore-Bradley Democratic primary debate. The IATSE strike led me to this research, because I was curious about how other voluntary associations might use campaign events as moments of opportunity. I had no idea how many organizations would be drawn to the campaign events or how difficult it would be for them to realize their goals. The stagehands managed to use a campaign event as leverage to accomplish a goal in a way that most of the associations I went on to study did not. IATSE did not succeed because it had media attention; it succeeded because it had the management of the Apollo Theater in an impossible position. In other words, the stagehands used a *political strategy* that attracted media attention. Disrupt and so many other activist groups tried the inverse: they used a *media strategy* they hoped would attract political attention.

Voluntary associations, as publics, are valued because they provide communal spaces for marginalized groups to safely articulate their needs and goals, but also because they allow participants to develop strategies to amplify their voices when they enter mainstream public arenas. The experiences of the groups in this book demonstrate that while such strategizing abounds, attempts to expand mainstream dialogue are profoundly limited. Most associations strive to enter the larger public arena by courting the news media, rather than by reaching out via their own media or through face-to-face discussions with potential supporters. When meaningful news coverage fails to materialize, the associations are left involuntarily enclaved, unable to reach mainstream audiences.

This disempowers activist groups, but it also diminishes the quality of political discourse in general. For example, during the 2004 campaign cycle, John Kerry worked to counter the fear that a Democrat in the White

House would make the United States vulnerable to terrorist attacks by presenting himself as tough on defense. As a result, the voting public heard militaristic rhetoric from both sides. There were some media accounts of antiwar activities, but most included information about permitting issues, arrests, and what the marchers were wearing, excluding the substantive arguments underneath the activists' antiwar position. With little coverage of antiwar political figures (e.g., Rep. Dennis Kucinich), and virtually no issue-based coverage of the many peace groups active around the campaign events and throughout the election, readers and viewers of the mainstream news were left with little exposure to alternative interpretations and arguments. While many would have likely found the peace groups' arguments unpersuasive, the ideas and information proffered by these groups may have altered others' priorities or behavior in the voting booth. This impoverished discourse isn't simply a disappointment for marginalized groups hoping to sway the public. On the contrary, narrowing the dialogue challenges the very premise that undergirds democratic elections: that of informed citizens making educated decisions on their own behalf.

We are left looking at news media that privilege one set of political actors and expressions over others; at a set of voluntary organizations so narrowly focused on courting these media that they fail to communicate with real people, and even debase their own group life in the frenzied pursuit, that media attention; and ultimately at an election process quite distant from the vision of pluralism recounted in high-school civics classrooms, in which interest groups have a seat at the table and advocate on their own behalf, while the state serves as a neutral mediator. If those in power, candidates for public office, or the voting public take the self-articulated interests of politically vocal voluntary organizations into account, the associations introduced in this book do not appear to be among them.

Presidential elections do more than elect presidents. Recognizing and celebrating that elections inspire participation, and working to broaden the dialogue to make room for that involvement, would strengthen the legitimacy of the democratic process. Dwelling on voter turnout rates, which implicitly chides those who fail to vote, does not hold accountable a process in which earnest attempts to participate in the electoral process before the final hour appear futile. The chasm that exists between voluntary associations and broader publics is a significant concern, and the challenge is to create avenues that facilitate connections between multiple publics and broader participatory arenas.

Epilogue

Web 2.0 and Election 2008

THE 2008 PRESIDENTIAL election felt different somehow, ripe with possibility for activist voices. New information and communications technologies (ICTs) supporting self-publication and group coordination had flooded into the mainstream since 2004, and the news media seemed to be interested again in activism, eagerly covering the young activists mobilized by the Obama campaign. Yet a closer look reveals that the new ICTs do little to resolve the issues of marginalization that haunt activist organizations or to unseat (old) media-centrism. What's more, the heightened visibility of activism was actually the heightened visibility of electioneering, showcasing the work of party and candidate volunteers, while the groups analogous to those examined in this book remained at the periphery.

2008: Hope and Change

The 2008 campaign cycle was among the most electrifying in American history, not only because Barack Obama was an unusual candidate—a young, charismatic orator of African decent—but also because the election coincided with the mainstreaming of new technologies that created innovative ways for average people to participate in the electoral process. And they did get involved, in droves, particularly young people. Under the guidance of the sociologist Marshall Ganz and others, the Obama campaign merged new technological tools with a model of political organizing that emphasized mass participation, interaction, and relationship building. The combination of an electrifying candidate with door-to-door field organizing and the proliferation of new ICTs that lowered the bar for participation, proved powerfully mobilizing. The Republican nominee, John McCain, was no stranger to new media either, having used Internet campaigning to his advantage during his fight for the nomination a full eight years prior, and yet the contrast between the McCain and Obama campaigns in 2008 was striking. Technology alone did not ensure success.

The web-based liberal advocacy group MoveOn is in some ways the Obama 2008 campaign equivalent in the realm of voluntary organizations. MoveOn offers a noteworthy case in which the possibilities of Internet activism are showcased, but the organization is best understood as an illustrative exception to the way most activist groups worked to shape the 2008 presidential election. Although new ICTs have been incorporated into the repertoires of activist groups—there is a qualitative difference in the web presence of groups active around the 2000/2004 elections and those active in 2008—Internet activism has done little to help these organizations influence political discourse in the mainstream public sphere.

ICTs and Political Life

The year 2008 felt like a watershed moment for the use of ICTs in the context of political campaigns, but the relationship between digital media and electoral politics has been evolutionary. Indeed, the Internet has played a role in presidential campaigns since the 1990s. In 1996, candidates had relatively simple, billboard-like websites, but this electronic brochure model was being reimagined as early as 1998, when Jesse Ventura's Minnesota gubernatorial campaign began experimenting with supporter e-mail lists, newsgroups, and chat rooms. John McCain's presidential campaign in 2000 transitioned campaign-related web use from unidirectional communication to an interactive space of fund-raising and volunteer coordination. In an effort to harness volunteer energy during the primary season, McCain's director of Internet operations, Max Fose, instructed web developers to find ways to engage the donors and volunteers visiting the website. In response, they designed low-time-commitment opportunities, such as the ability to participate in virtual phone banking and election-related e-mail campaigns—all this at a time when Bush strategist Karl Rove was quoted as saying, "We don't need the Internet" (as it turns out, he was correct; see Rapaport 2000). And Howard Dean is well-known for his innovative web presence in 2004, ripe with synergy between his campaign website, the social networking site Meetup.com, and supportive bloggers, which combined to catapult him from long shot to contender for the Democratic nomination. In other words, the Internet work choreographed by the Obama campaign, while effective, was more advance than invention. The same is true of Internet activism. For example, although MoveOn was ubiquitous in 2008, the organization was founded in 1998 and had been active in the 2000 and 2004 elections and around other projects/issues between election cycles. In addition, many voluntary organizations across the associational spectrum (from the AARP to anarchist collectives) have been using the Internet since the mid-1990s, some in quite innovative ways.

This gradual evolution reflects the development of ICTs themselves. New social media tools thought to have been so critical in 2008 had actually been in use for a decade prior to the election, and indeed had been utilized in earlier presidential campaigns, including those documented in this book. In 2004, while Facebook was still limited to Harvard affiliates and Twitter had yet to be born, blogs were widely used,[1] and were even in use—if in their infancy—during the 2000 campaign. They had been gaining in popularity since the late 1990s, when LiveJournal and Blogger introduced user-generated content (UGC) platforms featuring WYSIWYG editing, making it possible to blog without computer-programming skills.

For activist groups seeking visibility, the rapid expansion of UGC vehicles—wikis (1995); blogging platforms such as Blogger (1999) and LiveJournal (1999); social networking sites such as Meetup (2001), Friendster (2002), MySpace (2003), and Facebook (2004); video-sharing venues such as Vimeo (2004) and YouTube (2005); and photo-sharing sites such as Photobucket (2003) and Flickr (2004)—was a pivotal technological advance. These UGC vehicles extended the ability to publish information online—which had long been feasible for corporations, political parties, and other organizations able to employ web developers—to groups with far more modest means. Publishing still requires resources such as Internet access, technological proficiency, and time, which are unequally distributed, but these newer platforms substantially reduce prior inequities. Publishers need not even pay for web hosting space as they can utilize other websites (e.g., Indymedia, YouTube, Blogger) as free distribution networks. What's more, the social nature of these platforms, replete with opportunities for commenting, creating groups, and open, asynchronous discussions, offer tremendous potential for organizing and mobilizing groups.[2]

Activist Groups and New ICTs in the 2008 Election

The activist groups in this book used the Internet primarily for "brochure-ware" and "online facilitation of offline activism" in their work around the 2000 and 2004 elections. "Brochure-ware" refers to one-way, cause-related information distribution via organization webpages, akin to an electronic pamphlet, as the name suggests. Groups engaging in "online facilitation of offline activism" use the web to coordinate face-to-face events such as rallies, marches, and so forth (Earl et al. 2009). The organizations described in this book, then, generally used the web to provide cause-related information or details about the times, dates, and meeting places of planning sessions and events in the host cities.[3] The depth of information varied from fairly thin, static pages to information-rich, frequently updated websites including a variety of elements, such as logistical information, profiles of group leaders/staff, mission statements, organization histories, information about recent successes and challenges, links to outside resources (e.g., like-minded groups or Independent Media Centers), and newswires containing relevant stories from mainstream media outlets.

The 2000/2004 groups very rarely created spaces for the other forms of Internet activism identified by Earl et al., "online participation" and "online organizing." An activist group creates space for online participation when it presents opportunities for supporters to be virtual activists, as by signing online petitions, participating in e-mail campaigns, or engaging in more disruptive Internet activities (e.g., "hacktivism," such as efforts to shut down websites). Groups engaging in online organizing conduct entire campaigns online. These groups place online participation at the core of their work, and rarely if ever attempt to coordinate face-to-face efforts. They may also have leaders who are geographically dispersed.

How did the large-scale mainstreaming of new ICTs that transpired between 2004 and 2008 shape the 2008 mobilizations? Since I was not in the field in 2008, and the dearth of reporting on activism at the perimeter of elections makes it difficult to identify the universe of active organizations, it was not possible for me to take a purposive sample representing the range of mobilizing groups. Instead, I examined the organizations whose campaign-related activities were the most visible online and in the news. For the RNC, I examined the web presence of Protest RNC 2008, a large umbrella coalition coordinating protests in Minneapolis, and the cheekily named RNC Welcoming Committee, an anarchist group interested in disrupting the convention proceedings. For the DNC, I examined web material from Recreate68, a coalition of antiwar groups, and Unconventional Denver, a local antiauthoritarian group affiliated with Unconventional Action. As the earlier chapters suggest, choosing "visible" groups introduces important biases. Most significant, the media usually highlights those working to coordinate a sizable presence in the streets, and this was the case in 2008 as well. As a result, the web work of these organizations may or may not be indicative of the choices made by other voluntary associations, but they are still helpful for exploring potential changes between 2000/2004 and 2008.

The integration of new ICTs in the 2008 web work is noteworthy. The groups most visible around the DNC worked with social media including Facebook (Recreate68), MySpace (Unconventional Denver), and blogging (Unconventional Denver). Protest RNC 2008 provided an option for interested parties to receive updates via SMS (text message) through their website, as well as links to the group's Facebook and MySpace pages. The Protest RNC 2008 website also included a blog and a discussion forum, where visitors could start new discussion threads and contribute to ongoing dialogue. Chat rooms, discussion forums, and blogs were available in 2000 and 2004 but were not used by groups in my sample, even those with richer web presences. The RNC Welcoming Committee posted a clever video "trailer," titled "We're Getting Ready," on YouTube in order to guide people to their website for more information.[4] Looking at the web work across the three campaign cycles, there is no question that activist groups in 2008 were working with a new set of tools.

And yet these new participatory communication environments did not necessarily alter the role of Internet activism in the campaign context. Given the widespread interest in communicating with outsiders, it seems plausible that activist groups might use these tools to self-publish with an eye toward reaching outsiders, as an alternative to depending on the mainstream news media. And yet three of the four groups I examined used these media simply as additional spaces to post logistical information for supporters. Facebook and MySpace were used as staging grounds for future demonstrative mobilizations, rather than as a new avenue for demonstrative action. Even the RNC Welcoming Committee, which did something quite innovative with their video trailer, positioned it toward potential participants. Naturally, the public nature of this form of publishing means that others can and sometimes do access the activists' content, but the substance—logistical information for participants—indicates that it is not intended as demonstrative work. In other words, the 2008 organizations used their web presence to post information and facilitate offline activism, very much in keeping with the groups active in 2000 and 2004.

This tendency to focus internally would be a net gain if the new tools were used to support richer internal communication. As the previous chapter demonstrates, the internal life of many groups mobilizing around major campaign events suffers as a result of (old) media-centrism. Platforms that facilitate many-to-many communication have the potential to connect group members and to connect those members to the group itself, but the groups whose web work I reviewed did little to foster these connections. For example, the blog portion of the Protest RNC 2008 MySpace page might have contained posts in which the authors addressed questions about planning the mobilization, long-term priorities, differences in opinion or preferred strategies among member organizations, political philosophy, why protesting the RNC is important, issues of inclusion, concerns about policing, and so forth. Instead, the largely idle blog functioned as frequently updating brochure-ware, including meeting dates, times, and locations, but devoid of discussion about why someone should attend or what the event might accomplish politically. The same was true of the blog portion of the Unconventional Denver MySpace page. Unconventional Denver's posts were more detailed and included information about the organization's goals, but they effectively read as author-less, disconnected announcements rather than as starting points for conversation or as a means for more inclusive organizing. As a result, comments (i.e., interaction) were extremely rare.

Social media need to facilitate many-to-many communication among group members in order to expand dialogue effectively, and they are certainly capable of doing so. The commenting feature available on most blogs and video- and photo-sharing sites is one of the spaces where these digital conversations can unfold. Facebook and MySpace have built-in areas for such exchange, and websites can include elements such as a forum section, discussion board, or a chat room.[5] Yet I did not see organizations working to deploy such tools in this way, nor did I see evidence of the sort of internal virtual conversations or debates that are fostered in some online political fora.[6]

The Protest RNC 2008 Facebook page contained some multidirectional information sharing on the Wall and in the Discussions section, such as people posting relevant links and announcements about offline activist opportunities. But because these pages attract snipers as well as supporters, the informative posts were overshadowed by crass exchanges riddled with vitriolic insults, name calling, and mockery between provocateurs who disagree politically or strategically and incensed group members who feel under attack, and periodically between activists on the same side of the issue. The venom is remarkable, marked by rampant use of the f-word and lesser expletives, as well as instances where people were referred to by vulgarities such as douche, pussy, or bucket of piss, and politicized insults such as Nazi, fascist, or socialist. One poster even challenged another to a physical fight. While the often-astonishing incivility is noteworthy in terms of evaluating the extent to which these new media support internal communication, the central issue is that flame throwing complicates the possibility of productive exchange between members of the group by making participants feel leery of posting (for fear of harassment or ridicule) as well as through sheer distraction. Organizations need to create codes of conduct and see that participants abide by them in order to create safe spaces for discussion and connection online. This is not to say that everyone must agree or be ideologically compatible, but rather that the most outrageous forms of incivility (e.g., the use of obscenities or threats) should not be tolerated. At the same time, facilitators should find ways to encourage positive involvement (e.g., open threads or poll questions). Despite the problems with the Facebook pages, they were at least active spaces, unlike the primary websites, which were nearly dormant. Interestingly, the dialogue on YouTube in response to the anarchist trailer was the most extensive and substantive that I witnessed.[7] Certainly, there was sniping and frustration, but there were also more measured attempts to critique, clarify, and defend the group's political choices.

New ICTs, Old Media-centrism

New digital tools that democratize self-publishing online seem revolutionary for activists hungry for a platform, and yet they do little to disrupt old-media centrism. The forum section of ProtestRNC2008.org offers an insightful, if anecdotal, illustration. The forum contained only two discussion topics: "Why Protest the RNC?" and "Logistics." Under "Why Protest the RNC?," four threads were started, and although each thread in a forum is intended to be the start of a discussion, none of the initial posts elicited even a single response. Looking closely at these failed threads proves revealing. One, by a provocateur, offers, "Pack your bags and get the hell out of the U.S.A. if you don't like the country you call home. . . . Kook season opens the first week of November. Get ready. Putzes." Two of the threads contain reposted news stories without commentary. The fourth thread, however, offers an answer. Why protest the RNC? The post began, "This Republican National Convention could be about creating the *Greatest Peace Media Event Ever* [emphasis in the original]. The trick is to steal the media coverage, to have the biggest media story ever. Think Big, think the whole Twin Cities area, think the whole country." This impassioned and optimistic (old) media-centrism suggests a continuation of the themes in this book, rather than a departure from them. Removing the flame thrower's thread, we are left with three threads—two reposted news stories and one about the potential for media coverage—all media-centered. And the media-centrism doesn't seem to be transforming. It does not sound like Indymedia-centrism, or media-centrism in the web 2.0, do-it-yourself (DIY) or do-it-with-others (DIWO) sense, but rather like a continued focus on the traditional news media.

One forum on one website is not generalizable to all activism around the 2008 election, and noteworthy exceptions such as MoveOn certainly exist. But based on the people I've spoken with and the web work I've seen, the forum threads do somehow poignantly capture this moment of transition. Activist groups are steeped in new possibilities created by technological advances, but their explorations of how to use them are advancing in fits and starts. Despite the explosion of youth participation and the proliferation of potentially democratizing media tools, for most organizations the web remains a backstage region where activists plan for demonstrative actions still oriented around getting covered in the mainstream news.

New Media Tools, Familiar Challenges

This is not to say that attempting to use the web for demonstrative work targeting outsiders would necessarily make sense. On the contrary, DIY/DIWO social media, like independent media and alternative media before them, offer a place to publish information, but there is a critical difference between the ability to publish and the ability to draw an audience. In fact, if other campaign-related Internet patterns are any indication, we would expect reaching outsiders via activist group websites to be fairly unlikely. Research has shown that those visiting candidate websites tend to be supporters rather than undecided voters attempting to weigh their options (Bimber and Davis 2003; Foot and Schneider 2006). If the central challenge for the organizations in this book is to cross over, to move from parallel micro public to mainstream public, publishing alone is not enough. This is the intervening wrench in debates around the extent to which the Internet has been democratizing.[8] The changes are undeniable; the ability to post, participate, connect, and consume in highly individualized ways is groundbreaking. But what these new tools do best is facilitate the development of communities of interest, social networks; they excel at the social equivalent of narrowcasting, not broadcasting. For organizations hoping to enter the mainstream public sphere, self-publishing online is unlikely to yield access. Blogs, MySpace pages, Twitter feeds, and YouTube channels have the potential to reach a broad audience, but in practice most do not. They do little to support broadcasting except for those entities that already had heavy traffic in the web 1.0 era, such as major television networks, newspapers, and magazines. In fact, Hindman (2009) shows that the audience for the top blogs is even *more* heavily concentrated around a small number of top sources than the audiences for traditional media (e.g., magazines and newspapers), and that people from elite backgrounds overwhelmingly author the blogs that are most widely read. This supports earlier work suggesting that online political debates tend to be dominated by elites (Jankowski and van Selm 2000). Online, like offline, the challenge for activist groups is reaching the general public.

Thus the struggles online in many ways are the same as those found offline, but the opportunities transfer as well. The avenue of greatest potential for organizations mobilizing around the campaign events is the ability to recruit supporters from other ideologically compatible groups. Just as activist groups in the field found support for petitions and marches at convergence centers and in designated free speech zones, activists online may be able to bolster their ranks through overlapping social and virtual networks created through friending and following, and via the infrastructure of the blogosphere (e.g., blogrolls, trackbacks, and comment sections with links to commenters' own blogs). While this infrastructure does not grant immediate access to a mass audience, it offers an opportunity for connecting people with similar interests and priorities. It is possible that web work will connect activist groups to the mainstream public *indirectly*, via journalists, but some research suggests this is unlikely. Jha (2008, 717) found that although journalists described openness to and appreciation for websites erected by politicians, corporations, and public relations firms, "when it came to social movement websites, most respondents were admiring of the web sophistication of activist groups, but dismissive of the sites as sources of possible information, ideas, or contacts." This finding pertained to protesters specifically and might not hold true for other types of voluntary groups, although as chapter 4 showed, the likelihood of journalists seeking to cover the activism of those other groups is rather slim.

Activism Everywhere?

I was not able to conduct campaign-related fieldwork during the 2008 general election. In my absence, I hung on every word of the few people I knew who worked as journalists, staff, or security during the campaign, or who were engaged in activist work around the key events. I set up online news alerts to keep abreast of the stories emerging from the host cities, and regularly checked Indymedia.us for updates. I found a lot of activism in the news, but not the kind that I uncovered in 2000 and 2004. Non-protest-based activist work (i.e., "inside events") remained largely invisible, and although the news included some stories about protests (covered in predictable ways), the media were ripe with other stories of political participation. In particular, there were many stories about young people inspired by Obama: first-time voters working phone banks, college students driving to swing states to canvass, eager volunteers with stories that suggested the election was in their hands. The articles depicted the young people as individual volunteers, and included stories about why they felt moved to get involved. These American-youth-aren't-apathetic-after-all accounts could have been written about the young activists outside the conventions, but they weren't. The news as a whole left readers with a sense that there had been a new surge of activism in 2008, but it was a very particular form of political engagement—electioneering—and certainly not one that suggests the gap between voices at the margins had won inclusion in the mass-mediated public sphere.

For all the elements of the 2008 election cycle that felt new, there were others that felt hauntingly familiar. The twin development of social media and user-generated content platforms offered a new set of tools for voluntary associations, but they are a set best suited for building support, developing relationships, and facilitating communal organizing by allowing geographically dispersed members to contribute ideas and serve as sounding boards. Used to their full potential, this is an incredible resource. But this set of tools does not close the gap between these communities of interest and the mainstream public sphere. The Obama campaign succeeded for many reasons, but in part because it fused online organizing with a compelling message and old-fashioned face-to-face, door-to-door field organizing. This presents a useful lesson and reminder that media strategy is not a substitute for political strategy. But it is possible that activist groups could use these tools to shepherd in tangible political and cultural gains as they begin to explore the political strategies that open to them through new ICTs (e.g., moving away from the online coordination of media-centric offline activism, and experimenting with online activism and online organizing), and through capitalizing on the inherent strengths of many-to-many communication tools by using them to build stronger social and discursive spaces for members and supporters. Both of these possibilities are themselves media-centric, but they represent a transformed and productive type of (new) media-centrism that functions alongside the mainstream news media rather than being eclipsed by them.

Appendix

Methods

THESE FINDINGS ARE based on in-depth, semi-structured qualitative interviews with association members and journalists, as well as supplemental data from a variety of other sources: field notes from association events and meetings, literature distributed by voluntary associations, Internet materials produced by these organizations, and newspaper articles. I combined these information sources to weave together a multidimensional overview of each voluntary association in the sample.

Associations and Respondents

The 2000 sample was drawn from voluntary associations that organized activities that coincided with preplanned,[1] national-level campaign events during the general election in which one or more of the presidential candidates were present. There were five such events in the 2000 general election prior to Election Day: the Republican National Convention (held in Philadelphia), the Democratic National Convention (held in Los Angeles), and three televised presidential debates (held in Boston, Winston-Salem, and St. Louis).[2] The 2004 sample was drawn from voluntary associations that organized activities coinciding with the Democratic National Convention (held in Boston) and the Republican National Convention (held in New York City).[3] I traveled to each of these host cities to draw my sample of associations.

I identified associations for the sample via advance research on the Internet, by contacting community centers, looking in local newspapers, and canvassing the area immediately surrounding the official campaign event locations. In each city, I compiled a list of organizations with activities planned to coincide with the event period. Because I sought to understand mobilization, I excluded organizations engaged exclusively in their regular activities (e.g., monthly meetings), because I did not view questions about why organizations chose *not* to mobilize as particularly helpful (though I did ask many representatives to discuss any reluctance they felt in deciding to mobilize). I then took a purposive sample of voluntary associations in each city, which varied on a number of relevant characteristics pointed to by previous researchers. First, I sought out both *national and local organizations*, because the process of taking action might have different meanings and outcomes for these groups. Second, I chose organizations that had different *types* of activities planned (e.g., protests, fund-raisers, rallies, voter drives, meetings), recognizing that organizations that plan different types of activities may have different goals and experiences. Finally, I sought diversity in the axis of association; in other words, I selected groups whose *concerns* varied.

When choosing among the associations available at a given location, diversity along these three trajectories guided my choices. For example, after my first stop in Philadelphia, I realized that in seeking out organizations with diverging axes of association, I had overlooked scope. As a result, my sample at that point contained more local organizations than national ones, so I sought to correct this imbalance when I arrived at the next location. I evaluated my sample at multiple points during my fieldwork, often daily, in an effort to attend events planned by, and interact with members from, the full range of organizations active in the environment. I continued sampling until I reached saturation, at which point I felt I was no longer gathering new information by adding additional organizations to my sample.

In total, data were gathered on 50 different voluntary associations. Twenty-five of these organizations are national or international organizations, most quite large, and many with a sizable number of paid staff members. The remaining 25 organizations are local, statewide, or regional in nature, half of which have a small paid staff (generally one or two people, often part-time). The organizations in the sample planned an extensive range of activities, which included civil disobedience and protest, a debate watch in a movie theater, a full-sized concert in an arena, street performances, a forum about the Supreme Court with nationally recognized political figures, a $250-per-plate fund-raiser, marches, rallies in front of government buildings, leafleting, member meetings, petitioning, and a national voter education drive. The associations in the sample are organized around a variety of issues, including the war in Iraq, the death penalty, gun control, environmental concerns, women's rights, religion and morality, labor issues, campaign finance reform, global justice, voter turnout, senior citizen's issues, school vouchers, and nuclear weapons. Tables A.1 and A.2 provide a listing of the associations in the sample and their activities.

Voluntary Associations: Scope and Primary Axis of Organization 2000

Abolish	state	death penalty
American Adult Network	national	senior citizens' issues
Bootstraps	local	civic responsibility
Business Watch	national	responsible business
Christians for Families	regional	human rights
Citizens' Campaign Watch	national	inclusive government / campaign finance reform
Disrupt	local	wide-reaching costs of structural inequality
Envirolink	national	environment
Federation for the Freedom from Religion	national	separation of church and state
Feminists for a Socialist Future	int'l	women's issues / economic justice
GenNext	national	youth voter turnout
Income Gap Attack	national	economic inequality
Inequality Forever	regional[1]	wealth in politics
Land and Life Protection League	national	environment / global justice
MassCares	state[2]	protecting the public interest
National Union of Creative Artists	national	labor
NC Citizens for Smaller Government	state[3]	limited government
NC Parents Against Gun Violence	state	gun control
Network for Peace	national	nuclear disarmament / peace
Northeast Union of Professionals	regional	labor
Pro-Choice and Paying Attention (PCPA)	national	reproductive rights
Rights Now	int'l	human rights / global justice
School Choice, Family Choice	state	school vouchers / education
Stand-Up St. Louis	local	direct action / open debates
Students for Change	local	students' issues
The Freedom and Equality League	national	multi-issue progressive
United for Change	state	social justice
United Trades (local number withheld)	local[4]	labor
Young Adult Voters Association	national	youth voter turnout

1. At the time data were collected about Inequality Forever in 2000, it was a modestly sized regional organization, but in the years that followed it blossomed into a national organization.
2. This is the Massachusetts state chapter of a national organization.
3. This is the North Carolina state chapter of a national organization.
4. United Trades is a national labor union, but the data gathered for this research pertain only to the activities of one local branch.

Voluntary Associations: Scope and Primary Axis of Organization 2004

Alternacheer	local	broad anti-capitalism / anti-authoritarian agenda
Boston Pacificsts United	regional	peace and justice
Boston Resistance	local	anarchist / anti-authoritarian
Chinese Cultural Freedom Collective	int'l	religious persecution in China
Choice	local	reproductive rights
Conservatives for Reproductive Rights	national	reproductive rights / conservative women's issues
Electoral Gridlock	national	oppose two-party electoral system
End Contemporary Colonialism	national	peace / racial justice
Faith in Peace	regional[1]	peace
Guts Initiative	local	multi-issue progressive
Jews for Justice	local	racial justice / economic justice
Moms for New Leadership	national	anti-Bush
National Peace and Equality Coalition	national[2]	peace / social justice
Pre-born Protectors	national	pro-life
Progressive Activists Coalition	local	broad progessive agenda
Radical Grandma Chorus	local[3]	peace / social justice
Republican Freakshow	local	political corruption
Skilled Trades Union	local[4]	labor
Veterans Opposing War	national	peace
Women Against War	national	peace / social justice
Wrath of Christ	local	opposing homosexuality

1. Faith in Peace is a national religious organization, but the data gathered for this research pertain only to the activities of one regional group.
2. The National Peace and Equality Coalition is a large umbrella organization, with paid staff and volunteers, but individuals do not join the organization, rather entire groups become members. Their large numbers of volunteers qualify them as a voluntary association as defined in this research.
3. This is a local chapter of an international organization.
4. The Skilled Trades Union is a national labor union, but the data gathered for this research pertain only to the activities of one local branch.

From each organization in the sample, I subsampled one *typical member/participant* and one *core member/organizer/leader* for in-depth, semi-structured interviews.[4] Members who were instrumental in planning events were considered core members. In most cases, these were professional staff members, committee chairs, head volunteers, or officers of the association. Members who were not involved in planning the events but participated in or attended them were considered typical members.[5] The viewpoints of typical members and core members were each essential to the research. While both types of participants were able to share their (different) experiences and interpretations, core members had access to critical information about the symbolic and instrumental strategies and motivations of the organization, which typical members often lacked.

The first interviewee in each organization was selected in person, based on suitability, rapport, and willingness to participate. The subsequent respondents were recruited either via in-person solicitation or referral. This process yielded a total of 101 useable interviews. In two instances, I had the sense that I was not able to get a complete picture from the two initial interviews; in each of these cases, I conducted an additional interview. In another instance, I interviewed a core member but was never able to interview a typical member. I ultimately decided to include this organization in the sample, because I was able to obtain a substantial amount of information about the organization from other sources.

I also sampled a group of journalists (N = 33) covering the events. I used purposive sampling to recruit respondents who worked for both national and local news organizations. I made a significant effort to include journalists who attended (and in some cases covered) the activities of associations I sampled, but a few of the reporters attended or covered the activities of other voluntary organizations. Regardless, all were interested in or assigned to cover events transpiring outside the convention or debate.

Some of the interviews were conducted in person at mutually agreeable locations (e.g., the organization's offices or a coffee shop). Most association affiliates were incredibly busy preparing and carrying out their activities, and journalists were often on deadline, so a significant number of interviews were conducted by telephone, after the heat of the moment had subsided. Although I had some concerns about this initially, I think the telephone interviews introduced as many advantages as disadvantages. The face-to-face interviews permitted me to watch body language and to use nonverbal communication to probe, but I also often had to contend with interruptions and other distractions in these settings. There is an intimacy involved in extended telephone conversations that I felt contributed to the quality of the interactions, and I benefitted from being able to review my interview guide and jot notes without appearing uninterested to the respondent.

Supplementary Data

I supplemented the in-depth interviews with data gathered from field observations, newspaper articles, Internet materials, and literature distributed by the associations. The sample of field observations includes at least one member-gathering or public event organized by each of the associations, in addition to observations recorded on the way to and from these events, at the organizations' preceding meetings when possible, around the campaign event sites, and at designated meeting/protest areas.

In the field, I was open about my role as a researcher when asked. In general, my presence rarely surprised people—I seemed to fit in, but various people I encountered perceived me quite differently. Journalists often approached me, believing that I was an activist, perhaps because I appeared comfortable and periodically pitched in (e.g., setting up tables or handing out tape). Police officers often thought I was a journalist, probably because of my notebook and my social location (most journalists I encountered were also white, middle-aged, and middle-class). This turned out to be a mistake that benefitted me on many occasions, as I was not "cleared out" with pedestrians during difficult standoffs, but rather allowed to remain in the thick of things, mill about freely, speak to activists (even those waiting to be arrested), and ask questions of the officers. At closed-group meetings, activists usually knew who I was, but at large public meetings and events, I was sometimes presumed to be a journalist (they were often deflated to find I was just a sociologist), an undercover police officer (despite my denials), or a member of another organization. Passersby often approached me as if I were another passerby.

Overall, I was able to move freely from event to event and my presence rarely seemed to strike others as an oddity. This had much to do with the milieu. In the mobilization context, the setting and the faces are new to all involved. I was not disrupting a routine, because there was no routine. Two of the times that I did feel conspicuous were at large, clearinghouse meetings attended by association representatives. My lack of affiliation and my status as a researcher in these spaces made other participants leery, and they probably assumed I was with law enforcement. Because of this and the fact that I found the individual association/coalition meetings and events more informative, I only attended two of these large coordinating meetings. The only other time my presence seemed uncomfortable was at the Beverly Hills luncheon described in chapter 3.

The sample of newspaper articles includes all articles referencing the organizations (or their events) that appeared in the *New York Times*, the *Washington Post*, and the primary local papers published in the host city of each specific campaign event (*Philadelphia Daily News, Philadelphia Inquirer, Los Angeles Times, Los Angeles Daily News, Boston Globe, Boston Herald, Winston-Salem Journal, St. Louis Post-Dispatch, New York Daily News*). Articles published on the days of the conventions and debates have been included in addition to those that appeared on the two days before and the two days after the events.

The sample of Internet materials includes miscellaneous information from the organizations' official websites and from the discussion groups generated by these websites. Literature about the associations or their activities that was distributed at their meetings and events was also included. These materials are unquestionably incomplete, but they provided useful backstory as I acclimated myself to the settings and groups.

Taken together, I came to develop my analysis of these associations based on interviews from members and leaders, observations at their events, the materials they distributed on location and online, and from journalists' accounts via interviews and through their published work. It is a tremendous amount of information, from which I culled the story told in the pages of this book. While each association had a unique experience, the themes presented here represent my best attempt to identify patterns in association involvement in the campaign context.

Notes

1. Because several associations in the sample engaged in illegal activities, I changed the names of all subjects and the organizations with which they are affiliated.

2. Ferree et al. (2002). See chapters 4 and 6 for additional information.

3. See Sobieraj (2006) for an earlier formulation of these ideas.

4. Indeed, all legitimate democratic elections, save those that are uncontested, offer moments of liminality, but a presidential election offers liminality in conjunction with these other characteristics (particularly significance) in a way that a local or midterm election does not. See Herzog (1987) on elections as liminal stages.

5. Tocqueville ([1835] 2000) describes national elections in the United States as crises. This is discussed at some length by Wolin (2001) and revisited by Perrin et al. (2006) in their examination of postmodern electoral crises.

6. But Bennett et al.(2004) show that it is not so easy to hijack attention away from elites, finding that when activists' issues receive attention in the news media, it is often the result of elites' cues and comments.

7. Alexander (1998) describes the evolution of the concept as having three phases. Early modern versions (Ferguson [1767] 1995; Smith [1759] 1976; Rousseau [1762] 1968; Hegel [1821] 1967; Tocqueville [1835] 2000) understand civil society broadly as those realms of social life distinct from the state. Virtually everything outside the state (the market, legal structures, and the voluntary sector) is included under the umbrella of civil society, with the exception of the family. The second phase of the concept, most notably crafted by Marx, equates civil society quite narrowly with market capitalism. The third phase consists of more contemporary understandings of the sector, which separate civil society from the state and the economy in an effort to better understand the solidarities and activities that take place in the associational realm, and which also seek to concretize theoretical formulations by examining existing democracies (Alexander 1997; Cohen and Arato 1992). For a thought-provoking account of the history of the concept, see Seligman (1992).

8. Civil society influences and is influenced by the state and the economy, but its activities are analytically distinct. Much research on nonprofit organizations demonstrates that these three sectors are more accurately described as

interdependent than independent (Hall 1987; Moore et al. 2002), but for analytic purposes these distinctions are productive. As a result of its perceived or relative "independence," civil society is often understood as a counterweight to state and market power, a watchdog poised to intervene on the public's behalf, which allows groups and communities to assert their rights and political preferences.

9. See Eliasoph (1998), Fiorina (1999), Gutmann (1998), Lichterman (1999), Meeks (2001), and Sobieraj and White (2004, 2007).

10. Eley (1992), Fraser (1992), Meeks (2001), and Melucci (1996) address this contestation.

11. Alexander 1997, 1998

12. Cohen and Arato 1992

13. Walzer 1992

14. Calhoun 1991, 1993

15. See Dao and Van Natta (1999) for an account of this change.

16. This phenomenon is true not only in the present day, but historically as well. Skocpol (1999, 2003) shows that each of the major American wars, from the revolution through World War II, launched new voluntary associations and revitalized existing ones. Associational activity was also central to the rights-based movements of the 1960s. Competing publics formed by the marginalization of minorities from mainstream politics provided both the training ground and the solidarity building for the civil rights movement, the women's movement, and the antiwar movement. Mobilizing moments exist that stimulate associational activity. During the Montgomery bus boycott of the civil rights movement, daily mass meetings provided opportunities for strategizing, finding inspiration, and coordinating finances (Schudson 1998).

17. Those working in the traditional collective behavior paradigm (Smelser 1963; Kornhauser 1959) differ on the nuances of movement formation, but they share a view of social movements as nonrational, extra-institutional group activity generated by individual responses to the "strains" that accompany social changes. In contrast, resource mobilization theorists emphasize rationality, examining the role of political opportunity structures (McAdam 1982; Piven and Cloward 1977; Tilly 1978), mobilizing organizations (McCarthy and Zald 1977), or framing processes (Gamson 1975; Snow et al. 1986) in social movement emergence. Those working in this tradition share a belief that social movements form as a result of individuals and groups rationally pursuing their interests as resources and opportunities for collective action arise. Finally, new social movement theorists (Touraine 1985; Melucci 1996) argue that social movements develop to contest social norms, assert collective identity, and democratize civil society. Those working in these four prominent traditions disagree on the catalysts and goals of social movements, but they implicitly hold the view that mobilization is neither consistent nor continuous, a fundamental oversight in the civil society literature.

18. Walder (2009, 399) sees this as detrimental, making the case that the preoccupation with mobilization has in fact been so extensive as to limit the intellectual vitality of social movements research: "For more than two decades debates in this subfield have been about the role of organization, political opportunity, resources, strategy, collective identity, cognitive frames and emotions, all of them defined as complimentary or competing approaches to understanding group mobilization."

19. I leave answering these difficult questions to social movement scholars, who have developed an extensive and sophisticated set of insights. Some key pieces include Amenta et al. (2002), Amenta (2006), Baumgartner and Mahoney (2005), Giugni (2007), Meyer (2005), Olzak and Soule (2009), Piven (2006), Skocpol (2003), and Soule et al.(1999). See Amenta et al.(2010) for an excellent review of work on the political consequences of social movements.

20. The exceptions to this tendency (e.g., Fantasia 1988; Lichterman 1996; Polletta 2002, 2006) are incredibly useful and I return to them in chapter 6.

21. Consider, for example, a Take Back the Night march. These events are intended to raise awareness about violence against women, and to empower and support participants (particularly survivors).

22. These two campaign cycles occur in quite different political moments, culturally speaking. In 2000, I found organizations still elated from their recent victories in Seattle and optimistic about their political future, but in 2004, 9/11 and the Patriot Act loomed to create a climate far less hospitable to political dissent. This did not affect all groups in the same way. I elaborate more on the differences between 2000 and 2004 in chapter 2.

23. Some noteworthy examples include Eliasoph (1998), Lichterman (1996, 2005), and Fisher (2006).

24. See the appendix for a more detailed accounting of the methods utilized in this research.

25. Indymedia (Independent Media Centers) emerged in 1998 and began to flourish in 1999. By 2000 there were many Indymedia reporters circulating at the campaign-related activist events, but the activist groups expressed very little interest in publicizing their work via this channel. Although most activists supported and were enthusiastic about Indymedia, when representatives talked about attracting "media attention" or "news coverage," it proved to be synonymous with mainstream news media, preferably national.

26. Fraser (1992, 124) acknowledges that the inequities present in mainstream publics may be reproduced in counterpublics: "I do not mean to suggest that subaltern counterpublics are always necessarily virtuous. Some of them, alas, are explicitly undemocratic and antiegalitarian, and even those with democratic and egalitarian intentions are not always above practicing their own modes of informal exclusion and marginalization." Still, for Fraser these competing publics widen discursive space, because they emerge in response to exclusion; therefore, she argues that multiple publics are a step toward democracy, even if an imperfect one.

27. Aronowitz (1995), Gregory (1994), Jacobs (2000), Simone (2006), and Squires (2000) provide illustrations.

28. Noteworthy examples include Cohen and Arato (1992), Fung (2003), Habermas (1989, 1996), Tocqueville ([1835] 2000), and Warren (2000).

29. Habermas (1989, 1996) acknowledges the coexistence of multiple publics (in a break from his earlier work). Here he is presumably referring to a mainstream public sphere without implying that no other publics exist.

Notes to Chapter 2

1. A standoff (and subsequent negotiation) between protesters and police ensued as well, but I have omitted the details here.

2. Activists use the term *black bloc* to describe a particular type of affinity group within larger political actions, demonstrations, and the like. People utilizing a black bloc tactic generally include a subset of anarchist participants committed to a set of agreed-on principles that vary from group to group. Those self-identifying as part of a black bloc wear black and shield their faces with bandanas to conceal their identities. They often engage in some sort of property crime as part of their political expression, such as appropriating newspaper racks and garbage cans to build barricades or breaking corporate retailers' windows. Black bloc groups made up a tiny percentage of activists involved with the major actions around the 2000 conventions and debates, but police and journalists seemed disproportionately concerned with the behavior of such groups, whose perceived propensity for violent and erratic behavior seemed to take on almost mythical proportions. At the march I describe here, I saw a moderate-sized bloc, which was the largest I saw active in either 2000 or 2004. In fact, in Los Angeles, I only saw two other black bloc affinity groups, one with approximately five members present, and another with only three.

3. I know of no such constitutional guarantee, although the critique of the 15 percent threshold is a familiar one, as it allows the Commission on Presidential Debates (which has been run by former heads of the RNC and DNC since it formed in 1988) to virtually assure that only the two dominant party candidates will be able to participate.

4. The intersection of the major campaign stops with the ephemeral character of contemporary civic engagement (Sobieraj 2006; Wuthnow 1998) proved to be a productive climate for a special form of mobilization: the creation of entirely new associations. Ten of the organizations in my sample formed explicitly for the campaign year or these specific events. Mark, a core member of United for Change, a multi-issue progressive group, explained that his organization formed expressly because the Republican National Convention was coming to Philadelphia:

The news came on and said the Republicans had announced that they were coming to Philadelphia, and I just couldn't believe it. I thought, how stupid. I said, "What a great organizing opportunity! . . . Here's the Republican Party coming to town. We can find some way to mobilize people." So, I, just on a whim, put together a website and that evening had a website and sent out an e-mail to my friends and some colleagues. The next morning, when they announced that the Republicans were coming, they also had an article in the newspaper that said—and we hadn't done any media work on this, I don't know how they got the story—but this story said, "How long do you think it will take before the first protests are organized about the Republicans? How about already?" They gave the website and then we, almost immediately, had a couple hundred people on an e-mail list who wanted to start working on things.

The sparks that ignited at the announcement of the convention ultimately evolved into a large coalition of organizations that organized a massive permitted march. Six other organizations in my sample formed for legal political activity with such varied foci as creating awareness about the role of the elite in politics (Inequality Forever), supporting the passage of a school voucher initiative (School Choice, Family Choice), and working to prevent the reelection of George W. Bush (Moms for New Leadership). The remaining newly formed organizations (Boston Resistance, Disrupt, and Stand Up St. Louis) emerged to coordinate direct action. Two of the new organizations indicated that their groups hoped to endure beyond the campaign. The first of these, United for Change, has since dissolved. The second, Inequality Forever, germinated dozens of fledgling chapters across the country.

5. A breakdown of mobilized fundamental activities is not provided because all mobilized communal and demonstrative events require heightened fundamental activity, and by virtue of the sampling design, organizations that mobilized exclusively via fundamental action are not included in the sample.

6. For more on activist–political party interaction, see Heaney and Rojas (2007).

7. Abolish, the Freedom and Equality League, NC Parents Against Gun Violence, and Network for Peace in 2000, and Boston Pacifists United, Moms for New Leadership, National Peace and Equality Coalition, Skilled Trades Union, and Women Against War in 2004.

8. For excellent sources on the restrictions of nonprofit tax status, see Lunder and Whitaker (2006) and Berry with Arons (2003).

9. As I mentioned, these efforts did not represent mobilization for this particular organization. As a voters' organization, they routinely held such events. Still, I point to them in order to address their interest in holding events that are demonstrative in nature.

10. This is discussed in detail in chapter 4. See also Bennett et al.(2004), Gamson and Wolfsfeld (1993), and Gitlin (1980).

Notes to Chapter 3

1. A 14-month battle took place between the organization and the city of New York over permitting, centering on the organization's application to use Central Park as a rally location, which was denied, with the city citing concerns about damage to the grass. This upset the organizers, who took the matter to the courts, claiming a violation of First Amendment rights. This was one of several such lawsuits over Central Park, all of which failed to convince the sitting judge. The matter, which consumed a great deal of the organizers' energy, remained unresolved until just a few days before the march.

2. Events such as this one most clearly evoke what Tilly (2004) refers to as WUNC displays: efforts on the part of social movements to show that they are Worthy, United, Numerous, and Committed.

3. This famous statement, from a 1946 speech by the German anti-Nazi pastor, appears in many slightly varied versions in several prominent locations, including a carving at the New England Holocaust Memorial in downtown Boston, steps away from the marchers' path.

Notes to Chapter 4

1. See Ferree et al. (2002) for a more detailed synopsis of the role of the public sphere in democratic theory.

2. Groups and individuals can also enter this master forum involuntarily, when they are the subject of discussion. Many examples are relevant here, such as discourse about minority groups that have not shaped or initiated the discussion (e.g., immigrants, nonwhites, the poor) or dialogue about communities that do wish to be enclaved (e.g., the San Angelo, Texas, "polygamy raid" in April 2008).

3. These visions abound in theories of the public sphere and in work on media and democracy more generally. For some examples, see Bennett (2007), Curran (2002), Entman (1989), Gurevitch and Blumler (1990), Keane (1991), and Young (2000).

4. See Bennett et al. (2004), Gitlin (1980), and Habermas (1996) for examples.

5. The script in this case refers not only to the spoken words, the literal script, but also to the stage direction (blocking), lighting, signage, music, and even gestures planned in advance. No detail goes unplanned. See Panagopoulos (2007) and Pomper (2007) for more on contemporary conventions.

6. Debates have become increasingly controlled since the Commission on Presidential Debates took responsibility for them in 1988.

7. For example, "Except as provided in subparagraph (d) (viii) of this paragraph 9, TV cameras will be locked into place during all debates. They may, however, tilt or rotate as needed" (Open Debates 2004, 16).

8. Outsider is an accurate term in some ways and a misnomer in others. These associations are outsiders in the sense that they do not (for the most part) have an opportunity to participate in the political business that transpires at the conventions. They do not have a seat at the table. In contrast, many groups in the sample, such as labor unions and large membership organizations, are politically influential in their own right.

9. Although this term is dated and somewhat controversial in the United States, I use it to indicate the publications' national and international relevance, rather than as an indicator that these newspapers are either (1) complete reflections of the national landscape, or (2) somehow simply stenographic vehicles for the transmission of information. Indeed, the arguments of this book serve as testament to the contrary.

10. Although the *Wall Street Journal* has a substantially higher circulation than either the *New York Times* or the *New York Daily News*, it was excluded because its content is specialized. In addition, while the circulation of the *New York Post* rivals that of the *New York Daily News*, I included only the higher circulating paper, since no other city had three papers represented.

11. This is a highly selective archive, but I would argue that it is still a good barometer for news coverage more generally. Although newspapers are but one medium through which news circulates, they remain the foundation of all news: those who produce news in other venues (e.g., television or magazines) use newspapers as launching points for their own stories (McManus 1995). Analyzing televised news would have been useful as well, but logistical considerations prohibited me from doing so.

12. Bennett (2007) refers to the tendency for news to report events as threats to order as the "authority-disorder bias." The stories in this sample reflect this bias, emphasizing either disruption and subsequent arrest or the noteworthy peacefulness of a given event.

13. Indeed, these are politically important topics, but none of the associations I studied was active because it hoped to force issues of public space, for example, into public discourse. When these issues became relevant to the associations, as in the case of the highly restrictive protest zone in Boston in 2004, many associations did wish to call attention to the curtailing of free speech, but this kind of meta-political activity—political activism about political activism—was not the reason for entry.

14. Entman and Rojecki (1993, 2000) and others illustrate elsewhere the problem that emerges if we look exclusively at the frequency of representation without considering the context.

15. As a result of the norms of professional journalism, these associations are rarely represented as such, but instead are presented through members, participants, or spokespeople. See Bennett (2007) on the tendency for news to be a retelling of personal stories.

16. Gitlin (1980), drawing on an interview with Ben Bagdikian, describes three hurdles faced by activities transpiring outside of regular beats: the editor's decision that a setting or event is potentially newsworthy, the reporter's decision about what in that setting is worth noting, and the editor's decision about what the final story should look like and where it will be placed.

17. In extraordinary circumstances—Reagan's attempted assassination, the attacks of September 11, the Columbine High School shootings—news preempts scheduled programming and expands exponentially.

18. But far fewer had nurtured the long-term relationships with journalists, such as those described by Ryan, Anastario, and Jeffreys (2005).

19. Such images may be effective in another setting. For example, we can imagine journalists including these types of events in coverage of, say, the Iowa caucuses.

20. There is a circulating belief that including "why" amounts to conjecture about causality, and reporters maintain a commitment to approximating objectivity. Carey (1986) argues that while the "how" and "why" are often missing in individual stories, when journalism is taken as a whole—as a body of reportage made up of newspapers, televised news, documentaries, newsweekly articles, and other media—the answers are present. I take issue with this claim on several levels. First, his idea that the answer to the question "why" forms and comes to exist "out there" is true only if a story is alive in the news long enough to develop depth. Most news stories do not become the subject of documentaries, newsweeklies, or book-length journalism. Second, I see no reason why what Carey terms the "bare description" that makes up daily press cannot include a description of why an event transpired. A journalist need not insert his or her own presumptions about why someone did something in order to provide this information; they need only to ask a source and report the answer. Third, while journalism does indeed include a body of work on a given topic, approaching news "as a curriculum" is neither the habit of most consumers of news nor a luxury that most can afford. The most critical elements of the news—the how, what, where, when, why, and, I would add, *with what result*—need to be readily available, not requiring that consumers tease them out through prolonged immersion in an intertextual world of news.

21. This power dynamic can shift when a particular organization is highly sought out. For example, journalists were clamoring for official statements from the leaders of the organization that coordinated the massive march around the 2004 RNC, looking for insights about plans for the march, responses to decisions made by the police, projections for the number of attendees, and so forth. This shifts the balance, allowing an organization to have greater control over the flow of information to the press—who will speak, what they will say, when they will say it, and to whom.

22. Gans (1979, 140–41) describes beat reporters as being forced to be more polite to their sources, as they must establish and maintain rapport in order to complete their work, whereas general assignment reporters, who source "strangers," often can also press them with more challenging, provocative, and leading questions.

23. One notable exception was the subset of antiwar organizations active in 2004 that included groups who discussed the personal toll that the war had taken on their families (e.g., parents whose children had been killed, kids who missed their parents, soldiers who had returned from Iraq).

24. This calls to mind work the work of Ryan (2004) and Ryan, Anastario, and Jeffreys (2005), which demonstrates that social movement organizations can win the media negotiation.

Notes to Chapter 5

1. See Sobieraj (2006) for a more detailed discussion of citizen groups and civic engagement.

2. Eliasoph (1998) shows the shrinking space available to political dialogue, while Sobieraj and White (2004, 2007) demonstrate its centrality to political mobilization.

Notes to Chapter 6

1. See also Walsh (2004) and Sobieraj and White (2004) on the tangible impact of political dialogue.

2. The early planning for the RNC protests in February 2008 included an explicit rule that coalition members should avoid discussing issues on which there was not widespread agreement (interview with Betsy Leondar-Wright 2008).

3. The fire that ensued ultimately killed 5 children and 7 adults, destroyed 61 row houses, and left 250 people homeless.

4. See Wagner-Pacifici's fascinating *Discourse and Destruction: The City of Philadelphia Versus* MOVE (1994) for more on competing interpretations of MOVE.

5. Several groups worked in coalitions for select events while also coordinating independent efforts.

6. Research in social movements has given far more extensive attention to collective identity than research on voluntary associations. Polletta and Jasper (2001) offer an excellent review.

7. Wake Forest University, which hosted the Winston-Salem debate, allowed protesters on the university grounds under a series of remarkable restrictions. First, activists were required to meet security off campus in a parking lot for registration, where they were required to show ID and indicate which group they were with. The members of each group were then given a color-coded identification bracelet and cleared by security guards, who ensured that no one brought backpacks, bags, or anything that could possibly be construed as a potential weapon (e.g., a hairbrush). Once cleared, activists were shuttled by bus to campus and led to a soccer field— largely obscured from view of nonparticipants—that had been divided with orange construction fencing into square pens, one for each color-coded group in order to prevent mingling. And that is how they stayed for the duration of the event.

8. While some of these technologies existed in 2000, they were a more relevant and realistic option in 2004. In 2008, they entered the election setting in a more pronounced way, as I describe in the epilogue.

Notes to the Epilogue

1. Bloggers were mainstream enough by 2004 that the RNC and DNC both extended credentials to political bloggers, and the DNC even hosted a bloggers' breakfast for attendees, featuring a keynote from Howard Dean.

2. For an enthusiastic, almost romantic, take on these capabilities, see Shirky (2008).

3. The groups coordinating illegal activities offered logistical information about face-to-face meeting/planning sessions and convergence spaces, but the precise details of actual "actions" were not posted online.

4. The lighthearted trailer offered a campy, Pleasantville-esque vision of what Minneapolis might look like during the convention. It followed a person going about her daily routines in full anarchist garb: black head to toe, with a bandana as a facemask. Among other things, she showers (fully clothed), brushes teeth (under the bandana), gets the newspaper (which reads, "The Republicans Are Coming!") from a friendly neighborhood news carrier on a bike, picks up a packed lunch (from Food Not Bombs), and runs to the RNC convention center, all the while encountering only people dressed just as she is (including the news carrier, a neighborhood kid on a tire swing, someone pruning bushes with bolt cutters, and a neighbor who does some grilling with the help of a Molotov cocktail). It ended with the words "We're Getting Ready. What Are You Doing?" and a prompt to find out more information from their website.

5. For an unsettling example of an organization that promotes internal discourse in this way, see the forum section of white supremacist group Stormfront's website (http://www.stormfront.org/forum/). It contains the most extensive and active discussion board I've seen used by a voluntary association.

6. Pickard (2008), for example, describes considerable political debate on Democratic Underground and Free Republic, which are communities of participants who share broad ideological commitments.

7. This is especially interesting given YouTube's reputation for juvenile, combative, off-topic, and offensive comment threads.

8. I prefer not to rehash these rich debates here. My concern is not whether the Internet has been democratizing, but rather, far more narrowly, how the social media mainstreamed in the mid-2000s alter the opportunities available for activist groups hoping to intervene in electoral politics. For a few key writings on the Internet as a democratizing force, see Bimber (2003), Dahlgren (2005), and Margolis and Resnick (2000); for some less optimistic assessments, see Hindman (2009), Norris (2001), Sparks (2001), and Sunstein (2001). In addition, Flew (2009) offers a thoughtful analysis of new ICTs and citizenship.

Notes to the Appendix

1. Most events are preplanned to a degree, but many campaign stops are scheduled only days in advance and may not be well publicized, giving associations little opportunity to respond. Therefore, for the purposes of this research, preplanned is intended to mean planned well in advance of the scheduled appearance. I have used six months advance notice as an arbitrary guideline.

2. The vice-presidential debate could be considered a sixth event of this type, but because the presidential candidates are unlikely to be present at these events, I excluded them from the sample.

3. In 2000, there was a much greater level of activity coinciding with the conventions than with the debates (most likely because of their extended duration and the far larger numbers of political figures drawn to the events). As a result, in 2004, I omitted the debate sites from the research design.

4. I use the term *typical members* to refer to general members or participants in the events, and *core members* to refer to key members, leaders, or organizers of the association events; however, it is important to note that these categories are not restricted in any way to formal membership.

5. In other words, "typical" refers to non-leaders and is in no way intended to indicate that these members were perceived to represent the membership overall.

References

Alexander, Jeffrey C. 1997. "The Paradoxes of Civil Society." *International Sociology* 12:115–133.

———. 1998. *Real civil societies: dilemmas of institutionalization.* Thousand Oaks, CA: Sage.

Amenta, Edwin. 2006. *When movements matter: the Townsend Plan and the rise of social security.* Princeton: Princeton University Press.

Amenta, Edwin, Neal Caren, Elizabeth Chiarello, and Yang Su. 2010. "The Political Consequences of Social Movements." *Annual Review of Sociology* 36:14.1–14.21.

Amenta, Edwin, Neal Caren, Tina Fetner, and Michael P. Young. 2002. "Challengers and States: Toward a Political Sociology of Social Movements." *Research in Political Sociology* 10:47–83.

Aronowitz, Stanley. 1995. "Against the Liberal State: ACT-UP and the Emergence of Postmodern Politics." Pp. 357–383 in *Social Postmodernism: Beyond Identity Politics,* edited by Linda Nicholson and Steven Seidman. Cambridge: Cambridge University Press.

Baumgartner, Frank R., and Christine Mahoney. 2005. "Social Movements, the Rise of New Issues, and the Public Agenda." Pp. 65–86 in *Routing the Opposition: Social Movements, Pubic Policy, and Democracy,* edited by David S. Meyer, Valerie Jenness, and Helen Ingram. Minneapolis: University of Minnesota Press.

Belluck, Pam, and Marc Santora. 2004. "Mass Protests, Traffic Jams? None So Far and a Region Is Relieved." *New York Times,* June 27.

Benhabib, Seyla. 1992. "Models of Public Space: Hannah Arendt, the Liberal Tradition, and Jürgen Habermas." Pp. 73–98 in *Habermas and the Public Sphere,* edited by C. J. Calhoun. Cambridge: MIT Press.

Bennett, W. Lance. 2007. *News: the politics of illusion.* New York: Pearson Longman.

Bennett, W. Lance, and David L. Paletz. 1994. *Taken by storm: the media, public opinion, and U.S. foreign policy in the Gulf War.* Chicago: University of Chicago Press.

Bennett, W. Lance, Victor Pickard, David P. Iozzi, Carl L. Schroeder, Taso Lagos, and Courtney Evans-Caswell. 2004. "Managing the Public Sphere: Journalistic Construction of the Great Globalization Debate." *Journal of Communication* 54:437–455.

Benson, Rodney. 2006. "News Media as a 'Journalistic Field': What Bourdieu Adds to New Institutionalism, and Vice Versa." *Political Communication* 23:187–202.

Berry, Jeffrey M., with David F. Arons. 2003. *A voice for nonprofits.* Washington, DC: Brookings Institution Press.

Bimber, Bruce. 2003. *Information and democracy: technology in the evolution of political power.* Cambridge: Cambridge University Press.

Bimber, Bruce, and Richard Davis. 2003. *Campaigning online: The Internet in U.S. elections.* New York: Oxford University Press.

Blee, Kathleen M., and Ashley Currier. 2006. "How Local Social Movement Groups Handle a Presidential Election." *Qualitative Sociology* 29:261–280.

Bombardieri, Marcella. 2000. "In Preliminary to Debate, Demonstrators Take the Stage." *Boston Globe*, October 4.

———. 2004. "Boycott Is Planned for Free-Speech Zone." *Boston Globe*, July 25.

Calhoun, Craig J. 1991. "Indirect Relationships and Imagined Communities: Large-Scale Integration and the Transformation of Everyday Life." Pp. 95–121 in *Social Theory for a Changing Society*, edited by Pierre Bourdieu and James S. Coleman. New York: Russell Sage Foundation.

———. 1992. *Habermas and the public sphere.* Cambridge: MIT Press.

———. 1993. "Civil Society and the Public Sphere." *Public Culture* 5:267–280.

Carey, James W. 1986. "Why and How: The Dark Continent of American Journalism." Pp. 146–195 in *Reading the News*, edited by Robert Manoff and Michael Schudson. New York: Pantheon Books.

Castells, Manuel. 1997. *The power of identity.* Malden, MA: Blackwell.

Clines, Francis X. 2000."The Republicans: The Protesters; Demonstrators Try to Steal Some Thunder at Convention." *New York Times*, August 2.

Cohen, Jean L., and Andrew Arato. 1992. *Civil society and political theory.* Cambridge: MIT Press.

Curran, James. 2002. *Media and power.* New York: Routledge.

Dahlgren, Peter. 2005. "The Internet, Public Spheres, and Political Communication: Dispersal and Deliberation." *Political Communication* 22:147–162.

Dao, James, and Don N. Van Natta Jr. 1999. "NRA Is Using Adversity to Its Advantage." *New York Times*, June 12.

Darnton, Robert. 1975. "Writing News and Telling Stories." *Daedelus* 104:175–194.

Dayan, Daniel, and Elihu Katz. 1992. *Media events: the live broadcasting of history.* Cambridge: Harvard University Press.

Durkheim, Emile. 1995. *The elementary forms of religious life.* New York: Free Press.

Earl, Jennifer, Katrina Kimport, Greg Prieto, Carly Rush, and Kimberly Reynoso. 2009. "Changing the World One Webpage at a Time: Conceptualizing and Explaining 'Internet Activism.'" Paper presented at the annual meeting for the American Sociological Association, San Francisco.

Earl, Jennifer, and Alan Schussman. 2004. "Cease and Desist: Repression, Strategic Voting, and the 2000 U.S. Presidential Election." *Mobilization* 9:181–202.

Eley, Geoff. 1992. "Nations, Publics, and Political Cultures: Placing Habermas in the Nineteenth Century." Pp. 289–339 in *Habermas and the Public Sphere*, edited by C. J. Calhoun. Cambridge: MIT Press.

Eliasoph, Nina. 1998. *Avoiding politics: how Americans produce apathy in everyday life*. Cambridge: Cambridge University Press.

Eliasoph, Nina, and Paul Lichterman. 2003. "Culture in Interaction." *American Journal of Sociology* 108:735–794.

Entman, Robert M. 1989. *Democracy without citizens: media and the decay of American politics*. New York: Oxford University Press.

Entman, Robert M., and Andrew Rojecki. 1993. "Freezing Out the Public: Elite and Media Framing of the U.S. Anti-nuclear Movement." *Political Communication* 10:155–173.

———. 2000. *The black image in the white mind: media and race in America*. Chicago: University of Chicago Press.

Fantasia, Rick. 1988. *Cultures of solidarity: consciousness, action, and contemporary American workers*. Berkeley: University of California Press.

Ferguson, Adam. (1767) 1995. *An essay on the history of the civil society*. Reprint, Cambridge: Cambridge University Press.

Ferree, Myra Marx, William A. Gamson, Jürgen Gerhards, and Dieter Rucht. 2002. *Shaping abortion discourse: democracy and the public sphere in Germany and the United States*. Cambridge: Cambridge University Press.

Fine, Gary Alan. 2004. *Everyday genius: self-taught art and the culture of authenticity*. Chicago: University of Chicago Press.

Fiorina, Morris P. 1999. "Extreme Voices: A Dark Side of Civic Engagement." Pp. 395–426 in *Civic Engagement in American Democracy*, edited by Theda Skocpol and Morris P. Fiorina. Washington, DC: Brookings Institution Press.

Fisher, Dana. 2006. *Activism, inc.: how the outsourcing of grassroots campaigns is strangling progressive politics in America*. Stanford: Stanford University Press.

Fishman, Mark. 1980. *Manufacturing the news*. Austin: University of Texas Press.

———. 1982. "News and Nonevents: Making the Visible Invisible." Pp. 219–240 in *Individuals in Mass Media Organizations: Creativity and Constraint*, edited by James S. Ettema and D. Charles Whitney. Thousand Oaks, CA: Sage.

Flew, Terry. 2009. "The Citizen's Voice: Albert Hischman's Exit, Voice, and Loyalty and Its Contribution to Media Citizenship Debates." *Media, Culture, and Society* 31:977–994.

Foot, Kirsten, and Stephen M. Schneider. 2006. *Web campaigning*. Cambridge: MIT Press.

Fraser, Nancy. 1992. "Rethinking the Public Sphere: A Contribution to the Critique of Actually Existing Democracy." Pp. 109–142 in *Habermas and the Public Sphere*, edited by C. J. Calhoun. Cambridge: MIT Press.

Fung, Archon. 2003. "Associations and Democracy: Between Theories, Hopes, and Realities." *Annual Review of Sociology* 29:515–539.

Galtung, Johan, and Mari Holmboe Ruge. 1965. "The Structure of Foreign News." *Journal of Peace Research* 1:64–91.

Gamson, William A. 1975. *The strategy of social protest.* Homewood, IL: Dorsey Press.

Gamson, William A., and Gadi Wolfsfeld. 1993. "Movements and Media as Interacting Systems." *Annals of the American Academy of Political and Social Science* 528:114–125.

Gans, Herbert J. 1979. *Deciding what's news: a study of CBS evening news, NBC Nightly News, Newsweek, and Time.* New York: Pantheon Books.

Gitlin, Todd. 1980. *The whole world is watching: mass media in the making and unmaking of the New Left.* Berkeley: University of California Press.

Giugni, Marco. 2007. "Useless Protest? A Time-Series Analysis of the Policy Outcomes of Ecology, Antinuclear, and Peace Movements in the United States, 1977–1995." *Mobilization* 12:53–77.

Goldenberg, Edie N. 1975. *Making the papers: the access of resource-poor groups to the metropolitan press.* Lexington, MA: Lexington Books.

Goldstone, Jack A. 2003. "Bridging Institutionalized and Noninstitutionalized Politics." Pp. 1–26 in *States, Parties, and Social Movements,* edited by Jack A. Goldstone. Cambridge: Cambridge University Press.

Graber, Doris. 1993. *The mass media and American politics.* Washington, DC: Congressional Quarterly Press.

Grazian, David. 2003. *Blue Chicago: the search for authenticity in urban blues clubs.* Chicago: University of Chicago Press.

Gregory, Steven. 1994. "Race, Identity and Political Activism: The Shifting Contours of the African American Public Sphere." *Public Culture* 7:147–164.

Gurevitch, Michael, and Jay G. Blumler. 1990. "Comparative Research: The Extending Frontier." Pp. 305–325 in *New Directions in Political Communication,* edited by David L. Swanson and Dan Nimmo. Newbury Park, CA: Sage.

Gutmann, Amy. 1998. *Freedom of association.* Princeton: Princeton University Press.

Habermas, Jürgen. 1989. *The structural transformation of the public sphere: an inquiry into a category of bourgeois society.* Cambridge: MIT Press.

———. 1996. *Between facts and norms: contributions to a discourse theory of law and democracy.* Cambridge: MIT Press.

Hall, Peter Dobkin. 1987. "Abandoning the Rhetoric of Independence: Reflections on the Nonprofit Sector in the Post-liberal Era." *Journal of Voluntary Action Research* 16:11–28.

Hallin, Daniel C., and Paolo Mancini. 1984. "Speaking of the President: Political Structure and Representational Form in U.S. and Italian Television News." *Theory and Society* 13:829–850.

———. 2004. *Comparing media systems: three models of media and politics.* Cambridge: Cambridge University Press.

Hart, Roderick P. 2000. *Campaign talk: why elections are good for us.* Princeton: Princeton University Press.

Hart, Stephen. 2001. *Cultural dilemmas of progressive politics: styles of engagement among grassroots activists.* Chicago: University of Chicago Press.

Heaney, Michael T., and Fabio Rojas. 2007. "Partisans, Nonpartisans, and the Antiwar Movement in the United States." *American Politics Research* 35:431–464.

Hegel, Georg Wilhelm Friedrich. (1821) 1967. *Hegel's philosophy of right.* Translated by T. M. Knox. Reprint, Gloucestershire, UK: Clarendon Press.

Herzog, Hanna. 1987. "The Election Campaign as a Liminal Stage: Negotiations over Meanings." *Sociological Review* 35:559–574.

Hindman, Mathew. 2009. *The myth of digital democracy.* Princeton: Princeton University Press.

Jacobs, Ronald N. 1996. "Producing the News, Producing the Crisis: Narrativity, Television, and News Work." *Media, Culture, and Society* 18:373–397.

———. 2000. *Race, media, and the crisis of civil society: from Watts to Rodney King.* Cambridge: Cambridge University Press.

———. 2003. "Toward a Political Sociology of Civil Society." *Research in Political Sociology* 12:19–47.

Jankowski, Nicholas, and Martine van Selm. 2000. "The Promise and Practice of Public Debate in Cyberspace." Pp. 149–165 in *Digital Democracy: Issues of Theory and Practice,* edited by Kenneth L. Hacker and Jan van Dijk. Thousand Oaks, CA: Sage.

Jha, Sonora. 2008. "Why They Wouldn't Cite from Sites: A Study of Journalists' Perceptions of Social Movement Web Sites and the Impact on Their Coverage of Social Protest." *Journalism* 9:711–732.

Keane, John. 1991. *The media and democracy.* Cambridge: Polity.

Kornhauser, William. 1959. *The politics of mass society.* Glencoe, IL: Free Press.

Kurzman, Charles. 2008. "Meaning-Making in Social Movements." *Anthropological Quarterly* 81:5–15.

Lester, Marilyn. 1980. "Generating Newsworthiness: The Interpretive Construction of Public Events." *American Sociological Review* 45:984–994.

Lichterman, Paul. 1996. *The search for political community: American activists reinventing commitment.* Cambridge: Cambridge University Press.

———. 1999. "Talking Identity in the Public Sphere: Broad Visions and Small Spaces in Sexual Identity Politics." *Theory and Society* 28:101–141.

———. 2005. *Elusive togetherness: church groups trying to bridge America's divisions.* Princeton: Princeton University Press.

———. 2006. "Social Capital or Group Style? Rescuing Tocqueville's Insights on Civic Engagement." *Theory and Society* 35:529–563.

Lunder, Erika K., and L. Paige Whitaker. 2006. "501(c)(4)s and Campaign Activity: Analysis Under Tax and Campaign Finance Laws." CRS Report R40141, Congressional Research Service, Washington, DC.

MacCannell, Dean. 1999. *The tourist: a new theory of the leisure class.* Berkeley: University of California Press.

Manoff, Robert Karl. 1986. "Writing the News (by Telling the 'Story')." Pp. 146–195 in *Reading the News,* edited by Robert Manoff and Michael Schudson. New York: Pantheon Books.

Margolis, Michael, and David Resnick. 2000. *Politics as usual: the cyberspace "revolution."* Thousand Oaks, CA: Sage.

McAdam, Doug. 1982. *Political process and the development of black insurgency, 1930–1970.* Chicago: University of Chicago Press.

McAdam, Doug, John D. McCarthy, and Mayer Zald. 1996. *Comparative perspectives on social movements.* Cambridge: Cambridge University Press.

McCarthy, John D., Clark McPhail, and Jackie Smith. 1996. "Images of Protest: Dimensions of Selection Bias in Media Coverage of Washington Demonstrations, 1982 and 1991." *American Sociological Review* 61:478–499.

McCarthy, John D. and Mayer N. Zald. 1977. "Resource Mobilization and Social Movements: A Partial Theory." *American Journal of Sociology* 82:1212–1241.

McManus, John H. 1995. "A Market-Based Model of News Production." *Communication Theory* 5:301–338.

Meeks, Chet. 2001. "Civil Society and the Sexual Politics of Difference." *Sociological Theory* 19:325–343.

Melucci, Alberto. 1996. *Challenging codes: collective action in the information age.* Cambridge: Cambridge University Press.

Meyer, David S. 1993. "Institutionalizing Dissent: The United States Political Opportunity Structure and the End of the Nuclear Freeze Movement." *Sociological Forum* 8:157–179.

———. 2005. "Social Movements and Public Policy: Eggs, Chicken, and Theory." Pp. 1–26 in *Routing the Opposition: Social Movements, Pubic Policy, and Democracy,* edited by David S. Meyer, Valerie Jenness, and Helen Ingram. Minneapolis: University of Minnesota Press.

———. 2007. *The politics of protest: social movements in America.* New York: Oxford University Press.

Meyer, David S., Valerie Jenness, and Helen Ingram, eds. 2005. *Routing the opposition: social movements, public policy, and democracy.* Minneapolis: University of Minnesota Press.

Meyer, David S. and Debra C. Minkoff. 2004. "Conceptualizing Political Opportunity." *Social Forces* 82:1457–1492.

Minkoff, Debra C. 1997. "Producing Social Capital: National Social Movements and Civil Society." *American Behavioral Scientist* 40:606–619.

Molotch, Harvey, and Marilyn Lester. 1974. "News as Purposive Behavior: On the Strategic Use of Routine Events, Accidents, and Scandals." *American Sociological Review* 39:101–112.

Moore, Gwen, Sarah Sobieraj, J. Allen Whitt, Olga Mayorova, and Daniel Beaulieu. 2002. "Elite Interlocks in Three U.S. Sectors: Nonprofit, Corporate, and Government." *Social Science Quarterly* 83:726–744.

Mouffe, Chantal. 1999. "Deliberative Democracy or Agonistic Pluralism?" *Social Research* 66:745–758.

Myers, Daniel J., and Beth Schaefer Caniglia. 2004. "All the Rioting That's Fit to Print: Selection Effects in National Newspaper Coverage of Civil Disorders, 1968–1969." *American Sociological Review* 69:519–543.

Norris, Pippa. 2001. *Digital divide: civic engagement, information poverty, and the Internet in democratic societies.* New York: Cambridge University Press.

Oliver, Pamela E., and Gregory M. Maney. 2000. "Political Processes and Local Newspaper Coverage of Protest Events: From Selection Bias to Triadic Interactions." *American Journal of Sociology* 106:463–505.

Oliver, Pamela E., and Daniel J. Myers. 1999. "How Events Enter the Public Sphere: Conflict, Location, and Sponsorship in Local Newspaper Coverage of Public Events." *American Journal of Sociology* 105:38–87.

Olzak, Susan, and Sarah Soule. 2009. "Cross-Cutting Influences of Environmental Protest and Legislation." *Social Forces* 88:201–225.

Open Debates. 2004. "Memorandum of Understanding." http://www.opendebates.org/news/documents/debateagreement.pdf&pli=1.

Ostrander, Susan A., and Kent E. Portney. 2007. *Acting civically: from urban neighborhoods to higher education.* Hanover: University Press of New England.

Panagopoulos, Costas. 2007. *Rewiring politics: presidential nominating conventions in the media age.* Baton Rouge: Louisiana State University Press.

Patterson, Thomas E. 1993. *Out of order.* New York: Knopf.

Perrin, Andrew J. 2005. "Political Microcultures: Linking Civic Life and Democratic Discourse." *Social Forces* 84:1049–1082.

———. 2006. *Citizen speak: the democratic imagination in American life.* Chicago: University of Chicago Press.

Perrin, Andrew J., Robin Wagner-Pacifici, Lindsay Hirschfeld, and Susan Wilker. 2006. "Contest Time: Time, Territory, and Representation in the Postmodern Electoral Crisis." *Theory and Society* 35:351–391.

Peterson, Richard A. 1997. *Creating country music: fabricating authenticity.* Chicago: University of Chicago Press.

Pickard, Victor W. 2008. "Cooptation and Cooperation: Institutional Exemplars of Democratic Internet Technology." *New Media and Society* 10:625–645.

Piven, Frances Fox. 2006. *Challenging authority: how ordinary people change America.* Lanham, MD: Rowman and Littlefield.

Piven, Frances Fox, and Richard A. Cloward. 1977. *Poor people's movements: why they succeed, how they fail.* New York: Pantheon Books.

Polletta, Francesca. 2002. *Freedom is an endless meeting: democracy in American social movements.* Chicago: University of Chicago Press.

————. 2006. *It was like a fever: storytelling in protest and politics*. Chicago: University of Chicago Press.

Polletta, Francesca, and James M. Jasper. 2001. "Collective Identity and Social Movements." *Annual Review of Sociology* 27:283–305.

Pomper, Gerald. 2007. "The New Role of the Conventions as Political Rituals." Pp. 189–203 in *Rewiring Politics: Presidential Nominating Conventions in the Media Age*, edited by Costas Panagopoulos. Baton Rouge: Louisiana State University Press.

Putnam, Robert D. 1995. "Bowling Alone: America's Declining Social Capital." *Journal of Democracy* 6 1:65–78.

————. 2000. *Bowling alone: the collapse and revival of American community*. New York: Simon and Schuster.

Rapaport, Richard. 2000. "Best of the Web: Net vs. Norm." http://www.forbes.com/asap/2000/0529/053_print.html.

Richardson, Franci, and Doug Hanchett. 2000. "Debate Attracts Hordes of Activists: Police Arrest 16." *Boston Herald*, October 4.

Roberts, Laurie. 2004. "Format Wrecks Gammage 'Debate.'" *Arizona Republic*, October 16.

Rohlinger, Deana. 2007. "American Media and Deliberative Democratic Processes." *Sociological Theory* 25:122–148.

Rousseau, Jean-Jacques. (1762) 1968. *The social contract*. Reprint, Baltimore: Penguin Books.

Russell, Jenna. 2004. "Protesters Reach Wary Acceptance of Police Role." *Boston Globe*, July 29.

Ryan, Charlotte. 1991. *Prime time activism: media strategies for grassroots organizing*. Boston: South End Press.

————. 2004. "It Takes a Movement to Raise an Issue: Media Lessons from the 1997 UPS Strike." *Critical Sociology* 30:483–511.

Ryan, Charlotte, Michael Anastario, and Karen Jeffreys. 2005. "Start Small, Build Big: Negotiating Opportunities in Media Markets." *Mobilization* 10:111–128.

Ryan, Mary. 1992. "Gender and Public Access: Women's Politics in Nineteenth-Century America." Pp. 259–288 in *Habermas and the Public Sphere*, edited by C. J. Calhoun. Cambridge: MIT Press.

Salzman, Jason. 2003. *Making the news: a guide for activists and nonprofits*. Boulder, CO: Westview Press.

Schudson, Michael. 1978. *Discovering the news: a social history of American newspapers*. New York: Basic Books.

————. 1982. "The Politics of Narrative Form: The Emergence of News Conventions in Print and Television." *Daedalus* 111:97–112.

————. 1998. *The good citizen: a history of American civic life*. New York: Martin Kessler Books.

———. 2000. "The Sociology of News Production Revisited (Again)."Pp. 175–200 in *Mass Media and Society*, edited by James Curran and Michael Gurevitch. London: Edward Arnold.

———. 2003. *The sociology of news*. New York: Norton.

Seligman, A. 1992.*The idea of civil society*. New York: Free Press.

Sexton, John. 2004. "Resolved: That Was No Debate." *Los Angeles Times*, October 8.

Shirky, Clay. 2008. *Here comes everybody: the power of organizing without organizations*. New York: Penguin Press.

Simone, Maria. 2006. "codepink Alert: Mediated Citizenship in the Public Sphere." *Social Semiotics* 16:345–364.

Skocpol, Theda. 1999. "How Americans Became Civic." Pp. 27–80 in *Civic Engagement in American Democracy*, edited by Theda Skocpol and Morris P. Fiorina. Washington, DC: Brookings Institution Press.

———. 2003. *Diminished democracy: from membership to management in American civic life*. Norman: University of Oklahoma Press.

Skocpol, Theda, and Morris P. Fiorina, eds. 1999. *Civic engagement in American democracy*. Washington, DC: Brookings Institution Press.

Smelser, Neil J. 1963. *Theory of collective behavior*. New York: Free Press.

Smith, Adam. (1759) 1976. *The theory of moral sentiments*. Reprint. Indianapolis: Liberty Classics.

Smith, Jackie, John D. McCarthy, Clark McPhail, and Boguslaw Augustyn. 2001. "From Protest to Agenda Building: Description Bias in Media Coverage of Protest Events in Washington, DC." *Social Forces* 79:1397–1423.

Snow, David A., E. Burke Rochford Jr., Steven K. Worden, and Robert D. Benford. 1986. "Frame Alignment Processes, Micromobilization, and Movement Participation." *American Sociological Review* 51:464–481.

Sobieraj, Sarah. 2006. "The Implications of Transitions in the Voluntary Sector for Civic Engagement: A Case Study of Association Mobilization Around the 2000 Presidential Campaign." *Sociological Inquiry* 76:52–80.

———. 2010. "Reporting Conventions: Journalists, Activists, and the Thorny Struggle for Political Visibility." *Social Problems* 57:508–528.

Sobieraj, Sarah, and Deborah White. 2004. "Taxing Political Life: Reevaluating the Relationship Between Voluntary Association Membership, Political Engagement, and the State." *Sociological Quarterly* 45:739–764.

———. 2007. "Could Civic Engagement Reproduce Political Inequality?" Pp. 92–110 in *Acting Civically: From Urban Neighborhoods to Higher Education*, edited by Susan A. Ostrander and Kent E. Portney. Hanover: University Press of New England.

Soule, Sarah, Doug McAdam, John D. McCarthy, and Yang Su. 1999. "Protest Events: Cause of Consequence of State Action? The U.S. Women's Movement and Federal Congressional Activities, 1956–1979." *Mobilization* 42:239–256.

Sparks, Colin. 2001. "The Internet and the Global Public Sphere." Pp. 75–98 in *Mediated Politics: Communication in the Future of Democracy*, edited by W. Lance Bennett and Robert M. Entman. New York: Cambridge University Press.

Squires, Catherine. 2000. "Black Talk Radio: Defining Community Needs and Identity." *Harvard International Journal of Press Politics* 5:73–95.

Sunstein, Cass. 2001. *Republic.com*. Princeton: Princeton University Press.

Thomas Jefferson Center for the Protection of Free Expression. 2005. "Jefferson Muzzles." http://www.tjcenter.org/muzzles/muzzle-archive-2005/.

Tilly, Charles. 1978. *From mobilization to revolution*. Reading, MA: Addison-Wesley.

———. 2004. *Social movements, 1768–2004*. Boulder, CO: Paradigm Publishers.

Tocqueville, Alexis de. (1835) 2000. *Democracy in America*. Translated by Henry Reeve. Reprint, New York: Bantam Books.

Touraine, Alain. 1985. "An Introduction to the Study of Social Movements." *Social Research* 52:749–787.

Tuchman, Gaye. 1972. "Objectivity as Strategic Ritual: An Examination of Newsmen's Notions of Objectivity." *American Journal of Sociology* 77:660–679.

———. 1973. "Making News by Doing Work: Routinizing the Unexpected." *American Journal of Sociology* 79:110–131.

———. 1978. *Making news: a study in the construction of reality*. New York: Free Press.

Van Dyke, Nella. 2003. "Crossing Movement Boundaries: Factors That Facilitate Coalition Protest by American College Students, 1930–1990." *Social Problems* 50:226–250.

Wagner-Pacifici, Robin Erica. 1994. *Discourse and destruction: the city of Philadelphia versus move*. Chicago: University of Chicago Press.

Walder, Andrew G. 2009. "Political Sociology and Social Movements." *Annual Review of Sociology* 35:393–412.

Walsh, Katherine Cramer. 2004. *Talking about politics: informal groups and social identity in American life*. Chicago: University of Chicago Press.

Walzer, Michael. 1992. "The Civil Society Argument." Pp. 90–107 in *Dimensions of Radical Democracy: Pluralism, Citizenship, Community*, edited by Chantal Mouffe. London: Verso.

Warren, Mark. 2000. *Democracy and association*. Princeton: Princeton University Press.

———. 2001. *Dry bones rattling: community building to revitalize American democracy*. Princeton: Princeton University Press.

Wolin, Sheldon S. 2001. *Tocqueville between two worlds: the making of a political and theoretical life*. Princeton: Princeton University Press.

Wuthnow, Robert. 1998. *Loose connections: joining together in America's fragmented communities*. Cambridge: Harvard University Press.

Young, Iris Marion. 1990. *Justice and the politics of difference*. Princeton: Princeton University Press.

———. 2000. *Inclusion and democracy*. Oxford: Oxford University Press.

Zelizer, Barbie. 1993. "Journalists as Interpretive Communities." *Critical Studies in Mass Communication* 10:219–237.

Index

Abolish, 36, 154

Abortion, 15. *See also* Anti-abortion; Pre-Born Protectors; Pro-choice; Pro-life

Abu Ghraib prison, 61, 62

Abu-Jamal, Mumia, 31

Action, 171; behind-the-scenes, 13–14; collective, in civil society, 12; fundamental, 14; group, 9; illegal, 41–42; journalists and, 89; marches/street protests, 53–57; member-focused, 53, 64–67; street theater, 30, 56–62, 101–2, 117–19; use of high profile speakers, 62–64. *See also* Communal activity; Demonstrative action

Active civil society, 9

Activism: characteristics of coverage, 74–80; civil liberties and, 33; demonstrative action and, 34–35; everywhere, 176–77; Internet, 168–70, 175; news coverage of, 71–80; newsworthiness, 88; presidential campaigns and, 2–3, 5–7; public displays, 112–18. *See also* Media-centered activism

Activists, 22, 73; animal rights, 78; as carnivalesque or colorful, 53, 76; collective identity, 158–60, 162; crime reporting model, 76–77; designated protest areas rejected, 34; distaste for, 60–61; enclaving, 106; excitement, 156–58; global justice, 47, 78; "good activists," 91–101; ICTs and, 170–73; inner lives, 96; news media and, 2, 72–103; presidential

debate Boston, 2000, 30–31; in public spaces, 23–34; 2008 election and, 170–73; voice, 79; "The whole world is watching" refrain, 1. *See also* Voluntary associations

Activists, rules for, 83–84; authentic activists, 91–96; authentic events, 84–91; polished appearances, 92–93; political acceptability, 96–100; shaping public appearances, 92

Activity classification scheme, 14

Advertising, 10

Africa, John, 146

African Americans, 58, 119

Agenda building, 44

Alternacheer, 37, 39, 50, 113

Alternative conventions, 161

American Adult Network, 36, 43–45, 124–25, 156–57; media training, 137–38

Anarchists, 15, 129–31

Animal rights activists, 78

Anti-abortion, 28, 37, 49, 133, 145

Anti-homosexuality, 28

Antiwar movement, 18, 72, 133

Anti-war protests, 53–54, 62–64, 63

Apollo Theatre, Harlem, 3, 16, 165

Arato, Andrew, 9–11, 20

Arizona Republic, 71

Associated Press, 78

Association representatives, 16

Association response, 21

Authenticity, 103; emergence, 84; journalists and, 83–87; self-interest and, 95–96. *See also* Inauthenticity

"Avoiding politics," 150

About the Author

SARAH SOBIERAJ is Assistant Professor of Sociology at Tufts University.